CU00747171

PLAID CYMRU

PLAID CYMRU

An ideological analysis

Welsh Academic Press

Published in Wales by Welsh Academic Press, an imprint of

Ashley Drake Publishing Ltd
PO Box 733
Cardiff
CF14 7ZY

www.welsh-academic-press.com

First Impression – 2011

ISBN
978-1-86057-116-9

British Library Cataloguing-in-Publication Data.
A CIP catalogue for this book is available from the British Library.

Typeset by Prepress Projects Ltd, Perth, Scotland
Printed by the MPG Books Group Ltd, Bodmin, Cornwall

CONTENTS

I	Introduction	1
II	Ideology and Nationalism	8
III	The Ideological Development of Early Plaid Cymru	33
IV	Modern Plaid Cymru and the Ideology of Nationalism	81
V	Other Ideologies Associated with Modern Plaid Cymru	102
VI	Concepts within Plaid Cymru's Ideology	143
VII	Ideological Debates within Plaid Cymru	192
VIII	Conclusion: A New Ideological Framework	199
	Bibliography	213
	Index	227

I

INTRODUCTION

This book will examine whether the rhetoric, statements, policies and general political philosophy of Plaid Cymru equate with the established conceptions of the ideology of nationalism. The automatic linking of nationalism and Plaid Cymru is a conventional assumption that has been generally accepted by those investigating both nationalism in Wales and the political content and ideological structures of Plaid Cymru, a political party that is generally regarded as being the foremost advocate of Welsh nationalism. However, whether Plaid Cymru's Welsh nationalism is a full, a distinct or an established ideology,[1] or simply a disparate collection of principles and political ideas whose primary focus may, or may not, be the nation, and the advancement of national causes, needs to be determined.

To enable it to do so, the model of what constitutes an ideology, as enunciated by Michael Freeden, the foremost analyst of political ideology, will be invoked. If it is not clear that nationalism is the sole ideology that pervades Plaid Cymru's morphology, or if claims that it is are refuted, then it will need to be determined whether it is possible to identify what specific set of ideas, or ideological concepts, constitute Plaid Cymru's ideology. Freeden's model will be operative from the start of this investigation but it will be conspicuous mostly in the chapters evaluating the party's genealogy, its ideology and its ideological concepts.

Plaid Cymru's ideology requires this rigorous and detailed investigation because, despite the ever more prominent role that the party is now playing in Welsh politics, there still appear to be some customary misconceptions, and a lack of clarity, regarding the party's political aims, its overall objectives and its general political philosophy. This is not to claim that this is a unique situation regarding Plaid Cymru alone, and it should not inadvertently lead to a besmirching of the party's organisational ability and its capacity to communicate the party's true essence to the general public. Equally, therefore, a parallel investigation could have been carried out on any political party that is generally recognised as being a repository for a certain political ideology (e.g. the Labour Party and socialism, or the Conservative Party and conservatism) but which may be sheltering a more diverse ideology beneath its facade. Thus, the framework and manner of this investigation of Plaid Cymru's ideology should be easily transferable for those who wish to consider the ideological bases of comparable political parties.

In a similar vein, although it is just Plaid Cymru that will be under the spotlight in this work, it must be recognised from the outset that the party does not operate in a political vacuum and, to this extent, Plaid Cymru is engaged in an ongoing dialectical process with other political parties – one in which it both proactively advocates policies knowing that other parties will counteract – favourably or not – while reactively formulating responses to any developments that arise from the political parties and pressure groups that surround it. Furthermore, Plaid Cymru also shares, or has shared, certain political convictions with other political parties (i.e. an environmentalist agenda with the Green Party, a decentralisation agenda with the Liberal and Liberal Democratic parties and a broadly welfarist agenda with the Labour Party); indeed, within the world of Welsh politics, and within the aforementioned dialectical process, Plaid Cymru's turbulent relationship with the Labour Party, in particular, is of interest, especially since the arrival of coalition government in 2007 under the One Wales agreement. Whilst Carwyn Fowler has commented on how 'Plaid Cymru and Welsh Labour share a broadly similar public policy platform',[2] other commentators, such as Laura McAllister, have noted the 'issue of a symbiosis between Labour and Plaid.'[3] This is observable at a level of voter identification and affiliation, transference of membership and in some areas of ideology.[4] These aspects were most conspicuous, according to Peter Harries, on 14 July 1966, when 'Gwynfor Evans' by-election victory in the Carmarthenshire constituency … was helped by redundant miners in the Gwendraeth and Amman Valleys switching their support from Labour.'[5] Furthermore, and to add to the case for seeking close identification between the two parties, Evans had defeated the 'strongly nationalist Labour candidate, Gwilym Prys Davies.'[6]

Whilst acknowledging that there are undoubtedly a number of areas of overlap and coexistence, some of whose ideological content and status will be explored at a later stage, this examination does not intend to engage in any comparative debates in regard to the nature of individual political parties as it will seek to focus on the unique characteristics that are associated with, and are contributing factors towards, the ideology of one particular party, namely Plaid Cymru. Nevertheless, it must be recognised from the beginning that Plaid Cymru may share several ideological concepts or, moreover, actual ideologies with other political parties. These will be noted if, or where, they become evident.

If, hopefully, a clearer understanding of Plaid Cymru's ideology transpires, then any attempts to further investigate the comparative nature of party politics in Wales – be it from a structural or an ideological position – should be made easier as more detailed knowledge and analyses of individual party ideologies emerge. Furthermore, it is worth re-emphasising that the methodology and the Freedenite ideological model that will be employed here could be equally applied to the Labour Party in Wales, or indeed any other political party throughout the world. Thus, although it is Plaid Cymru that is being dissected, it should not be seen as being a cocooned or isolated study of one party or one theoretical paradigm alone.

What will be contended is that, for the last eighty years or so, nationalism has been used as a motif – a flag of convenience, in other words – by Plaid Cymru and its observers alike, without any particularly extensive ideological underpinning, or any detailed understanding about the usage of nationalism within political vocabulary. Similarly, the possible consequences of associating the ideas of Plaid Cymru with the ideology of nationalism appear to have been put to one side. Hence, a thorough investigation of these matters needs to be embarked upon. To these ends, as nationalism is not a full ideology, according to the Freedenite model, and as other ideologies and ideological concepts noticeably arise, if any detailed reading of the party's political outlook is undertaken, then the ideological variations at work within the party need to be analysed and assessed in order to uncover the precise ideological framework of the party, and its conceptual constitution.

To perform this task, therefore, this book will initially look at the structure of ideology and nationalism, and the contention by Michael Freeden that nationalism is not a full political ideology. It will then focus upon the genealogy of the political thought that fed into Plaid Cymru, along with its formative ideational development and the evolution of Plaid Cymru as a political party offering an alternative ideological voice. After a study of the party's ideological shape, and its apparent *raison d'être*, is considered, the various ideologies and ideological concepts that have arisen within the party, since its formation, will be appraised. What this examination seeks to uncover, therefore, is the exact nature of Plaid Cymru's ideology, or, to use Freeden's terminology, its 'thought-practices'.[7]

A Distinctive Approach?

Hopefully, the distinctiveness of this book will be its challenge to what appears to be the perceived notion that, in the minds of many of those writers who have considered it, Welsh nationalism as a political ideology, positioned primarily, though by no means exclusively, in the political party known as Plaid Cymru, is somehow incontestable. Being incontestable, according to these party observers, Plaid Cymru's ideological underpinning – nationalism as these writers invariably see it – is generally assumed to be all-embracing enough for the purposes of studying this particular party to a sufficient degree. Whilst the actual nature and shape of Plaid Cymru's nationalism is put, sporadically, under the spotlight, the question of how nationalism and ideology should be defined in this context has remained, for the most part, unchallenged. This book will contest the idea that both Plaid Cymru itself, and those who have written about the party, are correct in their use of nationalist ideology, and what customarily amounts to nationalist ideology alone, to describe the thought-practices that exist within the party; even though the party has modelled itself as nationalist on many occasions, and Plaid Cymru is usually perceived by the public at large to be a nationalist political party. This latter point arises, arguably, because, in both a pragmatic and a simplistic sense, nationalism has been the most expedient description for proponents, opponents and political commentators to adopt.

Since its formation in 1925 the membership of Plaid Cymru has adopted a plurality of political ideas and standpoints. Hence, it is erroneous to assume that the party denotes any single all-encompassing political position or that in its political pronouncements it reaffirms, time and again, one grand narrative. The myth in relation to Plaid Cymru over the last eighty-five years has been the tacit assumption that the party has championed its policies and principles, which have long been assumed to be the prime elements of a coherent philosophy and ideology, under what appeared to be the most appropriate label, namely that of nationalism. But, it can be argued, there are ideological complexities within the structure and fundamental principles of Plaid Cymru as an organisation, and in the thought-practices and agendas of individuals within that organisation, that cannot be overridden by simply labelling these political ideas as nationalist, or as Welsh nationalism, without due care and attention being paid to the definitions of nationalism and an analysis of what this apparent Welsh version of nationalism is, and how it fits into the arrangement of political ideologies. If it is not at all clear that what is represented here is nationalism – as it will be argued later that nationalism is a set of ideas and not merely a political theory or a concept within an ideology – then questions arise as to how clear Plaid Cymru's message can be if it is aligning itself as a nationalist political organisation.

As this exploration is not a standard work of political science, psephology or political history – though all three may be summoned in due course – any answers, and indeed further questions, arising out of it may have to be addressed at another time. Consequently, the prime concern of this work is political ideology and the exegesis of the ideological make-up of Plaid Cymru. With this in mind, it must be stressed from the beginning that it is Plaid Cymru itself that is the focus for this exploration and not the wider implications that a study of the more extensive issues regarding nationalism in Wales, in its various guises, would encounter; though naturally a certain amount of political, social, historical and theoretical overlap is inevitable in a study of this nature.

To commence this examination, therefore, Plaid Cymru's genealogy has to be scrutinised. As Michael Freeden has observed, 'the history of an ideological tradition, the conventions through which it is understood and perceived, and its spatial diversities, must also play a central role in attributing meaning to the ideology in question.'[8] An analysis of Plaid Cymru's genealogy will help to explain the party's ideologically fractured or pluralistic nature. It should become clearer, through analysis, whether this fracture is dysfunctional and debilitating, certainly as far as any attempt by the party to declare ideological uniformity is concerned, or whether it merely represents a pluralistic body of opinion, epitomised by individual party members or, intermittently, by factions who are seemingly content to operate within inexact ideological parameters. Subsequently, only through scrutiny will it be possible to declare that Plaid Cymru's ideology is an established, distinct or full ideology, or whether the nationalism that has been attributed to Plaid Cymru is merely a flag of convenience that has been adopted by Plaid Cymru strategists in the hope of stimulating an electoral impetus or uniting an otherwise divisive coalition within its ranks. Alternatively, it could be the case that nationalism is a label attached to Plaid Cymru by its political opponents. All political parties implement a degree of political propaganda in order to tarnish their opponents. Hence, the distinction between propaganda and scientific or theoretical evaluation needs to be remembered whenever Plaid Cymru's adversaries describe the party's political make-up.

Whilst bearing the above in mind, it is nevertheless fair to add that if the flag of convenience argument is to have credence then it needs to be established whether any attempt by Plaid Cymru to use the emotive iconography that comes with talk of the nation and national sentiment – to engender a heightened sense of awareness about all things Welsh

– is a deliberate policy strategy, or whether it has shown itself through individuals within the organisation who have pushed for a more overtly Welsh-centric basis to the party's social and political policies. Hence, in order to create a more transparent picture of where those within the party sit on these matters, it is important to analyse the set of political beliefs, narrow or extensive, that are currently residing underneath the banner of Plaid Cymru, first and foremost, and, as an appendage, Welsh nationalism. It must be made clear, however, that the set of political ideas that could be termed Welsh nationalism, or nationalism in a Welsh context, is very much secondary in this investigation to an analysis of the ideology of Plaid Cymru. Therefore, although they cannot be dismissed totally, other Welsh nationalist parties and organisations will not receive close scrutiny. However, their presence, and their possible influence on Plaid Cymru, may be acknowledged at points throughout.

It should also be noted that this book will not lay too much emphasis on trying to explain Plaid Cymru's thought-practices as somehow an appendage of its natural development or maturing as a political party. All political parties, from birth, develop at a different pace depending on a variety of factors such as initial membership numbers, financial potency, the level of political experience and expertise at its disposal, and the gamut of extraneous factors that either have led to the party's formation in the first instance or weigh heavily against its prospects for longevity. Whilst accepting that Plaid Cymru faced its own particular challenges on these fronts, this analysis does not wish to overplay the ways in which this process of maturing has shaped the party's ideology. This is because many of the aforementioned factors are essentially non-ideological and could be labelled strategic or managerial. Party structures, occasional internal reorganisation and, in recent years, the process of rebranding and taking on board the demands of multifaceted twenty-four-hour news media, hungry for political information, have all enabled the party to strengthen its base and broaden its appeal as it attempts to present itself as a professional political organisation. Nevertheless, a line must be drawn as to the influence of ideology on these practical matters. Therefore, this work will engage with the debate on the party's maturing as a political party – and change therein – but it will leave the above-mentioned factors to one side in order to concentrate on ideological developments alone.

Similarly, the issue of Plaid Cymru being a broad church that sweeps up the nationalistic, patriotic, cultural preservationist, and non-Labour soft left vote in Wales is far too simplistic a basis on which to launch an investigation of the party's political ideology. Broad church theories can be applicable to any mainstream political party that has to encapsulate views that may not be overtly or excessively rigid in their doctrines – unlike, arguably, fascism – and has to seek some form of general consensus on policy and actions, as opposed to the unbendable, totalitarian-style acceptance that may be commonplace within fringe or peripheral movements. Labelling Plaid Cymru's morphology as broad church may be fine if, on a fairly casual basis, it is accepted that there is a range of opinion within the party and that the party itself can be placed within the mainstream of politics. Nevertheless, the task here is to go beneath the surface of some of these general labels to uncover what ideologies and ideological concepts are identifiable. The broad church description, in this instance, is of little use as it may merely act as a smokescreen. Further comments on the broad church approach are noted at a later stage in the section on distinctive approaches.

Notes

1. Michael Freeden, 'Is nationalism a distinct ideology?', *Political Studies*, vol. XLVI, 1998, p. 750.
2. Carwyn Fowler, 'Nationalism and the Labour Party in Wales', *Llafur*, vol. 8, no. 4, 2003, p. 97.
3. Laura McAllister, *Plaid Cymru: The Emergence of a Political Party* (Seren: Bridgend, 2001), p. 140.
4. See Denis Balsom, 'The first Welsh general election', in J. Barry Jones and Denis Balsom (eds), *The Road to the National Assembly for Wales*, 2000, pp. 211–228.
5. Peter Harries, 'Cwllynfell colliery: an early attempt to form a workers co-operative', *Llafur*, vol. 7, no. 2, 2002, p. 51.
6. Charlie Kimber, *Wales: Class Struggle and Socialism* (London: Socialist Workers Party, 1999), p. 40.
7. Michael Freeden, *Ideology: A Very Short* Introduction (Oxford: Oxford University Press, 2003), p. 21.
8. Michael Freeden, *Ideologies and Political Theory* (Oxford: Clarendon Press, 1996), p. 5.

II

IDEOLOGY AND NATIONALISM

Before any exploration of nationalism or Plaid Cymru can commence, the concept of ideology, its definition and utilisation, nationalism's role as an ideology and Michael Freeden's interpretations require some examination.

Freeden and Thought-Practices

So as not to imbue ideology with any restrictive, or non-essential, baggage, this examination will use the term 'ideology' to denote actual ongoing 'political thought-practices.'[1] This is the conceiving and application of political ideas which, rather than being the preserve of a selective few, is instead 'a communal activity taking place in social space and recurring over time.'[2] Furthermore, ideologies act as instigators for human activity within society. This dynamic occurs because ideologies are 'the arrangements of political thought that illuminate the central ideas, overt assumptions and unstated biases that in turn drive political conduct.'[3]

To undertake a study of an ideology, therefore, it is important that an analysis takes place in order to be able to categorise and dissect the ways in which this communal activity occurs, and to observe how these arrangements of political thought are structured. In addition, any analysis must focus upon how those involved in this communal activity not only 'intentionally practice the art of political thinking'[4] but also 'unintentionally express the social patterns which that kind of thinking has developed.'[5] On this reading, therefore, thought engenders practice whether the practitioners realise it or not. Hence, the individual's thought and practice does have an effect, however small, on the direction of social events. Nevertheless, it should be recognised that the structures within society that are represented by changing social patterns – causal determinants – cannot be dismissed out of hand. Consequently, and for the purposes of this exploration of Plaid Cymru's thought-practices, any assessment of ideology using individual cases alone would turn out to be unfeasible, given the knowledge that a political party that incorporates a mass of people, albeit with individual ideas, is under scrutiny.

Following on from this, therefore, it is sensible to conclude that the categorisation of ideologies is vital in order to aid our understanding of how we have arrived at a juncture wherein political ideologies are identifiable as distinctive and symbolic blocs of policy and thought. Without categorisation – without, that is, the placing of these sets of political ideas into blocs or clusters – each and every distinctive form of thought, of each and every human being, could be labelled as an ideology-in-itself, and would have to be categorised as such, given that there is a contention that ideologies are thought-practices that anybody can partake of. For practical purposes, however, it is easier for political analysts to contend with tens of ideologies, as blocs of thought, as opposed to talking about the six billion ideologies on earth.

The question that follows on from this, however, is whether individuals respond to ideological concepts, ideologies or ideological blocs that are already operational, or whether individuals contribute effectively to the process of ideological formation. The answer would appear to be both. This is because there is continuous interplay between individuals and the ideologies, or ideological concepts, which they endorse. If this did not occur then stagnation would be instant, as there would be no mechanism for driving forward ideas within the group configuration. Though, within democratic societies and institutions, this may strike the observer as obvious, there must nevertheless be a high level of interplay between individuals and particular ideological blocs, even within closed societies or totalitarian parties. Therefore, even taking into consideration the worst case scenarios, there must still be some channels, albeit perhaps exceptionally limited, through which people can react to, and influence, social and political events and decision-making.

There is also the question of the legitimacy that each and every social and political authority requires in order for it to be effective; legitimacy is used here in a democratic rather than a non-democratic sense, whereby it can be attained through involvement in the political process and political discourse in general, as opposed to the legitimacy of authority coming about through fear of persecution. Thus, the individual has far more ability to affect outcomes than is normally imagined, although the space available in which to display this ideological independence is more likely to be restricted in non-democratic societies. The individual is also in the fortunate position that he or she is not tied to any singular ideological position. Whilst not failing to acknowledge methods such as brainwashing, and political or educational inculcation, most individuals do have room to manoeuvre and rationalise, and the individual can change his or her opinions at a moment's notice. This is because, importantly, most societies do not have structures that bind individuals and restrict their freedom to rationalise as individuals. This unprecedented degree of choice and free will does not exist, to the same degree at least, for the institution or political organisation. This is because there are laws, constitutions, conventions and practices that severely limit their operation. There is also a utilitarian rule of thumb for these bodies that privileges the opinions of the majority over the minority. Therefore, while the individual can act in an unencumbered manner, those aligning themselves to political organisations are more ideologically restrained.

This unencumbered torrent of thought-practices, however, is an ideal scenario. The reality is quite different. What really occurs is not ideological free thinking but rationalising that is limited by factors such as a person's socio-economic climate. Thus, other restraining factors such as 'cultural, temporal, spatial and logical constraints'[6] also come into play. Likewise, many individuals are restrained by the exertions of history. This is noticeable, for instance, in black political thought, wherein the practice of slavery plays a key psychological part in the thought-practices of those advocating political and cultural advancement. Nationalist discourse, similarly, is constrained to a certain degree through the fact that it is shaping discourse in a certain way. To exemplify this, it is evident in nationalist discourse that the setting of the nation, and its historical development, is a major component. So, similarly, is geographical positioning, with the factor of the other, often a neighbour or some colonial force, featuring highly in its discourse and reckoning.

If we translate this idea of the aforementioned individual free thinkers into a Welsh nationalistic setting, then it would seem unfeasible that there could be genuine freedom of thought and practice. This is because Welsh nationalist thought is influenced by and, moreover, is beholden to, a perceived historical grievance. This ensures that it is attempting to operate whilst under both the constraints of the past – its historical grievance – and the constraints from adopting the concept of the other – its nationalist justification. Thus, Plaid Cymru, presuming that its position does not vary too much from this nationalist rendition of grievance, would seemingly be constrained in certain ways. It would appear from this deduction, therefore, that the individuals within Plaid Cymru cannot claim to be truly rational and unhindered in their thought.

When, later in this book, a more detailed assessment of Plaid Cymru is made these issues will have a bearing on that party's ideological structure, and the part played by individuals within that organisation. While looking at this interplay between individuals and their ideological bloc, in this case the ideological bloc being the thought-practices of Plaid Cymru, it will be important to determine what constraints, if any, are put on individuals, and on the party itself, by referring to themselves as Welsh nationalists, or through aligning themselves with the body of opinion known as nationalism. So the question of self-image and self-expression needs to be considered. Moreover, when examining whether nationalism is a full ideology, or some other manifestation of opinion, the practical ramifications of that outcome will have to be scrutinised in order to evaluate how that pertains to Plaid Cymru and the individuals that constitute it.

The Pejorative View of Ideology

Because this book is dealing with a political party, Plaid Cymru, whose *raison d'être* is the attainment of a sufficient level of governmental power to enable it to administer its political programme, any purely abstract and hypothetical interpretation and analysis of ideology would be ultimately insufficient. The view of ideology as an abstraction that is somehow disengaged from the everyday social and political world is the pejorative or negative view of ideology that has been forwarded by conservatives such as Ken Minogue.[7] The contention that ideologues speculate about events that are entirely disengaged from the real world would appear to be defeating the objective of translating, or at least applying, political thought and discourse into realistic propositions that may subsequently transpire through political action. This is because political thought, in whatever form it manifests itself, has as its objective an ideal scenario, or at the very least a propitious outcome, that is rooted in the concrete political world. Notably, this thought does not inevitably have to involve a transformative programme of political action, as even a desire to maintain the status quo, regardless of its conservative and anti-ideological connotations, is still an ideological vision of an ideal scenario or a propitious outcome.

Somewhat surprisingly, the conservative interpretation of ideology has certain similarities – albeit rather marginal ones – with Marx's view of ideology. This is because contained within each interpretation there is the idea that ideology somehow operates in a separate domain from everyday politics. Hence, in a conservative reading of ideology, ideologies may be portrayed as 'metaphysical digressions',[8] although this is still in itself an ideological position, whereas a Marxist could argue that ideologies are 'a distorting or illusory epiphenomenon'[9] which make interventions into concrete political actions. The most practical way of approaching and studying ideology, therefore, and the one that will be adopted here, is to regard ideology as both theory and practice – theory as the formulation of ideas, practice as the application of those ideas – in a 'mutual relationship of interdependence'.[10]

Although it is important to remember that each ideology has its own relationship of interdependence with other ideologies and political concepts, it must also be acknowledged that each ideology has its own distinct features. Also, each ideology acts in an independent manner at certain times in order to achieve its aims, as nationalism does in the case of national self-determination, or to further its objectives, as socialism does in the case of the redistribution of wealth within socialist societies. Ideologies, therefore, have a complexity about them, and they are certainly not the monolithic entities that they are sometimes portrayed as being. The idea, for instance, that the ideology of Soviet-style communism was monolithic, as portrayed by American conservatives in the Cold War era, best exemplifies the negative representation of ideologies as immovable, intransigent and leviathan-like structures.

The Use of Ideology in this Analysis: Why Choose Freeden?

The concept of ideology that will be favoured in this study of Plaid Cymru's thought-practices – that proffered by Michael Freeden – refutes this depiction of ideologies as entrenched and inflexible entities. This refutation seeks to explain how ideology is evolutionary, in the sense that ideologies are thought-practices that are forever in motion. To this extent, there is a healthy unpredictability about their dynamic that prevents them from stalling or becoming vapid. This mode of progression within ideologies also ensures that there is no limitation to their interpretation or application, and this allows restricted scope for those who seek to oppose ideology, albeit from an ideological viewpoint, to point out any negative connotations inherent within. All in all, therefore, the fluidity within ideologies has the effect of allowing a constant reassessment to occur. However, rather than turning the ideology into an amorphous mass through this fluidic process, the opposite transpires as an equilibrium is maintained. This happens because the fundamental elements of the ideology – its core concepts – stay put while marginal elements of the ideology are reappraised and, on occasions, reshuffled. This process, in its entirety, ensures that ideologies never settle into what could be deemed to be a monolithic state.

It can be contended that, in broad conceptual terms, there are three streams of ideological thought: the Marxist, the liberal, and the anti-dogma, or conservative, stream. Michael Freeden has cultivated his theory firmly within the liberal conception. Freeden's analysis represents a developing school of thought within the study of ideologies.

Moreover, the liberal, and non-restrictive, nature of Freeden's method allows for both variety and originality in application. Hence, while observance is paid to other ideological streams, the approach adopted here contends that there is a certain malleability within the Freedenite model that enables a more lucid and in-depth examination of individual ideologies to occur.

Furthermore, adhering to Freeden's construal is preferable as his model of the ideological concepts – concepts that may be pooled to constitute an ideology – is also of great benefit when analysing ideologies as sets of ideas. This is because there are, encompassed within each ideology, ideological concepts that operate at varying levels of importance and ideational substance. These varying levels – Freeden's tripartite conceptual system – will be explained in more detail later. It is interesting to note at this stage, however, how the functions performed by Freeden's tripartite conceptual system – the classification of concepts as core, peripheral or adjacent with regard to the depth of their relationships to the ideology being observed – could be seen in similar terms to Thomas Hobbes's remarks, in *Leviathan*,[11] on the state and its components parts, such as the Commonwealth, resembling a living organism. The analogy could follow that Freeden's core concepts are akin to Hobbes's notion of the backbone or spine, in that they are essential to the survival of the corpus or ideology. Peripheral concepts, meanwhile, could be said to have similar functions to our fingers or toes. They play crucial roles and they form an important part of our body. Unlike the loss of the backbone, however, we could, survive without them. Adjacent concepts, on the other hand, are akin to our hair or skin colouring. They add to our, or an ideology's, overall make-up and present a particular angle or flavour. Ultimately, however, they merely complement the core elements but are not crucial for our survival or, for the purposes of this analysis, an ideology's survival.

The depth and extent to which these ideological concepts operate within the thought-practices of Plaid Cymru can be gauged using Freeden's model. These concepts will be rigorously examined later, and, as Plaid Cymru's morphology is discussed, the views of individuals within the party as to their endorsement or rejection of these concepts will be highlighted. Overall, therefore, it was calculated that, for the purposes of this examination, Michael Freeden's consideration of ideology would be the most analytically useful.

Nationalism as a Thought-Practice

Although it is important to recognise that there are both universal and particularistic aspects to nationalism in general, and each and every individual case of nationalism to be precise, it is an assessment of the depth and linkage between nationalism and ideology that is of primary concern. First and foremost, it is imperative to establish whether or not nationalism is in fact an ideology. To do this it is important to initially present some contemporary views of nationalism as ideology before moving on to the more detailed and specific argument advanced by Michael Freeden as to how the entities of nationalism and ideology should be considered and how any assessment needs to contemplate the configuration of an ideology. If, using Freeden's reasoning, nationalism is found to be a full ideology, it should have a recognisable structure and a consistent core of beliefs. However, if it is found to be less than a full ideology, can nationalist sentiment and practice still promote itself as political opinion, albeit in what may be an ideologically erratic manner? Or, as is more likely to be the case, in a manner wherein it blends with other thought-practices? An example of the latter point may come about, for instance, if a study is made of third world national-ism, or developing world nationalism, of the type advanced by Frantz Fanon[12] and the New Left in the 1960s. Here it becomes evident that, at its core, this form of nationalism witnessed a fusion of nationalism and Marxism. Similarly, as will be highlighted later, Welsh nationalism started off as an expression of cultural sentiment. It then borrowed from ideologies such as liberalism and socialism. Into this environment Plaid Cymru was born. This goes some way to explain how it has no instantly recognisably coherent ideology at its nucleus. Given these examples, the question could be asked as to why most scholars still think that there is a coherent and identifiable ideology called nationalism, and why, in particular, those writers who have assessed Plaid Cymru's thought-practices, insist on seeing nationalism as the overriding ideology.

Nationalism and Ideology: Correlation and Contradiction

Historians and political analysts who have studied nationalism have invariably sought to use ideology as a catch-all term to sum up all the elements of what may be described as nationalist, or nationalistic, thought and practice. In contrast, Michael Freeden's article 'Is national-ism a distinct ideology?'[13] offers a critical examination of the conceptual structure of both nationalism and ideology. Freeden's consideration on ideology was not 'the pejorative Marxist usage of ideology as distorted consciousness, reflecting exploitative and alienating power relation-ships that can be overcome in a socialist society'.[14] Rather, Freeden focused upon what could be termed a more descriptive, as opposed to prescriptive, account of ideologies. This is because Freeden views ideologies as 'thought-patterns of individuals and groups in a society that relate to the way they comprehend and shape their political worlds.'[15] Freeden's analytical preference, therefore, could be described as being bottom up as opposed to top down or imposed, as it is inclusive and open-ended and seeks to incorporate all individuals and organisations, whether politically active or not, in a form of dialectic that involves channels of discourse and avenues for personal and combined practice.

Freeden's Ideological Distinctions

When Freeden progressed to explore whether nationalism is a distinct ideology, he stated that if nationalism was to be perceived, in the first instance, as 'an established ideology within a loose framework of family resemblances it will have to manifest a shared set of conceptual features over time and space.'[16] If, after that, nationalism was to be assigned to a category that was to be found further into the nucleus of the species of ideology, by registering itself as a distinct ideology, 'the core of nationalism, and the conceptual patterns it adopts, will have to be unique to itself alone.'[17] Furthermore, and most important of all in terms of the subject matter under consideration, Freeden commented that 'in order to be a full ideology it will need to provide a reasonably broad, if not comprehensive, range of answers to the political questions that societies generate.'[18] As this examination is exploring the ideological depth of Plaid Cymru's nationalism, and Plaid Cymru's thought-practices in general, in whatever form they may take, then it is envisaged that Freeden's classifications, given the aforementioned inclusive and non-exclusionary nature of his theoretical model, should provide the best basis from which to undertake this particular course of inquiry.

While Freeden delineates ideology along a spectrum that could be described as ascending from soft to hard conceptions, with increasing levels of commitment to comprehensiveness, further explanation of these various depths at which an ideology may be present needs to be recorded. First, an established ideology is one in which core concepts are observable. These interplay with, and are affected by, peripheral concepts and adjacent ideologies. Whereas a core concept is 'one that is both central to, and constitutive of, a particular ideology and therefore of the ideological community to which it gives inspiration and identity'[19]– for example liberty is a core concept in liberalism – a peripheral concept has two substructures that interface with the core. Freeden has defined the first of these peripheral concepts as the margin.[20] Concepts can drift from the core to the margin and back again. On this point, Freeden has cited 'natural rights gravitating from a core to a marginal position in liberal morphology whereas violence gravitated from a marginal to a core position in the development of fascism.'[21] These marginal concepts can have a detrimental effect on the efficacy and progression of an ideology; for example, the adherence to a moralistic Christianity – a concept on the margin – almost certainly impaired the neo-liberal ideology of the 'New Right' in the early 1990s.

The other kind of periphery is referred to as the perimeter.[22] The perimeter components of an ideology are often 'specific ideas or policy-proposals rather than fully fledged concepts'.[23] For example, proposals for the decriminalisation of cannabis, as part of a general philosophical stance on drug use, could be bracketed as a perimeter component of an ideology such as liberalism. Although these perimeter components are not essential to the survival of an ideology, they do provide ideologies with a 'layering of meaning'.[24] In other words, they can add substance to an ideology but they are not likely to be cancerous or outmoded in the sense that some concepts on the margin may be. Reverting back to the case of an established ideology, therefore, it is evident that it can be influenced by, and could possibly even be reliant upon, the movement and shaping of other concepts or ideologies. Hence, it can be said to be at the more malleable end of the spectrum of ideologies.

Identifying Adjacent Concepts

Also evident within ideologies are adjacent concepts. According to Freeden, 'the existence of concepts adjacent to the ideological core is essential to the formation of an ideology.'[25] Within these adjacent concepts there is a division between logical adjacency and cultural adjacency.[26] If, for instance, a notion of non-constraint is an ineliminable component of the notion of liberty, then logically adjacent concepts to non-constraint would include 'autonomy, self-determination, self-development, and power'.[27] These notions are what Freeden has referred to as 'necessary options and permutations which are invariably brought into play by any concretization of non-constraint'.[28] So, logically adjacent concepts are variations that help to make a concept less indefinite. If the logically adjacent concept of self-development is removed from the above list, it does not fatally weaken the concept of non-constraint. Its inclusion, however, offers another option and a chance to enhance the concept of non-constraint by enabling a degree of latitude in which self-development may be appropriated and incorporated.

Although logical adjacency increases choices on one level, sometimes those choices have to be set against social constraints. Hence, any decisions taken by groups or individuals will be 'socially mediated through the notion of cultural adjacency, which imposes further constraints on the morphology of political concepts.'[29] Freeden has pointed out that there are two types of cultural adjacency. The first operates within the existing framework of logical adjacency, so that a decision may be made to favour one aspect of logical adjacency over another, as this is the most apt preference given existing cultural, or individual, practices in any chosen society. In this instance, therefore, there is an internal restraint on choice.

The second type of cultural adjacency can be said to be a mechanism through which external restraint plays a part. This occurs when 'ostensibly paradoxical logical features may be culturally pressed into one concept.'[30] For example, the belief in the right to life for all human beings, whatever the circumstances that certain individuals may find themselves in, could be considered a logically adjacent concept within liberalism. In this setting, a belief in the sanctity of human life could tie in with the notion of non-constraint. However, if operating within a polity that has capital punishment on its statute book, then the external restraint upon the logically adjacent conception of the right to life would not be allowed to flourish. This could occur in a society that has, for all intents and purposes, a liberal polity that has the freedom of the individual as a core concept of its political ideology.

Moving on from an assessment of what constitutes an established ideology, a distinct ideology is a specific body of concepts that has its uniquely identifiable structure, techniques and dynamics. For an ideology to be distinct, it has to go-alone on certain issues. It has the channels to do this as it develops independently. However, there has to be a distinctive pattern to its development and in this sense it decontests concepts in a way unique to itself. Within distinct ideologies there is also a sense of genealogy – a sense of its own origins – that established ideologies do not necessarily contain. A prima facie analysis of what constitutes a distinct ideology could, therefore, view this type of ideology as stronger than the type of ideology labelled as established.

Critics and criticisms of distinct ideologies can, nevertheless, be found. For a Marxist such as Georg Lukacs, for example, the genealogy required for a distinct ideology to unfold would, inevitably, be wrapped in bourgeois historical practice. If, as Lukacs has argued, 'intellectual genesis must be identical in principle with historical genesis,'[31] it is a logical step to equate hardened ideological structures – which a distinct ideology would need to be a part of – with being producers of false consciousness. While accepting that that is a Marxist judgement on the bourgeois influence and practice of ideologies, the criticism that a distinct ideology can be construed as being an enclosed and narrow

ideology, in the way that it can decontest concepts using its own for-
mula and genealogical precedents, is without doubt a valid one.

Ascertaining the Nature of a Full Ideology

If criticism can be made of a distinct ideology, then the case against
excessive adherence to an ideology becomes ever more acute if a full
ideology is examined. This is because a full ideology offers a far greater
range of concepts and solutions. To anyone professing an anti-ideology,
or ideo-sceptic, position, therefore, a full ideology can present itself
as a frightening prospect. But it is only the content on offer that really
threatens, as a full ideology is merely a vessel containing a comprehensive set of views. The full aspect is specified by the range and breadth
of the actual thought-practices. Its content is simply a series of propositions, not a directive, and there are exigencies in any liberal democratic
system that narrow the scope for that ideology's practice; in liberal
democracies, for example, the government does not tell individuals
whom to marry or how to spend their money. This is because there is
a public–private divide that is not touched upon, aside from in certain
exceptional circumstances, even by those who advocate full ideologies.
In the liberal democracies, therefore, there is little fear of a full ideology – such as liberalism or socialism – adopting totalitarian tendencies.
One thing that does occur in these liberal democracies, however, is
that political parties have to present to the general public their ideas
for governing the state. Hence, they need to submit a comprehensive
doctrine of their aims and intentions. However, the question invariably
arises as to whether that comprehensive doctrine sheds light on whether
that particular political party's thought-practices satisfy the conditions
for being referred to as an ideology, full or otherwise.

Sectors that a full ideology may comprehensively embrace – sectors,
conceivably, that may not be covered under the other variants of ideology – could be areas such as the economy or the notion of citizenship.
With regard to an issue such as the economy, a full ideology would
look to provide a thorough set of justifications for economic policies
that would be conducted under the remit of that ideology. For instance,
the reorganisation of the economy and the redistribution of wealth
generated within that economy are concepts within the morphology of
socialism. Being a full ideology, socialism's tentacles reach into virtually every aspect of social and political life and socialist policy tends
to be universal in its application. Conversely, feminism, for example,
which cannot be granted the same full ideology label, is restricted as
an ideology because it is 'often indifferent or even silent when it deals

with some political concepts – justice, democracy, rights, political obligation, to name a few – to which many women and men, not solely liberals, attach importance.'[32]

The idea of an active citizenship, and citizenship rights, is another way in which a full ideology, in particular liberalism, may be evident. Citizenship can be seen to be an increasingly important component within contemporary liberalism. Active citizenship, in its purest sense, would involve every citizen making decisions and working within a community structure in order to achieve some goal, or to implement an agreed set of standards. Although citizenship as a sense of civic duty can be juxtaposed with the belief in, and practice of, education in liberal societies – as citizenship is invariably endorsed through educational establishments – in an anarchist society, for example, citizenship would have more moral substance to it than the rational explanation for it offering a conception of the good, as presented by liberals and liberalism. This is because the idea of the free-thinking autonomous individual, represented through libertarianism, is even more central to anarchist ideology than it is to liberal ideology. It is also because, as a rule, liberalism advances the state as a mechanism for keeping individuals under a certain restraint, in a rational and legalistic sense, while anarchism relies on individual moral judgement. However, both liberalism and anarchism have strands of opinion within them that would take issue with this assessment. So, even within full ideologies, there is still a variance of opinion as to what are considered to be core concepts.

Although ideologies are professedly unencumbered, enabling them, in theory, to attempt to construct a resolute and ideologically compatible opinion to each political conundrum that arises – and thus, supposedly, leaving no room for political vacuums – the fact remains that if one body of opinion can be so capacious in its analysis it could be construed as having an intensely totalitarian ring about it. Freeden cited an example of liberalism – a full ideology – feeding off one of its core concepts of liberty through self-development to take it on a journey through peripheral and adjacent concerns, such as the right to welfare and education for all.[33] This appears to be something of a conceptual error on Freeden's part. A full ideology cannot infringe upon each specific conceptual bloc as it so wishes. If it does so, then it surely reverts to being merely an established ideology. Given Freeden's descriptions of the various levels of ideology, a distinct ideology would be more potent than a full ideology. It would be less comprehensive in outlook but it would be less prone to influences from perimeter and adjacent concerns.

Evaluating Nationalism's Morphology

If nationalism is to be registered, to whatever degree, as an ideology, it must display 'one of two structures';[34] that is it must have either a full or a thin-centred morphology. A full morphology, while containing 'a general plan of public policy that a specific society requires',[35] must also embody 'particular interpretations and configurations of all the major political concepts'.[36] This is the comprehensive agenda most observably represented by the aforementioned full ideology. Alternatively, Freeden put forward the notion of a thin-centred morphology, which he believed would incorporate 'a restricted core attached to a narrower range of political concepts'.[37] Freeden continued by citing the absence of welfare policies from nationalist pronouncements as an indication that nationalism should be regarded as a body of thought more in tune with his description of a thin-centred morphology than a full morphology. As he claimed, 'a thin-centred ideology is … limited in ideational ambitions and scope.'[38] In Freeden's view, therefore, thin-centred ideology does not specifically address what counts as a political issue. So, offering a thin conception suggests ideological content without necessarily being a coherent or comprehensive ideology. This could prove to be important when considering Plaid Cymru's ideology.

Although there may appear to be a certain unfairness in describing nationalism's objective to press for national self-determination, and the placing of the nation at the centre of political life, as ideationally circumscribed, it is nevertheless accurate to describe nationalism's paucity of ideas in the field of domestic politics and public policy as limited in scope. This 'structural inability to offer complex ranges of argument'[39] is evident in what Freeden termed 'narrow nationalism'.[40] Consequently, 'the many chains of ideas one would normally expect to find stretching from the general and abstract to the concrete and practical, from the core to the periphery, as well as in the reverse direction, are simply absent.'[41] One could argue that Freeden, by using the term narrow nationalism, was eliminating civic and liberal nationalisms from his field of inquiry. But then it could also be asked whether nationalism really has a goal beyond the procuring of national self-determination?

It could be stated by nationalists, in their defence, that the civic and liberal strands of nationalism do at least attempt to fashion a society using a more comprehensive plan of action than that used by other narrower, and more extreme, forms of nationalisms: forms that content themselves with offering a compressed focus for opinion against whosoever, in their eyes, represents the Other. Freeden's rejoinder to this was that nationalism – and he judges civic and liberal forms of nationalism as indications of its chameleon-like nature rather than an indication that

this provides proof of weightier and more extensive ideological mani-
festations – 'fails to meet the criteria of a comprehensive ideology.'[42]
This is because nationalism's 'conceptual structure is incapable of providing on its own a solution to questions of social justice, distribution
of resources, and conflict-management which mainstream ideologies
address.'[43] Strands of nationalism are thus trapped. It is open to debate
as to whether they can or cannot open up to a more comprehensive
all-embracing agenda as long as they maintain the core concepts that
register them as nationalist. One who believed they cannot was Lord
Acton. He noted that, because of their limitations, nationalisms 'cannot
serve as a basis for the reconstruction of civil society … but they may
influence it with advantage.'[44] The advantage for nationalism in a circumstance such as this would be in the fact that, having gained the position from which it is able to influence with advantage, the civil society
that Acton cited would be reconstructed using concepts borrowed from
other ideologies. What would be in place, however, would be the framework of a polity that had nationalism, with its core concepts of prioritising the nation and the nationality represented thereof, as an omniscient
presence. Having reached its goal of national self-determination, a set
of policies from either left or right of the political spectrum could then
be pursued. In strategic terms, at least, this could be something that may
please Plaid Cymru's political leaders and theoreticians.

Problems arise if, or when, nationalism is used as the sole vehicle to
embrace and express the full range of policy matters. For instance, any
form of civic or liberal nationalism, having been strongly influenced by
the thought-practices of liberalism, could never take on a comprehensive mantle as long as it adheres to the core concepts of nationalism.
Therefore, nationalism has to oscillate between what Freeden called
'the second and third possibilities',[45] namely 'between being a distinct
thin-centred ideology and being a component of other, already existing, ideologies.'[46] Although Freeden admitted that complexity existed
within the various instances of nationalist thought and practice, he
saw core concepts as 'necessary for identifying any given instance as
belonging to the family of nationalisms.'[47] It is important, therefore,
to consider what Freeden believed nationalism's core concepts to be,
some of which may be applicable to Plaid Cymru.

Freeden's Core Concepts of Nationalism

First, Freeden identified the prioritisation of the group element, the
nation, as 'the key constituting and identifying framework for human
beings and their practices.'[48] This element – the nation, heralded, as it is,

as both the bedrock of power and the source for inspiration – cannot be modified. Without the structures and ideas, both concrete and abstract, which constitute the already existent nation, or the conception of the nation that is to be attained through nationalist thought and practice, nationalism would be a redundant ideology. However, it is important to acknowledge that this nation, when conceived and then assembled, is not duty bound to reflect, in its socio-political make-up, any one group of concerns.

The view of nationalists, and nationalist thought as a whole, is that what is of primary importance is the fact that a communal body exists that is recognisable as the nation; the nation, for nationalists, being composed of a group of people who share, according to Karl Deutsch, 'a heritage of common meanings and memories',[49] and who have a sense of geographical demarcation and historical alignment along ethnic, cultural, linguistic or political grounds. On the other hand, theorists such as Alan Finlayson have argued that the social values that prevail within nationalist discourse – the discourse of community, communal values, etc. – are a construct of political discourse. Following on from this, Finlayson maintains that the nation is 'the product of meaning systems and a meaning system in itself, a principle of internal cohesion.'[50] The differences between these two positions is in the way that many nationalist commentators portray communities as given or set, as if almost preordained, whereas the view of Finalyson was that the nation encompasses elements that have evolved through social interaction and the discourse of individuals for whom any concept of the nation would have been a purely abstract notion.

Returning to the concrete reality, through an acknowledgement that the nation, as the space in which a specific mode of politics operates, does exist, the debates as to whether the nation is to comprise a polity that is essentially liberal or illiberal, pluralistic or homogeneous is one for the various strands of nationalist thought to undertake. What is relevant here, however, is how the thought-practices of Plaid Cymru takes into account the possibilities offered up through these various strands of opinion.

Having thought up and constructed the nation, nationalists assign to their nation a 'positive valorisation'.[51] It is here that the border between a reasonable and non-discriminatory level of patriotism and pride in the achievements of one's homeland or place or birth comes into contact with xenophobic behaviour and fear of external forces. Although Freeden was correct to emphasise positive valorisation, as this indeed is an essential element within nationalism, any endorsement of the supposed fortitude of the nation as being intrinsically positive in its function is contentious. Here, splits again occur between nationalists representing the civic and narrow parameters of nationalist thought. Whereas those on the civic parameter may take an egalitarian or non-hierarchical viewpoint of the valorisation of one's own nation – mindful that the international political system operates principally along nation-state lines and recognising that, in theory at least, the claims and aspirations of each nation in international terms is equally valid – those favouring a narrower nationalism may find this egalitarian and non-hierarchical position far less appealing and, consequently, they would vigorously endorse the positive valorisation aspect as a core concept within nationalism. Therefore, as is evident within this second core concept, nationalism is forever inducing its own internal debates that require consideration and clarification.

The third core concept supervenes, and is engendered by, the first two core concepts. It is the 'desire to give politico-institutional expression to the first two core concepts.'[52] This is essential because nationalism cannot operate solely as a hypothesis. Although an abstract conception of an ideal society is a perfectly valid theoretical tool for advocates of nationalism to employ, ultimately, however, a process must exist in order to translate nationalist thoughts into nationalist political practices. The third concept, therefore, shores up nationalist ideas and grounds them in actual political practices and pragmatic aspirations. This is fundamental because in the final reckoning 'all types of nationalism seek institutional recognition.'[53]

The fourth Freedenite core concept within nationalism is that 'space and time are considered to be crucial determinants of social identity.'[54] What is evidenced here is that these crucial determinants act as signifiers. This is important because nationalism has a distinctive story to tell for a particular place. To try to show how crucial determinants act in each specific case the following example may prove insightful. It is sensible at this point not to cite an example of a man born in Wales as the issue of bilingualism – fluency in both the Welsh and English languages – is far more likely to come into contention than it is in the example proffered. Furthermore, the Welsh language, as a determinant for Welsh nationalism, and as a concept within Plaid Cymru's ideology, will be considered in some detail at a later stage.

A white man born in Leeds, for example, considers himself English, and is seen as such by others, because he is the holder of certain characteristics that are identifiable in space and time. These are, specifically, the fact that he is white – the pigmentation most commonly associated with English people – the fact that he is resident within the geographical space known as England and the fact that he has almost certainly spent the vast majority of his time within that geographical space and considers it to be his home. Having been educated in England, with English as his primary if not sole language, he will also have been immersed in the culture of that country and he will have been informed of his country's history at school, through the media and by his elders. Finding its way into this learning curve there will undoubtedly have been myths and stories about the glories of his nation's past (Hastings, Agincourt, etc.). All of this nurturing does not necessarily make that man a nationalist, but he has all of the components in place through which he could, if he so wished, make claims to be highly representative of the English nation, and possibly to be committed to the idea of an ultimate national destiny.[55] To turn these claims into nationalist ideological claims, however, he would need to exhibit the fifth core concept that Freeden has identified.

This fifth core concept is a 'sense of belonging and membership in which sentiment and emotion play an important role.'[56] Some difficulties can arise from this component, however, as sentiment, for instance, is a constituent part of each and every shade of political thought. We are not a community of abstract, dispassionate human beings and no single political doctrine is purely rational. Likewise, when addressing the issue of membership, there has to be a clear view of who is a member of whatever community or ethnic group, whose decision it is to say who belongs, who is refused membership and what the members who belong to the community are to make of those who do not.

As to the claims for this concept overall, then our aforementioned man from Leeds is an interesting case in point. He could display all of the characteristics required of someone purporting to be an English nationalist but, at the same time, he may be uncaring or unemotional about the nation in which he resides, and to which, nationalists would insist, he belongs. So sentiment and emotion are vital to the equation in order to provoke a nationalistic fervour that is identifiable both on an intensely personal level and as an everyday source of motivation and encouragement for the individual and the community as a whole. In this sense, emotion and belonging can be reified by nationalists in order for these dispositions to be utilised as instruments of policy.

Similarly, sentiment is a vital cog in the machinery of nationalism because 'nationalism is a rare instance of enlightenment-generated rational political thought that acknowledges the political importance of emotion when pointed in certain directions.'[57] Interestingly, all theories rely on emotion but nationalism, in this instance, actually acknowledges it. As for the charge of rationalism, although this is not true of all nationalisms as the rational aspect is more peculiar to civic than ethnic nationalisms – ethnic nationalisms being remnants of the counter-Enlightenment – this onus on sentiment and emotion induces a commitment to the nation – viewed, as it is, in concrete terms by adherents of nationalism – which is calculably greater than any feeling of loyalty to abstract notions such as civil society, or indeed any sense of universalism that would dampen any fear of 'the other'. Summing up this emotionally charged sense of political obligation, Heinrich von Treitschke commented that 'in all my life I have never once thought of my moral obligations towards [civil] society, but I think constantly of my countrymen, whom I seek to honour as much as I can.'[58]

These core concepts are not set in stone, however, and neither are they 'sufficient to account for the complexity of all forms and instances of nationalism.'[59] What the core concepts manage to do, nevertheless, is to provide a yardstick from which any given set of ideas purporting to be, or already classified as, nationalist can be scrutinised in order to ascertain whether or not they do actually qualify for entry into the 'family of nationalisms'.[60] Also, Freeden did not claim that those core concepts are invariant. The core concepts of nationalism are open to various readings and interpretations depending on how they adapt to social and historical change and how they interact with adjacent and peripheral concepts. Despite the acknowledgement that this adds to the 'richness ... and irreconcilable diversities'[61] found within varieties of nationalism, Freeden pointed out that 'the core concepts of nationalism cannot rival the possibilities available to the mainstream ideologies such as conservatism, liberalism or socialism – all of which have core conceptual structures which permit a far fuller range of responses to socio-political factors.'[62] These socio-political factors are crucial players as far as Freeden is concerned because it is they that forge the 'extraneous proximities'[63] that decide whether or not the nationalist core constitutes a thin-centred ideology or whether it is 'assimilated into existing ideological factors.'[64] It would appear, therefore, that nationalism's core concepts are open to influence from the vagaries of contingent factors to a far greater degree than the core concepts of other ideological families.

Nationalism's exposure to adjacent and peripheral concepts, and other contingent factors that force it to re-evaluate or react accordingly, can be examined more closely. Liberty is one useful example. If liberty is applied in the emancipatory sense of liberty from colonial domination, then the nationalist can use it with full justification because it is the Freedenite core concept of the nation that is the body that is being liberated. If liberty is being applied in a civil or domestic sense, then again this is relatively uncontroversial if, in nationalist parlance, the identifiable members of that nation – its populace – are allowed the liberty to live their lives as nationals, and, if they so wish, nationalists, in a contractarian-style agreement with both their fellow nationals and their nation.

Where problems may arise, nevertheless, is if liberty, in the form of freedom of movement and expression, is executed in a manner that may be detrimental to non-nationals or non-nationalists. One example of this could be institutionalised discrimination against ethnic minorities or refugees. Liberty can also cause difficulties for nationalists, if advocated in a universal or supranational sense. An instance of this application of liberty could be a legal decision that may be determined by a body higher than a national government or judiciary (e.g. the European Court of Justice). Despite the inevitable protests from those who maintain that there should not be any higher authority than the nation-state, or those nationalists for whom any external interference is tantamount to a denial of nationhood, and is thus an infringement on their rights as citizens of their nation, then as long as the nation-state is a signatory to any international or supranational agreements that legal decision will be binding upon the nation, and all those within its borders.

All of the above examples of liberty in practice are feasible or factual scenarios. However, the last two examples are specific examples wherein liberty can have negative connotations for anyone professing to be a nationalist. Nationalism, as a body of ideas, is therefore put under pressure when an adjacent concept such as liberty is adapted in various ways. Adherents to nationalism may well have to counteract the last two negative conceptions of liberty – negative in the eyes of the nationalist that is – by either standing firm in the face of rulings that have an external source or, more realistically, accepting that they must soften their nationalist stances to incorporate these eventualities. When these issues arise, other concepts, such as internationalism, democracy, human rights and egalitarianism, enter the forum. Advocates of nationalism are then left with three choices. They can adapt their position to absorb these other concepts, or engage them in a dialectic process, or they can maintain an intransigent position that immediately compresses the expanse of ideas and concepts that are available for nationalism to utilise. When this choice arises, nationalism seeks expression in what are known as its 'host-vessels'.[65]

The Notion of Host-Vessels

Host-vessels are other ideologies that accommodate, and to varying degrees absorb, nationalist thought-practices. However, these host-vessels maintain their own identities because their core concepts and objectives differ from the core concepts and objectives evident within nationalist or other contending ideologies. Could it be argued, then, that nationalism has limits in both an ideational and a practical sense? For instance, if a certain brand of nationalism is advancing liberationist or secessionist claims, then it has a definite objective. However, 'once the goals of nationalism are attained it has, like a realized utopia, nowhere to go.'[66] This, though, supposes that nationalism is a political goal that is embedded in a particular form of socio-cultural thought-practice at a certain point in time. If this political goal were achieved, then, bereft of ideas to propel it forward, nationalism would attain 'longer life only when contained in larger vessels.'[67]

If Freeden's thesis is true, then how does nationalism show itself within its host-vessels? Freeden has remarked on how nationalist concepts can be found within liberal ideologies. Liberalism, with its conception of liberty and respect for each and every individual, and liberal multiculturalists, with their onus on group rights and representation, provoke nationalists into considering a reassessment of the concepts of nationhood and identity. As homogeneity is on the wane, the existence of states in which multiple identities are a reality presents nationalists with a series of dilemmas. Do these nationalists incorporate liberal and multicultural positions into their belief systems while concurrently maintaining that the nation remains the paramount centre from which identity and inspiration can be attained? Consequently, if there is a compromise, or a synthesis of nationalist and liberal opinion, championing an additional national identity and a sense of solidarity may be feasible for minority ethnic groups who 'want to feel at home in the society to which they or their forebears have moved.'[68] However, this does not have to entail a surrendering of minority claims or identities. It is possible for ethnic minorities within any heterogeneous society to adopt this commonality and sense of national purpose while simultaneously 'preserving formative elements of their separate identities.'[69] This acceptance can be termed inclusivist and it is a stance that is adopted by those of a liberal or civic nationalist disposition. Alternatively, other host vessels can be summoned up that may not be as accommodating to non-nationalist voices.

Conservatism, Nationalism and Historical Continuity

It could be contended that conservatism strikes an immediate chord with nationalists in the sense that both make appeals to the past in the hope of finding justification for the present – more prominent in conservatism's case – and a path for the future – more apt in the examples of nationalisms that are attempting to construct a prototype nation rather than those that are merely consolidating the existing one. Whatever model is highlighted, nevertheless, the invocation of an 'organicist conception of community',[70] a conception that accentuates historical continuity, can often be found in both conservative and nationalist discourse. Occasionally both discourses draw near; a case in point being Edmund Burke's *Reflections on the Revolution in France*, which, as Alan Finlayson has commented, as well as being 'an advancement of the conservative view of evolutionary politics, is also a strikingly nationalist document.'[71] Although this organicist conception of community is undoubtedly a core concept for conservatives, for nationalists it is perceived as being more of an adjacent concept. In this sense, nationalists may find the organicist conception of community useful, but they may also be inclined to put it to one side if, through geographical or political realignment, they are attempting to develop a national identity and a sense of nationhood that is in its nascent stages. Likewise, liberal nationalists, for example, could play down the theme of historical continuity if they wished to incorporate recent ethnic additions or minority cultures into their scheme of nation building. While they can use socio-historical and geographical grounds for their nationalist bases, and conservative reasoning for the preservation of established communities, they can adopt liberal concepts when it comes to manufacturing political structures that take heed of cultural and demographic realities. In this example, therefore, a certain type of liberal, inclusive nationalism has moulded a fresh ideological position out of its involvement with its host-vessels of liberalism and conservatism.

If an inclusivist position is to be discarded by nationalists, then another host-vessel, fascism, could be instituted. Freeden has noted that, 'alone among the major ideological families, fascism recognises the nation as a core concept.'[72] But it is not merely confined to a simple recognition of the nation as the focal point for social and political expression, such as may be attributed to a nationalist reading, because fascism 'attaches the concept of the nation to an extreme valorization of one's own nation.'[73] This extreme valorisation is far more pronounced and activist than the positive valorisation that was earlier specified as being a core concept of nationalism. Furthermore, this extreme valorisation 'necessitates the concept, as well as practice, of violence as a manifestation of political will and power.'[74] What needs to be assessed when nationalism and fascism are held up for comparison, or if a specific type of nationalism is dubbed fascist, is the extent to which valorisation of one's nation is positive or extreme. The use of violence as a political instrument to consolidate the valorisation is one measure, but that may be just a gauge of xenophobic or radical nationalist activity as opposed to an indisputable representation of fascist ideology.[75]

Although Freeden preferred to leave socialism outside his list of host-vessels, this particular analysis will include it, as the concept of community, while not being a core concept of nationalism, does indeed link socialism and nationalism. Furthermore, the socialist state, in practice if not so much in theory, is a nation-state and is thus defined, and defended, as such. Although it must be noted that any ideological conjunction of socialism and nationalism is tenable in a conceptual sense, two instances that can be cited – albeit that they are of somewhat incoherent practice – are those of Ceausescu's socialist nationalism in Romania and Stalin's nationalistic socialism, or socialism in one country, in the Soviet Union. The socialist belief in common ownership places the community as the guardian and executor of economic control. This is invariably managed at a state level and thus places economic and social goods, however regionalised or compartmentalised, onto a national platform. The nation is therefore the highest form of community though, given a socialist interpretation, it may be viewed in a more material, instrumentalist sense rather than a symbolic and emotional one. Nevertheless, the notion of community, which features prominently in socialist ideology – its components and its importance to the cultivation of national characteristics – will also be a key factor when the thought-practices of Plaid Cymru are discussed in more detail later.

What arises, therefore, from this and other examples, is a supposition that although nationalism has its host-vessels, and although there is interplay and a certain dialectical engagement between the various ideologies, nationalism deserves to be regarded, at the very least, as a cogent body of opinion – if not as a full ideology – as its ideas and principles extend across, and are influential across, the political spectrum. The structure of this distinctive body of opinion is most visible when the nation is centred. Peter Alter noted this when he commented on how nationalism assigns a superior and more universal significance to the nation than 'other bodies of joint social action such as class, religious community or the family.'[76] Forging a sense of national consciousness that is mediated by education and party organisation is another essential component of nationalism's structure. Once tapped into, national consciousness can then act in both an inclusive and an exclusive sense. It can reinforce bias and a sense of tradition and continuity among the national group, or it can act as a barrier to local or universal appeals that could entice people to look elsewhere for a sense of reassurance and political solidarity. This also applies when nationalism seeks to keep out ideologies, such as communism or anarchism, whose core components issue a challenge to nationalism's prioritisation of the nation above class organisation or individual liberty.

When considering the extent of Plaid Cymru's nationalism, and whether that nationalism can be labelled as an established, a distinct or a full ideology, it is important to record the manner in which Plaid Cymru views the nation and how it seeks to prioritise the ethnic group known as the Welsh over and above other ethnic bodies, if that is indeed what the party intends to do. The extent to which issues such as the language and the socio-cultural recognition of Welshness take centre-stage in the ideational development of the party will also come into play as a tool for analysing the depth of Plaid Cymru's commitment to a nationalist agenda.

The next chapter will focus upon the genealogy of the party and its morphology in its formative years, what this assessment will term its early period. In this and subsequent chapters, the political pronouncements and ideological stances taken by the party, and its individual members, will be analysed in order to gauge if there is continuity of opinion, or, alternatively, to assess whether there are ruptures and disruptions in the thought-practices of Plaid Cymru. To do this, certain key theoreticians, people within the party leadership and some of the party's community activists will be focused upon in order to estimate any emerging patterns or variations in thought and practice; however, it must be noted from the outset that these are individual reflections and may not be indicative of party thought as a whole.

Notes

1. Michael Freeden, 'Practising ideology and ideological practices', *Political Studies*, vol. 48, 2000, p. 304.
2. Ibid.
3. Michael Freeden, 'What is special about ideologies?', *Journal of Political Ideologies*, vol. 6, no. 1, 2001, p. 6.
4. Ibid.
5. Ibid.
6. Michael Freeden, *Ideologies and Political Theory* (Oxford: Clarendon Press, 1996), p. 14.
7. Michael Freeden, 'Practising ideology and ideological practices', p. 303.
8. Ibid.
9. Ibid.
10. Ibid., p. 302.
11. Thomas Hobbes, *Leviathan* (London: Penguin, 1993).
12. Frantz Fanon, *The Wretched of the Earth* (New York: Grove Press, 1963).
13. Michael Freeden, 'Is nationalism a distinct ideology?', *Political Studies*, vol. XLVI, 1998, pp. 748–765.
14. Ibid., p. 749.
15. Ibid.
16. Ibid.
17. Ibid., p. 750.

18. Ibid.
19. Terence Ball, 'From "core" to "sore" concepts: ideological innovation and conceptual change', *Journal of Political Ideologies*, vol. 4, no. 3, 1999, p. 392.
20. Michael Freeden, *Ideologies and Political Theory*, p. 78.
21. Ibid.
22. Ibid.
23. Ibid., p. 80.
24. Ibid.
25. Ibid., p. 78.
26. Ibid., p. 68.
27. Ibid.
28. Ibid.
29. Ibid., p. 69.
30. Ibid., p. 71.
31. Georg Lukacs, *History and Class Consciousness* (London: Merlin Press, 1990), p. 155.
32. Michael Freeden, *Ideologies and Political Theory*, p. 525.
33. Michael Freeden, 'Is nationalism a distinct ideology?', p. 750.
34. Ibid.
35. Ibid.
36. Ibid.
37. Ibid.
38. Ibid.
39. Ibid.
40. Ibid.
41. Ibid.
42. Ibid., p. 751.
43. Ibid.
44. Ibid.
45. Ibid.
46. Ibid.
47. Ibid., p. 752.
48. Ibid.
49. Peter Alter, *Nationalism*, 2nd edn (London: Hodder Arnold, 1994), p. 6.
50. Alan Finlayson, *Ideology, Discourse and Nationalism* (London: Routledge, 1998), p. 107.
51. Michael Freeden, 'Is nationalism a distinct ideology?', p. 754.
52. Ibid., p. 752.
53. Ibid., p. 754.
54. Ibid., p. 752.
55. Ibid., p. 754.
56. Ibid., p. 752.
57. Ibid., p. 754.
58. Ibid., p. 761.
59. Ibid., p. 752.
60. Ibid.
61. Ibid.
62. Ibid.
63. Ibid.
64. Ibid.

65. Ibid., p. 759.
66. Ibid.
67. Ibid.
68. David Miller, *On Nationality* (Oxford: Oxford University Press, 1995), p. 138.
69. Michael Freeden, 'Is nationalism a distinct ideology?', p. 761.
70. Ibid., p. 762.
71. Alan Finlayson, *Ideology, Discourse and Nationalism*, p. 105.
72. Michael Freeden, 'Is nationalism a distinct ideology?', p. 763.
73. Ibid.
74. Ibid.
75. Ibid.
76. Peter Alter, *Nationalism*, p. 11.

III

THE IDEOLOGICAL DEVELOPMENT OF EARLY PLAID CYMRU

Introduction

This chapter will, initially, look at the genealogy and development of nationalist thought in Wales. This genealogical survey is important as it is, rightly or wrongly, nationalism that is the ideology with which Plaid Cymru is primarily associated. Therefore, tracing nationalist thought in Wales should prove more productive for this investigation into Plaid Cymru's morphology than, for instance, a study of environmentalism or social democracy in Wales. Hence, although both environmentalism and social democracy may be found to have had some impact on Plaid Cymru's ideology, it would be unrealistic to trace the genealogy of every ideology present within Wales. To these ends, therefore, this chapter will examine how certain social and political events of the last 800 years or so have acted as catalysts out of which nationalists took inspiration and how these historical events aided the development of ideological concepts within nationalism, such as myth-making, language prioritisation and conservation, and the positive valorisation of the nation. Furthermore, the formation of Plaid Cymru in 1925 will be analysed to discover if there was an ideological vacuum that made the founding, and introduction onto the Welsh political scene, of a nationalist political party an apposite action.

When considering Plaid Cymru's determining political philosophy, the party's key theoretician in its formative years, and one of its great intellectual figures, Saunders Lewis, will be closely scrutinised, using Freeden's ideological classifications, in order to understand what Lewis's exact ideological standpoint was, and how his views helped to configure the party's ideology. This is not to say, however, that Lewis was the only person to influence and arrange Plaid Cymru's thought in the early years of its existence. Hence, other leading figures in Plaid Cymru at that time will also feature in order to see how their approach either complemented or contradicted the views of Saunders Lewis.

Nevertheless, Lewis remains a key figure in many respects, and therefore his name and his viewpoints will predominate in this discussion.

Any assessment of ideology after the stewardship of Saunders Lewis, however, cannot take place unless an examination of the party's initial political ideology takes place. This will set the scene for a far more detailed dissection of the ideologies associated with the party and the core and peripheral concepts that amalgamate to form Plaid Cymru's ideology that will occur in the later chapters.

Origins and Genealogy of Nationalist Thought in Wales

Before an assessment can be made as to the ideological stances of leading party figures – the policy-making elite that becomes representative of the party's persona – within Plaid Cymru, the genealogy of nationalism, and nationalist thought, needs to be ascertained. It would be difficult, without this assessment, to establish the socio-economic and cultural worlds from which the individuals who helped to shape Plaid Cymru's ideology evolved their political ideas. To commence, therefore, it is valuable to consider the work of Thomas Combs on the development of nationalism in Wales, not least because Combs saw the development of nationalism occurring in phases. If this is so, then ideological breaks must have taken place over the course of time. This is insightful not only because it provides a series of epochs in which assessment can take place, but also because it pre-empts one of the lines of argument that will be developed, namely that the ideology of Plaid Cymru, arguably Welsh nationalism in its most conspicuous political guise, has also evolved in phases, specifically early and modern, with a contemporary or late modern phase, in which the party currently resides. Although it could be argued that these phases are merely part of a maturing process or simplistic evolution, this exploration will maintain that different personalities operating at specific times, and having to react to unique sets of circumstances, create new ideological directions or breaks from which new policies and thought-practices emerge. Combs's writings on the genealogy of nationalist thought in Wales, therefore, may prove insightful on several fronts.

Combs's Pre-political Phase

Thomas Combs identified four stages of development for nationalism in Wales. These were 'the pre-political phase; the Liberal Party phase; the Labour Party phase; and the contemporary phase associated with the electoral success of Plaid Cymru.'[1] Although each feeds into contemporary nationalist thought and practice, and each can claim to be a progenitor of contemporary Welsh nationalism, it is reasonable to maintain that it is the pre-political phase that is the vital one. This is because it is this phase that was the myth-maker: the historical epoch that offers nationalists space in which to transpose their stories about a golden era or, alternatively, a period of domination by an outside force. Both these myths seek to reinforce, or offer reasons for, the adherence to the idea of ourselves in contention to the, not to be trusted, other. This interpretation is vitally important to notions of nationalism worldwide. Hence, it is not a feature of any Welsh model alone.

The 1536 Act of Union is a symbolic date in this pre-political phase as it laid provision for a schism in Welsh society along linguistic lines. Whereas the Welsh economic elite adopted English as the language of law and business, the overwhelming majority of Welsh people continued to communicate through the medium of the Welsh language. What was created in 1536, therefore, was a sense of linguistic opposition: opposition to the rule of law, primarily, as speaking Welsh in government circles, or any other official environment, was perceived to be in breach of legal norms. This estrangement between the languages, and what each represented in the eyes of the other, continued until the 1990s. Although there still remain fragments of dissent on either side, the reality of a bilingual Wales has been recognised, de jure, only since the Welsh Language Act of 1993 and, de facto, by politicians and public alike in the last decade or so. What must be reasserted here, however, is that these events depict the genealogy of nationalism and nationalistic events in Wales and are, therefore, not solely attributable as the basis for Plaid Cymru's formation and subsequent political positioning. Nevertheless, the references to how the language played its part in contemporary Welsh politics, through, most notably, Gwynfor Evans's stance on the establishment of a Welsh-language television station, and its resultant effects on the ideology and standing of Plaid Cymru, will be addressed at a later stage.

So while the Act of Union of 1536, and the subsequent 1543 Act, were actual, as opposed to mythological, junctures that occupy the minds of Welsh nationalists, there is little doubt that the events around this period, and the centuries of English incursions beforehand, have helped to establish a grudge mentality in some Welsh people, who see the troubles of Wales bound up with what they regard as these unwanted impositions. Indeed, it could be argued that any residual Welsh grievances that surface today have their roots in the defeat of the last native Prince of Wales, Llywelyn ap Gruffydd, in 1282, and the subsequent incorporation of Wales by England, endorsed by the Statute of Rhuddlan in 1284. The Statute affirms that the country of Wales and her inhabitants would be put 'under feudal authority and annex and unify the said country with the crown of the Kingdom (of England) in one political body.'[2] Despite the fact that the Statute of Rhuddlan was repealed in 1887 under the Statute Law Revision Act,[3] the years 1282 and 1284, along with the dates of the Acts of Union, 1536 and 1543, remain potent reminders of Wales's suppression as an independent nation. It is understandable, therefore, to observe how nationalists have focused in on these dates in order to build up nationalist opinion. Subsequently, how these dates and events have acquired folklore status for some within Wales becomes explicable.

This pre-political phase, therefore, has resonances to this day. Although the Welsh language provides a line of transmission from one era to another, the myth-making element, stemming from the pre-political phase, is exemplified in the case of Owain Glyndwr. Whilst acknowledging that Glyndwr actually existed, it is nevertheless evident that the liberationist, or anti-English Crown, deeds performed by Glyndwr have been romanticised over time in order to create an iconic figure that contemporary Welsh people can find inspirational – the notion of the heroic figure who had a vision of a flourishing independent Wales. Hence, Glyndwr's aspiring Welsh nation of the early fifteenth century provides a paradigm, however tenuous, for nationalists in modern-day Wales.

Language, Myth-Making and Freeden

Having identified language and myth-making at this early pre-political phase, it is important to link these two concepts to Michael Freeden's interpretation of nationalism's principles to establish whether or not he regards them as core values. It is practicable to make a judgement that the myth-making element can be extrapolated from both the fourth and fifth core concepts of nationalism, as exemplified by Freeden. The fourth core concept identifies a particularism that nationalism must highlight if it is to appeal to its intended audience. This particularism must be justified 'in terms of competing notions of national space – geographical, linguistic, cultural, biological.'[4] Myth-making celebrates this particularism – be it factually based, semi-authentic or entirely mythical – and adorns it with a vitality from which people engaged in the politics of national liberation can take heart. Freeden continued his analysis of the fourth concept by citing 'the evolving cultural domain of language'.[5] As the Welsh language was the dominant language of Wales at the time of the noted period of particularism that feeds into our myth-making epoch (i.e. the era of Owain Glyndwr's rebellion), a clear line of argument can be established in which Welsh nationalism can be rooted.

Language evolves over geographical space and time and as it does it coincides with, and can be a marker of, a nation's fortunes. In the historical sense, therefore, Freeden's fifth concept – that which refers to sentiment and emotion – can be easily interwoven into this pattern of identification. While Freeden noted that all human beings experience a sense of excitability and emotion when considering things that they cherish, he remarked how it is in nationalism alone that 'the role of emotion becomes an overriding "consciously" desired value.'[6] Although it would be reasonable to contend that Freeden could have added fascism to this evaluation, as that too asks people to engage with a particular ideology for the same emotional commitment, there is undoubtedly a sense in which nationalism does seek to foster passionate, if not arguably irrational, sentiments. If an attempt is made to incorporate these core concepts into the arena of Welsh nationalism, and nationalist development, then one area that may be identified as an inducer of passion and emotion is the fostering of eisteddfodau as showcases for the Welsh language and Welsh culture. Nation builders within Wales pinpointed the adoption of a National Eisteddfod – stretching back to 1176, but whose modern-day instigator, Iolo Morgannwg, reinvented the Gorsedd of Bards at the Carmarthen Eisteddfod of 1819 – as a vehicle out of which the Welsh people could gain emotional attachment, and from which the idea of a coherently united Welsh cultural, linguistic, and possibly political, framework would emerge. In similar terms, Scotland also witnessed comparable periods of cultural invention and reinvention, and the Highland games stands as an example of a communal event that was fostered to induce solidarity and to engender a heightened awareness of one's identity and belonging.

Interestingly, in the Welsh instance, Gwyn Alf Williams identified this period, which saw the rebirth of the National Eisteddfod, as significant in the development of a modern Welsh identity. Linking Welsh political thought, and radicalism in particular, into the Zeitgeist of international political upheavals, Williams saw an alternative society arising in Wales. For Williams, 'the first modern Welsh "nation" was born with the American and French revolutions.'[7] By the 1790s, political and religious tracts dominated Welsh-language publications, and this created a wellspring out of which nineteenth-century patriots, inspired by the events in revolutionary France in 1789, 'tried to root a Wales which was to be a radical and total breach with the immediate past.'[8] That immediate past, which could plausibly be called a post-Act of Union era, would be replaced, in Williams's opinion, by a reincarnation of 'a remote past re-lived in romantic, utopian and increasingly millenarian spirit.'[9]

Although these views and tendencies may have incited Welshmen and women to opt for nationalism as their salvation, it does not necessarily follow that that is the course on which they actually progressed.

If one wishes to consider Williams's interpretation of the growth of radical consciousness at this time, or what, alternatively, may be termed national consciousness, it needs to be pointed out that utopian thought, for instance, eschews nationalism in favour of a pacifistic universalism. On closer inspection, indeed, Williams's theory regarding the emergence of a tentative national, and nationalistic, consciousness appears to be consumed by its need to inflate the substance of Welsh life at that time – its language, religion and class divisions – into the instruments through which nationalistic political activism emerged.[10] Although certain Welsh people undoubtedly did use the aforementioned realities as channels through which dissent against the status quo could be registered, Williams failed to mention the societal conservatism that linguistic adherence, religious observation and social stratification can also engender. It may be more enlivening to play up the radicalism of the age, but it is probably true to say that revolutionary inclinations, and nationalist intentions, were not as widespread around this time as some historians would have us believe.

Whilst not denying that there was a rise in nationalist sentiment, and an understanding of the possibilities attached to national self-government, it is feasible to argue that these views were held by a coterie of predominantly well-educated and politically motivated individuals but were not indicative of the population at large or of any coherent social movement within the wider public realm.

If the above observation proves to be accurate, then this vanguard seeking independent political control for Wales may have resonances when applied to Plaid Cymru. This is because the party shows signs of being an organisation – although numbering tens of thousands of members since its inception – which has been steered throughout its eighty-five-year history by a relatively small number of motivated people, as, indeed, it could be argued that most, if not all, political parties are. Possibly there are similarities between the ruling elite throughout Plaid Cymru's existence and what Gwyn Alf Williams described as 'the first spokesmen for this new "nation" … its "preacher-journalists".'[11] Whilst trying not to fall prey to the claim of generalisation, it is fair to say that in historical terms, and by taking occupation and status as a guideline, the people within the various communities within Wales who have advocated nationalism, certainly in its numerous mainstream guises, have invariably come from the professional classes – people who are perceived to have a certain level of standing within their communities.

Hiraeth and Welsh Nationalism

One fascinating area in which emotion, nationalism and Wales can be contextualised is through the Welsh expression *hiraeth*. This expression is unique in that it has no unambiguous meaning in translation. When used in Welsh it can mean longing or desire, but it can also express passion and emotion. *Hiraeth* is a term often used at eisteddfodau and other cultural and sporting gatherings. It offers identification and attachment to all of those people who associate with, or have a love for, Wales. It is not, however, a uniquely nationalistic term. It is used by people of all political creeds to express their views on their homeland. It would be wrong, therefore, to link it with nationalism alone. What is exceptional, nevertheless, is how this expression is used, by nationalists and non-nationalists alike, to denote something peculiarly Welsh. It shows how, if nothing else, the use of language and, as in this instance, a specific term within that language, does offer something to the user that is unique. The extent to which it is employed to summon up passion and patriotism, and whether this acts as a conduit into what would be seen as identifiably nationalistic views, is naturally open to interpretation as each case arises. It does, however, show the significance of one singular word within a language: a word that has a certain symbolism, particularly to those advocating the ideology of nationalism.

Regardless of the debate as to whether a term such as *hiraeth* has nationalist connotations or not, it would be fair to claim that it is possible, albeit in a tangential way, to match up the dominant features of Thomas Combs's pre-political phase, language and myth-making, with the fourth and fifth concepts that Freeden believed were fundamental values of nationalist ideology. Does this, therefore, firmly set the foundations for a nationalist ideology that would come to fruition with the formation of Plaid Cymru? Though early indications would point in this direction, there are still the other phases of development to assess, as outlined by Combs, along with the identification, or otherwise, of nationalism within Plaid Cymru once the party had been established.

The Liberal Party Phase

When moving on to an analysis of the Liberal Party phase,[12] as Combs titled it, nationalism can be viewed at a time of social, economic and political change associated with the epoch of industrialisation and the growth of urbanisation. It is during this period that dissent against the perceived iniquities of British authority, be it in a religious or political sense, became far more conspicuous. Socialist writers, such as Gareth

Miles and Rob Griffiths,[13] however, have disputed Combs's account of this Liberal Party phase as a burgeoning nationalistic period. Attacking the Liberal Party-inspired and -dominated Cymru Fydd (literally meaning the Wales that will be but often incorrectly translated as Young Wales) pressure group – a body that attempted to mirror the Scottish Home Rule Association and the Irish Home Rule movement – Miles and Griffiths maintained that the Liberals merely toyed with home rule. They pointed out that the concept of home rule, and the vision of a politically and economically independent Wales, was, in the words of Saunders Lewis, 'the spare time hobby of corpulent and successful men.'[14] This is undoubtedly a harsh assessment of this period in Wales's political history, as it claims that radical thought should be the preserve of the industrial working classes – a persistent argument that is forwarded by left-inclined writers. However, the Liberal Party phase, and liberalism itself, as a driving force for the development of nationalism in Wales, and the opening up of the political arena to allow for Plaid Cymru's formation and flourishing, needs more critical analysis than that offered by Miles and Griffiths alone.

Although the Liberal Party's policy on devolved rule in a federal Britain can be pinpointed to its radical programme of 1885, wherein it announced that it would 'entrust Wales, Scotland and Ireland with the free and full administration of their internal affairs',[15] it was the association of some Liberal Party members with the setting up of Cymru Fydd and the campaign to seek the disestablishment of the Church in Wales that was of greater importance. The one Liberal Party politician of this period who was most associated with Wales, and the aspirations of Cymru Fydd, was David Lloyd George. Indeed, Peter Beresford Ellis, paraphrasing a subheading of an article in the *Young Wales* magazine from June 1896, even went as far as calling Lloyd George the 'apostle of Welsh nationalism'.[16] By this time, Lloyd George had been advancing the notion of self-government for Wales for three decades. While it would be impolite to deny that Lloyd George was patriotically inclined, and only fair to acknowledge that he did desire a greater voice for Welsh people, the extent to which he represented a distinctly nationalist front is open to interpretation. His radical credentials cannot be denied, but Peter Berresford Ellis is one commentator who has sought to highlight the criticism levelled at Lloyd George within Wales when Lloyd George turned his attention away from the home rule issue and began making speeches on the Boer War.[17] Lloyd George even endured criticism from *Young Wales*, whose editorial line somewhat exaggerated matters by claiming that Lloyd George had turned his back on his fellow Welshmen.

Henry Richard's Nationalism

With this slightly unflattering representation of Lloyd George's over-all commitment to matters Welsh under the spotlight, it is perhaps understandable how contemporary Plaid Cymru activists, such as the former Ceredigion MP, Simon Thomas,[18] praise Lloyd George's fellow Liberal, Henry Richard, MP for Merthyr, as a far greater influence on Wales's distinctive brand of nationalism than the undoubtedly more well-known, and iconic, former prime minister. Similarly, but in a somewhat revisionist analysis of the individuals under consideration, Henry Richard is viewed as a member of parliament who was more in tune with traditionalist Welsh values such as non-violence and moral rectitude. These were traditionalist values in the sense that they stemmed from the religious convictions held by the church-attending majority. This contrasts sharply with the more lax attitude attributed to Lloyd George on this latter issue. Although a nationalistic tinge can be attributed to both men, the fact that Lloyd George let himself be corrupted by what some Welsh nationalists would refer to as English values (i.e. moral laxity) adds to the romanticised, if not chimerical, nature of nationalist thinking about social mores within Wales.

Praise for Henry Richard among some of the present generation of Plaid Cymru members can be said to have come about because Richard embraced the causes that certain people within Plaid Cymru claim as Welsh causes, namely Christian (or humanistic) pacifism, Chartism and workers' representation, and the coexistence of a patriotic and internationalist outlook. Relating Richard's perspective on affairs to present-day thinking, Gwyn Alf Williams stressed the internationalism advanced by Henry Richard. Bypassing a narrow jingoistic or xeno-phobic standpoint, Williams claimed an innately acquired point of view for Richard. He became, Williams has argued, 'a good internationalist precisely because he was a good Welshman.'[19]

Williams has also contended that Richard became 'what the late Raymond Williams called himself in his last years, a Welsh European.'[20] This Welsh European, and internationalist, vision is a viewpoint that has come to the fore in recent years as the debates about devolution, regionalism and decentralisation have reached a peak, and as the steady process of Europeanisation continues relatively unabated. This is an area that will be covered in more detail in subsequent chapters. The importance of what can be described as nationalist viewpoints within the Liberal Party, as Thomas Combs observed, are nevertheless evi-dent. So the Liberal Party phase, owing to its absorption of the salient political concerns of the period, does appear to have its place in the development of nationalism in Wales.

The Role of Liberalism in Freeden's Model

Before analysing Michael Freeden on this matter, it is worth noting how liberalism and nationalism have been interwoven in the eyes of another writer on ideologies. Erica Benner has observed that 'many of the concepts that have come to be identified as "core" elements of nationalist ideology – nation, national identity or "consciousness", and national self-government – began to acquire an important place in liberal and democratic thinking during the Nineteenth Century.'[21] The then fashionable desire for the relatively new portrayal of liberty, both individual and collective, and an attempt to understand one's own purpose within the wider structure of community – what became known as self-identification – can be put forward as reasons for discovering ideological linkages between liberalism and nationalism. In a similar vein, the upsurge in the level of discourse regarding the concept of freedom, traceable to the French Revolution of 1789, cannot be played down as it resonated in the minds of both liberals and nationalists. Looking at the way in which Freeden underscored liberalism in his analysis of nationalist ideology it is evident that the link that Benner made can be fitted in to this discussion on the Liberal Party phase.

As stated previously, Freeden regards liberalism as a host-vessel in which nationalist discourse can reside. It is reasonable to ask, however, whether it is really feasible, in assessing the genealogy of nationalist thought in Wales, to claim that nationalism was just residing within the biggest purveyor of liberal values, the Liberal Party, before it broke out of its skin to present itself to the world in the guise of Plaid Cymru. Although the more radical agenda of liberalism, pursued by the Liberal Party, would appear to be more conducive to nationalists who sought to alter the constitutional status quo, as opposed to the conservatism of a Tory Party intent on making only minor, if any, constitutional adjustments, the question that needs to be asked is 'Why did nationalism use liberalism rather than conservatism as a host-vessel?' One answer to this could lie in Combs's assertion that 'The Liberal Party was … the only alternative within the present political structure to correct the injustices which existed.'[22] If the praxis of liberalism, demonstrated by the Liberal Party, is indeed seen as a route out, or alternative, there is little wonder that nationalists favoured this course of progressive action to unsettle the status quo.

Liberals, as Freeden has noted, would not have had any qualms about accepting these nationalists into their ranks, as liberals respect people's self-identification and, bearing this in mind, 'liberalism must include respect for a sense of national identity and belonging.'[23] Whatever reservations liberals have about nationalism, and they have many with regard to the way in which certain more extreme or authoritarian forms of nationalism are seemingly dismissive of individual rights and claims, they do at least accept that nationalism 'sanctions the principle of self-government.'[24]

But to what degree did nationalist views emerge within the nucleus of Liberal Party opinion during the phase that Combs saw as important to the development of nationalism within Wales? By returning to Freeden's five core concepts of nationalism it can be shown that, as stated above, the identification of the nation is not a core of liberalism, and, hence, despite the appeals for home rule by Lloyd George and Cymru Fydd, the prioritisation of the particular group – the nation – is not a salient feature of liberalism at this, or any other, point in time. Nevertheless, this does not mean that nationalism was completely ignored by those holding liberal views during the period under discussion. Indeed, there is evidence of 'structural tolerance'[25] to be found in the fact that nationalism was able to surface in liberalism, and the Liberal Party, in nineteenth- and early twentieth-century Wales. This acceptance possibly stems from the political idealism that pervaded liberal thought in this period. If idealist thought was generally accepted, and therefore there was a climate in which there was clear evidence of 'the complementary nature of the individual and social principles',[26] then nationalism would have been able to find a voice as long is it didn't infringe on, or attempt to dominate or suffocate, those who favour individual thought and practice in contrast to collective identification. This is a key conceptual point in any attempt to understand where nationalism fits in with liberalism and vice versa.

One area in which there would be obvious signs of tension for someone with a nationalist disposition operating in a liberal ideological environment is when the issues of particularism and universalism are raised. In his discussion on this area of tension, Michael Freeden cited Lord Acton's contention that a pluralist liberalism can be adopted that is 'put in the service not of freedom as self-development, but of freedom from the unnecessary intervention of government.'[27] If this line of reasoning existed at the time, then nationalists could find an ideological home, albeit not ideal, in a Liberal Party whose core concept of liberty could be adapted by nationalists to embrace their desire for unrepressed national self-expression. The particular/universalist debate could then be managed in a way that would allow a synthesis to develop that stretches the use of the concept of liberty to embrace both camps. If this is done, and it is fair to argue that this is what appears to have happened in the case of nationalism and the Liberal Party in Wales, then a coexistence can, and clearly did, exist.

Conservatism and Organic Change

The Conservative Party, being the standard bearer of conservatism, could not offer the same conditions for nationalism to flourish for several reasons. This, however, does not mean that nationalists within Plaid Cymru have not borrowed some ideological concepts from conservatism, as will be demonstrated later. One of the core concepts of conservatism is 'an insistence on controlled organic and natural change.'[28] Any person advocating Welsh nationalism would have great difficulty in reconciling themselves with this conservative core as natural change would not bring about the substantial modification to the governmental structures that would be required in order to create the countrywide awakening that nationalists desire.

If it were just a case of nationalism fostering resurgence, and a greater recognition or understanding of what being involved with your nation should entail, then conservatism could act as its host-vessel as this resurgence could come about through organic and natural change. However, accepting a transformation along the lines desired by Welsh nationalists would require a more revolutionary and far-reaching stance. This is because, and here another reason why nationalists rejected the Conservative Party enters the debate, conservatism, as represented by the Conservative Party, upheld the laws, customs, conventions and values of the Union; a Union that held the component parts of the United Kingdom together and did not advocate any radical change to this system of governance in the foreseeable future.

For the Conservative Party there was immense symbolism in the construct that was, and still is, the Union – a symbolism of a potent, even nationalistic, expansionist and imperialistic Britain – and this was an image that the Conservative Party did not wish to relinquish. Conservatism, therefore, dampened internal nationalist demands because nationalism, not only in Wales but also in Ireland and Scotland, threatened the continuation of the existing socio-political configuration, and its accompanying imagery. Unsurprisingly, it is evident to see why Welsh nationalists would, in this instance, shy away from the Conservative Party, as its value-system and ideological framework would not have advanced nationalism in Wales. If this attachment to liberalism, and the Liberal Party, as opposed to conservatism and the Conservative Party, appeared to be the most conducive vehicle for nationalists in this Liberal Party phase then why did some nationalistically minded individuals seek to establish a distinctive political party, and what, in ideological terms, did they hope to achieve? Subsequently, therefore, it becomes apparent that other thought-practices – for instance, it could be contended that socialism was one – must have played some part in influencing the people who were to form the new political body that was Plaid Genedlaethol Cymru.

Ideologies and Political Developments Pre-1925

Thomas Combs mentioned the development of Welsh nationalism entering its third phase, what he labelled 'The Labour Party phase',[29] in 1922. While it is possible to understand the reasons why Combs choose this date for his third phase, as it saw the demise of Lloyd George's government and the manifestation of Labour as a mass party capable of taking power, there is also a case to be made for an earlier date to be put forward, and the Labour Party phase title could be replaced by a more generic designation such as the burgeoning Socialist phase or even the working-class recognition phase. One of the reasons for this reappraisal of Combs's titling of his separate phases is that in consideration of this stage of development, and although there are no reasons to deny or denigrate the prominent role that the Labour Party played in the development of Welsh politics, and partly in the development of Welsh nationalism, it would be unfair to attribute socialism merely to the Labour Party. This is because socialism had infused itself over the course of time into a variety of organisations and political movements.

Freeden's Core Concepts of Socialism

With the above observation in mind, therefore, and before an historical assessment is made, Freeden's view on the relationship between socialism and nationalism needs to be considered. The socialist core, according to Freeden, contains five concepts. These are 'the constitutive nature of the human relationship, human welfare as a desirable objective, human nature as active, equality, and history as the arena of (ultimately) beneficial change.'[30] While core concepts two, three and four can be adjudged peripheral to any nationalist concerns, it is the first and last concepts that could prove the most attractive to any nationalists who deem themselves to be left-leaning. For socialists, the first concept – the constitutive nature of the human relationship – is often illustrated as an organic master–slave association that not only features in the works of Marxist and socialist philosophers but whose general theme can also be located in the writings of philosophers as diverse as Rousseau, Mill and Nietzsche.[31] Furthermore, using the language of contemporary social capital,[32] vertical linkages are clearly visible within the structure and organisation of virtually every society. Herein the master–slave and employer–employee relationship is conspicuous. Socialists accept this and see the challenging, and breaking down, of these vertical linkages as a key objective.

Eventually, therefore, horizontal linkages, as opposed to vertical linkages, should be fostered so that the fourth core concept of socialism, namely equality, can be enacted. Here, liberalism varies from social-ism in that liberals maintain that, by advancing the notion of universal values, horizontal linkages – treating your fellow man or woman on a moral, if not an entirely legalistic, equalitarian basis – are enacted without having to engage in class struggle or regime change. Whilst this eye to eye notion of horizontal linkage would attract a nationalist, who would apply it on a particularistic basis, it may be more appropriate to contend that the espousal and application of nationalism would only exacerbate the vertical linkage tradition. This is because nationalists, of whatever shade, view the nation in a special light.

The nation has an esteemed place in the conceptual framework of nationalism, as it is the nucleus whose position and maintenance pro-vides nationalists with their key *raison d'être*. Nationalism without the nation is implausible. Nationalism without other ideological concepts that define a person's identity and position within society – class strati-fication, egalitarianism, etc. – is feasible. Here, therefore, it could be proposed that it is easy to evaluate that the liberal notion of individual identity could be surpassed by the desire to ferment a communal iden-tity; a communal identity that allows all within the construct that is the nation to relate, using vertical linkages, to that very nation. Socialism, it would seem, has more in common with nationalism on this concept than liberalism does, albeit socialism seeks to eradicate the vertical link-age whereas nationalism – so as not to dethrone or depower the nation itself – is happy to maintain at least the semblance of a vertical linkage between the individual and the nation to which he or she has attachment or allegiance. Certainly, nationalism would seek to generate an *esprit de corps* that would give a sense of horizontal linkage and equality. Indeed, it could be maintained that the flowering of that *esprit de corps* may well prove to be imperative if a nationalist ideology is to have any chance of attaining a certain status, and then subsequently maintaining its appeal. Nevertheless, and not withstanding the fact that solidarity may be achieved through this venture, the vertical linkage would still remain in place as the concept and idea of the nation takes pride of place. Thus, there is always going to be a certain level of subordination in any political environment that is underpinned by nationalism.

The Conception of History and Political Change

In keeping with Freeden's model, the fifth core concept of socialism, history as the arena of (ultimately) beneficial change, can be related to nationalistic visions in several ways. First and foremost, socialism and nationalism both envisage, and require, change as both a mechanism and a productive force. From Karl Marx's 'the history of hitherto existing societies is the history of class struggle',[33] through to Benedict Anderson's concocted 'imagined communities',[34] an historical epoch is summoned up in which radical restructuring has either occurred or is set to occur: Marx's belief in historical materialism and the inevitable collapse of capitalism at some given point in time being an obvious example.[35] For nationalists, the summoning up of *la belle époque* means that there may be an overlap with socialism as both ideologies advance what could be described as a romantic vision, as they seek to either create or recreate an historical or epoch-making era. In both ideologies this process of creation is classified by Freeden, albeit through differing descriptions, as a core concept. Given this justification, it is feasible to understand how somebody advocating an alternative socio-political course to the incumbent one could fluctuate between socialism and nationalism. This is because both are vehicles for social change and both offer a revolutionary, transformative route to societal advancement through the use of history as an arena of beneficial change; be it via the emphasising of certain historical events or through a glorification of what may be portrayed as a golden era, factual or mythical.

In light of all this, it is certainly possible that, pre-Plaid Cymru, nationalists in Wales, without a recognisably nationalistic vehicle in which they could operate in an unimpeded manner, would have to resort to inhabiting socialist groupings, especially as this period saw a major advancement in socialist theory and socialist political practice. At the end of the nineteenth century and start of the twentieth century, the socio-economic culture of Wales was locked into a blue-collar economy that encompassed the heavy industries of coal, iron and steel in the south, and the slate industry in the north. At the same time, mid and rural Wales was predominantly reliant on agricultural production. Taken as a whole, therefore, the working classes dominated the demographic map of Wales with few home-grown middle-class professionals or members of the upper classes in existence. For the majority of the population, at this point in time, the Liberal Party was the party of choice; certainly that was the case, in electoral terms, after the 1868 Reform Act. Meanwhile, in organisational terms, the trade unions provided a political release valve, if not an altogether coherent voice, until the advent of the Labour Party at the end of the Victorian age. In societal terms, consequently, a slow but sure process of collectivisation was occurring; a process that would see socialism become a major political force and one that would eventually oust the Liberals, with their soon to be outmoded political and economic philosophy of individualism.

Radicalism and the Role of the Welsh Language

In conjunction with this, the politics of direct action, be it through the Rebecca Riots, the Merthyr Rising of 1831 or the bloody Chartist advance on Newport in 1839, was imprinted upon the minds of Welsh radicals by the end of the nineteenth century. Though regularly portrayed as working-class, socialist-inspired activism, a nationalistic element can be attributed to all three of these actions, as each took place in large part, though not exclusively, through the Welsh language. One example of this is presented by Thomas Phillips, mayor of Newport at the time of the Chartist insurrection, who said that it was 'Welsh in its origin and character ... contrived by persons who communicated with each other in a language not understood by the authorities.'[36] Equally, in a move that summoned up historical passion, the essayist Harri Webb remarked that 'when the ragged Chartists marched from the valleys of Gwent, the radical John Frost called on the name of Glyndwr to inspire them.'[37]

In all of the aforementioned instances, therefore, it would be feasible to claim that the Welsh language acted both as a binder and as an alienator, and was successfully manipulated for this purpose by the insurrectionists themselves, as the commanding ranks of the armed forces and the judiciary who took action to quell these rebellious acts could not interact with the rebels in their mother tongue. The fact that extrinsic forces seemed to be putting down the actions of the indigenous population added to the folklore of resistance that nationalists used as a supplement to their armoury of grievances. Hence, these actions became part of the myth-making process, which is a vital ingredient for fostering nationalism. Although this is rarely commented on by historians or political commentators, it is reasonable to add that this division of languages cannot be underplayed. This is because language, like myth-making, can be a prime motivator within nationalism and, albeit subconsciously or certainly not in any premeditated sense, the linguistic divide was nurturing a sense of political nationhood – a sense of nationhood that theoreticians within Plaid Cymru would later allude to.

One commentator who has noted the relevance of language in fostering nationalist sentiment is Jane Aaron. In her National Eisteddfod lecture of 2003, Aaron noted how the Blue Books, the infamous government report on education in Wales in 1847 that attempted to 'shame the Welsh and persuade them to adopt the language and culture of the Englishman as a higher civilisation than Welsh culture,'[38] actually backfired on the commissioners. Aaron continued on this theme by citing the historian Ieuan Gwynedd Jones who, commenting on the effects of the 1847 report, maintained that 'for the first time in the century Welsh people ... had to weigh and measure what their nationality meant to them in a painful but very effective manner.'[39] If nothing else, therefore, criticism of the Welsh language by English-speaking, London-based officials had induced a sense of patriotic feeling across Wales as, in the opinion of many people, an extraneous force was seen to be attempting to deny the birthright of the, mostly uneducated, masses. It could be argued that this sense of patriotism, and an allegiance to the Welsh language, aided the course and development of nationalism in the years ahead. Moreover, it undoubtedly helps to explain why, allied to a perceived threat to a Welsh tradition from outsiders, nationalists in Wales were to place such a huge emphasis on the continuation and survival of the indigenous language.

Overall, therefore, one could contend that the countless acts of rebellion that Wales witnessed over the course of the industrial age may well have had socialist, or at the very minimum peasant or proletariat, inspiration but, ultimately, what arose out of these actions was a deeper sense of nationhood and community solidarity that was to eventually find an ideological home within nationalist, and later Plaid Cymru, thought-practices. Hence, socialism as an ideology, and the socialistic and non-conformist environment in which the bulk of the working classes were functioning, acted as a breeding ground for nationalism in Wales. The linkages, or overlapping consensus, between socialism and nationalism in Wales, though vigorously denied by generations of Labour Party activists, is something that comes across as quite apparent through an analysis of modern Welsh political history.

If nationalist ideas were taking root within a socialist milieu, and simultaneously those nationalistic views were finding expression within the Liberal Party, many of whose members were campaigning for home rule for Wales and Ireland and the disestablishment of the Church in Wales, then the question must be asked as to why some people felt that the formation of a distinctly nationalist, or at least a distinctly Welsh, political party was required. The instinctive supposition would be that the people who formed Plaid Cymru saw weaknesses, structural or ideological, in the other political parties at that time. Certainly, in structural terms, it is a fact that the prevailing political parties operated out of London and, barring the constitutional concerns of the Liberals, these parties were not particularly Welsh focused even though, in the case of the Liberal Party and, upon its inception, in the case of the Labour Party, a great deal of electoral support and general goodwill was gained from Wales. Also, and perhaps somewhat ironically, many of the most prominent politicians and activists within those parties were themselves Welsh. To give an example of how far the issue of Welsh political autonomy had drifted away from the mainstream of Liberal Party policy, Gwynfor Evans cites Sir Ben Bowen Thomas, who said that when the old Cymru Fydd campaigner E.T. John 'rose on 11 March 1914 to present his Self-government for Wales measure, the few who were there listened to his voice as the cry of one risen from the dead.'[40]

On the Ideological Road to Pwllheli

Carwyn Fowler has observed how 'having witnessed the failure of Cymru Fydd to force a home-rule act for Wales, David Lloyd George turned his attention to UK matters.'[41] If Lloyd George's decision to concentrate on issues at a UK level is an accurate assessment, and with the nascent Labour Party taking the nation out of its political rhetoric in favour of concepts such as workers' control and internationalism, then it could be argued that there was now an electoral vacuum, and deeper than that an ideological vacuum, for those people in Wales desirous of some degree of Welsh political autonomy. In contrast to Lloyd George, some cultural and political activists felt that the time was imminent to turn their and other people's attention to singularly Welsh matters.

Although this investigation is concentrating on ideological aspects, it would be correct to state that, in electoral terms alone, the choice of 1925 as the date for the launch of a new political party would not appear to be the most appropriate. This is because Wales had three major political parties at that time – Labour, Liberal, and the Conservatives – and it would be fair to imply that, of these three, both the Labour and Liberal parties could certainly lay substantial claim to be the true representatives of Welsh political opinion and consciousness. The policies and ideologies encompassed by these three political parties ranged from Marxists in the Labour Party through to high Tory, and some far right, viewpoints within the Conservative Party. There were also varying degrees of nationalist sentiment within all three parties, and many individuals within the Labour and Liberal Parties made great claims about their Welshness, on individual, if not party, terms.

It was amidst this compact political marketplace that Plaid Cymru was formed at Pwllheli in 1925. In purely electoral terms it would be fair to contend that there was not a natural constituency of voters who appeared to be desperate for a political party to emerge in order to

sum up and represent their ideological position. If voters were seeking nationalism, socialism, liberalism or conservatism then there were
outlets available, though the depth to which these thought-practices
were actually represented within the existing political parties is another
matter altogether. Nevertheless, all of this was problematic for Plaid
Cymru. Thus, Gwynfor Evans's notion that the formation of Plaid
Cymru lit a candle that stood out 'in the blackness of the night around
them'[42] appears somewhat fanciful. The reality of it all was that it
would be a long time after 1925 before Plaid Cymru was to see signs of
progress in electoral terms.

Returning to matters strictly ideological, one individual who certainly did feel that the time was right to form a new political party
around this period was the writer and academic Saunders Lewis. As
it turned out, it was Lewis's political philosophy that went a long
way towards shaping the early thinking of Plaid Genedlaethol Cymru
(National Party of Wales) – the party's full, original title – although
Lewis cannot and should not be portrayed as the sole voice and ideological driver of the party at that period in time. However, Lewis was
party president from 1926 to 1939, and it is probably fair to conclude
that it is Lewis whom the general public predominantly associates with
the name of Plaid Cymru at this time.

As he was, arguably, a giant, or at the very least a dominant and
often contentious personality, in terms of Plaid Cymru's history and,
more importantly, in terms of its morphology when it came to ideological content and development, the political thought of Saunders Lewis
needs to be addressed. What must be remembered, however, is the
unmistakable fact that Plaid Cymru was not then, is not today and never
has been a one-man band. Hence, alternative ideological positions and
differing voices within the party cannot be sidelined in any discussion
about Saunders Lewis's role in the party's ideational development.

Seeing the Nationalist Light: Saunders Lewis's Wartime Conversion

Saunders Lewis's conversion to nationalism came about through his
reading of Maurice Barres's *Le Culte du Moi*.[43] This conversion occurred
in 1916, when Lewis was in the trenches of Belgium. One of Barres's
passages that was said to have inspired Lewis was the one in which he
claimed that 'he who cuts himself off from his own past, his own land,
is starving his soul and frustrating his own being.'[44] Consequently, there
is a clear instance here of a time and place setting mixed in with a large
degree of emotion. Given Lewis's predicament in the battlefield, this

would have undoubtedly been a poignant episode. It is also important to recall that these combinations of time and place and emotion are core concepts of nationalism. While it is impossible to deny the actuality of this conversion, it is probably reasonable to add that there must have been some embedded political viewpoints that Lewis brought with him into his nationalist conversion. What, undeniably, Lewis did bring into the arena that Barres was evoking was a literary romanticism. Referring to his introduction to nationalistic writings, Lewis revealed, in an interview in 1961, that it was 'through Yeats, Synge, Collum and other writers belonging to the Irish literary tradition that he first came to understand the meaning of nationhood and the experience of patriotism.'[45] This romantic view of the exigencies of modern life was to play a significant part in the early pronouncements of Plaid Cymru, and it remained an important part of the Lewis psyche throughout his life.

Eulogising about the profundity of Saunders Lewis, one leading Plaid Cymru activist of the early years, D.J. Williams, noted how there was a lot more going on within Lewis's mind and soul than just a simplistic conversion to nationalism through the reading of a book during a time of extreme stress and longing. Williams commented that Lewis's 'conversion to Roman Catholicism and Welsh nationalism seem to have taken place simultaneously within him, the ideal and the practical aspect of his being, each as it were a complement to the other.'[46] This must have been a stimulating coalescence, and Saunders Lewis's attachment to his religious ideals marks a significant strand within his own, and Plaid Cymru's, ideological development.

Religion as a leitmotif within Plaid Cymru is a conceptual issue that will be assessed in due course. Strikingly, where there is a notable absence of religion is in Freeden's classification of the core concepts of nationalism. In the reasoning of Freeden, and when applied to the particular case of Plaid Cymru, religion must, therefore, be viewed as a peripheral concept – one that influences the core but is not, in itself, an essential driver of nationalism. Where it is worthy of appraisal, and confirming the realisation that there are nationalisms in a plural sense, as opposed to just one set of ideas to be labelled as nationalism, is when it becomes evident that this categorisation could, and possibly should, be applied to Welsh nationalism; if it is the case that that is the label to be attached to the set of ideas exemplified by Plaid Cymru. In the case of Irish nationalism for instance, religion should be positioned as a core concept. This is a timely reminder, therefore, that this analysis is dealing with a specific set of ideas collectively registered, rightly or wrongly, as Welsh nationalism, and the subsequent portrayal, or filtering, of this Welsh nationalism through the views expressed by one particular political party operating within this political environment, namely Plaid Cymru.

Lewis, Conservatism and Nationalism

While Saunders Lewis brought both literary romanticism and religious conviction into the arena from which Plaid Cymru's ideology was to evolve, he also brought a certain tinge of conservatism to the ideological composition. In a speech given at Llandrindod Wells in 1923, Lewis presented his interpretation of nationalism, and what that nationalism could deliver for Wales. For Lewis, 'another name for nationalism is conservatism. In essence nationalism and conservatism are one and the same.'[47] To further exemplify this theory, Hywel Davies noted how, during the course of his address, Lewis 'pointed to the Conservative Party as being the English Nationalist Party.'[48] Considering what has already been outlined with regard to the liberal and socialist influences on the development of nationalist thought and practice, and the all-round challenge to the status quo that these bodies of opinion brought with them, it appears curious that Lewis summoned up conservatism as an inspiration, and even more so to equate conservatism with nationalism. That is not to contend that conservatism endorses the status quo as such, but conservatism's favouring of organic, evolutionary change ahead of a revolutionary or radical restructuring of the Welsh polity would not appear, prima facie, to offer a solution to the problems that Lewis and others claimed were in existence.

Michael Oakeshott's remarks on the disposition of conservatism, in contrast to Lewis's interpretation, would appear to show that there was a high level of contradiction between the principles of conservatism and the ideology of nationalism, and in turn, Plaid Cymru's thought-practices. For Oakeshott, 'to be conservative ... is to prefer the familiar to the unknown, to prefer the tried to the untried, fact to mystery, the actual to the possible, the limited to the unbounded ...'[49] Lewis's political vision, and the accepted line of thinking within Plaid Cymru, would appear to go against this Oakeshottian appeal for familial and societal familiarity in a carefully limited and rational political environment. This is because this reading of conservatism counters all of the ideals of romanticism, and all of the social, cultural and political restructuring of any given society, to which that particular nationalism is committed.

Furthermore, Michael Oakeshott also criticised any ideology or mode of thinking that implied that some form of 'utopian bliss'[50] was achievable. By any reckoning, nationalism, with its onus on creating or, at the very minimum, offering fortification to a society that has the positive valorisation of the nation, and the nation's key component parts, as one of its core concepts, must surely have some perception of what it believes to be a near-perfect, if not quite utopian, society; a society in which the values of the nation, according to the nationalist agenda, are initially promoted and then ultimately embedded. It was clear to Oakeshott[51] that conservatism, with its emphasis on promoting growth and change through organicism rather than teleology, could not countenance such idealistic, Enlightenment-style thinking as that on offer from nationalism.

Before applying the Freedenite analysis to Lewis's view, it is intriguing to consider the second segment of Lewis's Llandrindod speech. In this, Lewis claimed that 'the national movement is a reaction – an attempt to nurture a Welsh conservative party, and to safeguard the civilisation which we share.'[52] Remembering that this was a couple of years before the launch of Plaid Genedlaethol Cymru in 1925, it would be fair to assess that if Lewis did indeed view the national movement as a movement created as a reaction to events and whose destiny it was to act as the conservationists of Welsh society, then this reading rails against the radicalism of earlier interpretations and it also places Lewis's brand of nationalism in the reactionary camp.

Highlighting the conservative tendencies displayed by Lewis, Charlotte Davies, paraphrasing Saunders Lewis from *Egwyddorion Cenedlaetholdeb (The Principles of Nationalism)*,[53] has placed Lewis's view of Plaid Cymru's responsibility as not one of modernising Welsh society but rather one that attempted to 'seek its roots in a much older nationalist principle, that of the early Middle Ages, when respect for a diversity of cultures was combined with an acceptance of the international moral authority of the Christian Church.'[54] There is an interesting intersect here, with arguably quintessential conservative values – certainly in terms of Christian moral authority – being portrayed by Charlotte Davies as a nationalist principle. With this in mind, and to further examine the link between nationalism and conservatism, and to analyse the core concepts of conservatism, it would prove insightful to return to Freeden.

Freeden's Reading of the Conservative Core

Michael Freeden claims that the 'two main core notions of conservatism concern an insistence on controlled organic and natural change, and a belief in the extra-human origins and underpinning of the social order.'[55] Taking the first core notion to begin, it could be argued that if conservatism's reticence to allow dynamic change within society were accepted, then the insistence on controlled and organic change would almost certainly stifle new, non-conservative and non-organic, initiatives. Any change in these circumstances, and certainly any change that may offer Wales a fresh system of government and the creation of a radically different society, would appear to be unacceptable to conservatives. Rising out of this, a question must be asked as to how many nationalists, beside Saunders Lewis that is, would accept this tight organicist approach knowing that it would set them automatically on to a painstakingly slow, gradualist pathway to change. Freeden has noted how this organic system promoted by conservatism cannot counter change that is 'destructive of the past or of existing institutions and practices.'[56]

As Saunders Lewis must have realised that the arrival of a Welsh society that had a measure of self-government, and was sworn to preserving the Welsh language and culture, could not come about without a very substantial alteration to what were existing institutions and practices, it appears somewhat perplexing that he would endorse the tenets of conservatism. Certainly the more traditionally radical (i.e. left of centre) voices within Plaid Cymru in its early years, such as D.J. Davies and Wynne Samuel, wanted to distance the party from any hints of conservative practice at that time. This was predominantly evident in the economic field where D.J. Davies, in particular, wished to eschew existing economic conventions by promoting cooperativism in order to 'undermine capitalism and transform it from within.'[57] For Davies, this would lead to a new economic and social system that would be markedly different from what had gone before and it would be based not on any existing practices and institutions but on 'the unifying and inspiring forces of national feeling.'[58]

The second core concept that Freeden attributed to conservatism is that conservatives observe 'a belief in the extra-human origins and underpinning of the social order.'[59] This is one concept that Saunders Lewis, at least, could have feasibly accepted and embraced as part of his nationalist outlook. This was because Lewis's religious convictions provided him with the justification for a belief in the extra-human origins and underpinning of the social order. As a Christian, Lewis's moral foundation, and his social philosophy, would have emanated from the Ten Commandments and his acceptance of creationism. As Plaid Cymru was not then, and is not today, a religiously based political party, such as, for example, the Democratic Unionist Party within Northern Ireland or the Hindu nationalist BJP in India, there are no sectarian restrictions or obligatory declarations required for membership. Although religious adherence may have grown organically within conservatism as an ideology, and the Conservatives as a political party, no such demands were made on Plaid Cymru as an organisation. Although some people within Plaid Cymru may have shared Lewis's enthusiasm for religion, many did not and, thus, any belief in the extra-human origins and underpinning of the social order remained a personal matter and one that did not take centre-stage within Plaid Cymru's thought-practices. The fact that it never moved from being a peripheral concept to a core concept may indicate that Saunders Lewis, despite his intellectual leadership and skills as a political debater, did not have the overall influence and ability on moral matters to persuade or coerce the party down the road to accepting a religious underpinning for Plaid Cymru's thought-practices. Arguably, this shows that Lewis's views did not receive blanket approval from either the party's policy-making elite or its rank and file.

Another line of contention, and one that could have been used by Saunders Lewis in defence of his seeking compatibility between nationalism and conservatism, materialises when consideration is given to the unhealthy aspects of organic, non-liberal societies. For instance, the spectre of racism and xenophobia is often apparent within conservative societies whose reluctance to accept change overspills into a detestation of heterogeneity; conservative tendencies that are entrenched within some people in modern-day Britain, with the refusal to contemplate the inclusive nature of a multicultural society and, similarly, to accept parity with other nation-states within the construct of the European Union being contemporary examples. Lewis makes an interesting case study to assess at this juncture as his views were somewhat paradoxical on this matter. This was down to the fact that he rejected interference in Welsh socio-political and cultural life from the British state machinery whilst simultaneously offering Wales up as an archetypal European nation that was able and willing to play its part in the evolving social and political culture of Europe. Indeed, in Plaid Cymru's earliest political pamphlet, *Egwyddorion Cenedlaetholdeb* (*The Principles of Nationalism*), authored by Lewis in 1926, Wales is summoned to claim her place 'in the League of Nations and in the community of Europe, by virtue of her civilization and its values.'[60] Freeden's citing of the nationalist core concept of positive valorisation can be witnessed here as, in Lewis's view, Welsh civilisation and values are blessed with a virtuous essence. Fighting for the civilisation of Wales was a favourite theme of Lewis's throughout both his political and literary lives. That civilisation, according to him, though thoroughly Welsh in language and being, nevertheless had a European character. This viewpoint of Lewis's, and through association the viewpoint of Plaid Cymru, was sometimes pejoratively referred to by critics of the party as Plaid Cymru's 'Continentalism'.[61]

Saunders Lewis's perspective on Wales's position within Europe amalgamated with his views on nationalism, literary romanticism and religion to form a distinct personal philosophy, one that, as mentioned earlier, was undoubtedly influential but ultimately not overbearing in terms of Plaid Cymru's thought-practices. Gwyn Alf Williams described Lewis's view thus:

> His simultaneous commitment to an utterly intransigent nationalism and to a radical reappraisal of Welsh tradition through its literature was grounded in a firm and focussed ideology which saw Wales as a nation of Europe, and of a Europe defined in terms of Latin Christendom and the lost values of the Middle Ages.[62]

Where it is reasonable to disagree with Williams's assessment is through raising the contention that Lewis's ideology may have been firm and focused in his eyes but, to students of political ideology, Plaid Cymru was, at this stage of its development, on certain topics indecisive, and at other times indecipherable. Pinpointing this uncertainty, or lack of clarity, Dafydd Glyn Jones has said of Lewis that he tried to sell to the Welsh public and, it could argued, that he tried to sell to the membership of Plaid Cymru, 'a brand of nationalism which he must have known was too sophisticated for most people to understand.'[63] Sophisticated or not, Lewis was reaching out to other ideologies in order to forge his, and by association Plaid Cymru's, political perspective.

Lewis, Fascism and Nationalism

The other, and most contentious, host-vessel that Lewis's brand of nationalism brings into play is fascism. Freeden's model affirmed how fascism is the only ideology other than nationalism to recognise the nation as a core concept. But what of the other core concepts of fascism and how do they equate with Plaid Cymru's Welsh nationalism and, in this instance, with the ideology of Saunders Lewis? Fascism's other core concepts, according to Freeden, were 'leadership, totalitarian organicism, myth (determinist and/or anti-modernist), regenerative revolution, and violence.'[64] Leadership and totalitarian organicism can be dismissed from Plaid Cymru's line of reasoning from the outset as leadership in fascist terms is autocratic and unchallengeable. As is the case with most other political parties, Plaid Cymru, throughout its existence, has always had leaders who have driven policy and stamped their mark on the party. However, none of these leaders, not even the influential figure of Plaid Cymru's intellectual grandee Saunders Lewis, could be accused of autocratic rule. This was despite the fact that Lewis did envisage the benefits of a nationalistic vanguard – 'leadership by a responsible elite'[65] – taking Plaid Cymru's message out to the Welsh people.

It is reasonable to argue, thus, that not one of Plaid Cymru's theoreticians or leading lights would seek to countenance the notion of strong leadership in the direct fascistic terms enunciated by Freeden. Indeed, D.J. Davies's opposition to some of the directions and ideas emanating from Saunders Lewis were expressed in articles such as 'The insufficiency of cultural nationalism'[66] and 'The way to real co-operation',[67] wherein a more socialist, pluralist and egalitarian vision for Wales was sought to override any narrow cultural expressionism and oligarchical tendencies that some within the party might be showing signs of endorsing. The likes of D.J Davies, Kate Roberts, Wynne Samuel, Gwynfor Evans and others believed that the party's mission should be to aim to spread power throughout Wales – to make it a truly nationwide and representative phenomenon – rather than attempting to restrict it and centralise power in the hands of a select few. These views were to prove prescient as Plaid Cymru did adopt a more pluralistic stance as it developed over time. This is best summed up through analysing the party's thoughts on creating a decentralised society, which will be addressed later.

Totalitarian organicism is another core concept within fascism. This is also rejected by Plaid Cymru because, as will be expanded upon in ensuing chapters, notions such as subsidiarity, decentralisation and a democratic, and non-hierarchical, form of communityism are either core or peripheral concepts within the party's thought-practices. By its very nature of authoritarian discipline, totalitarian organicism denies pluralism and it would find repellent the form of individual or localised development – in community terms – advocated by Plaid Cymru. This is because the bottom-up personal and communal enhancement favoured by Plaid Cymru runs directly counter to the one size fits all centrally commanded, top-down system of organic growth put forward by proponents of fascist ideology.

The myth element is one that has already featured in this exploration. What is interesting when the notion of myth arises within the fascist core concepts is how Freeden bifurcates myth into determinist and/or anti-modernist positions. The determinist position – the Thousand Year Reich standpoint, as it could be characterised – has no precedent, certainly not in any vainglorious way, in Plaid Cymru's thought-practices. Nevertheless, where a determinist position could be applied – although the myth element here becomes very tenuous – is when Saunders Lewis's objective of a fully unilingual, Welsh-speaking Wales is presented for analysis. Lewis once pronounced that 'we cannot aim at anything less than to annihilate English in Wales … It must be deleted from the land called Wales.'[68] This use of language to create a fully Welsh Wales is a strategy used on occasions by nationalists – examples may be found in Spain within some of the thinking emanating from Catalan and Basque nationalists[69] – who seek to forge unity through a singular description, in this case language.

Tying this in with some of the theories of nationalism, it was Elie Kedourie who claimed that 'nationalism imposes homogeneity.'[70] Although it would be correct to maintain that any adherence to the nation and nationality must necessarily entail a degree of homogeneous acceptance, and although Kedourie's claim could be argued over at length, it is evident not only that Saunders Lewis moved along the same lines as the school of nationalist reasoning that Kedourie was assessing but that his tone in talking about the annihilation of the English language, and its deletion from Welsh soil, could be portrayed, as it was by his detractors, as fascistic.

As previously observed, the concept of language, as a driver and a motivator of political ideas, does appear from time to time among the rhetoric of nationalists in Wales and, in this particular instance, among the oratory of the prime theoretician of Plaid Cymru in its formative years. Perhaps, however, it is not surprising that language features so prominently in Lewis's pronouncements, or indeed in Plaid Cymru's early political philosophy, because, faced as the party's thinkers and policy-makers were with a Wales that was without the state institutions and developed civil society that was conspicuous in other, fully emblazoned, nation-states, the promotion of the Welsh language – whose very existence and status Tudur Jones called 'the most significant and valuable mark of our national identity'[71] – became the mission of Plaid Cymru from its inception.

With regard to the creation of a unilingual Wales, where there is some inconsistency in this line of argument is that it is possible to step easily into the conceptual region of totalitarian organicism – a line of thought that other competing concepts such as decentralisation and pluralism seek to refute. Arguing for the flowering of community values, on the one hand, while insisting on the prominence and, idealistically, the triumph of the Welsh language as the encompassing language, on the other hand, could leave Plaid Cymru open to charges of inconsistency of thought as possibly unattainable, or seemingly incompatible, ideals are woven together. This only adds to the contention that the political ideology of Plaid Cymru is strewn with competing notions that prevent ideological coherence and straightforward classification.

Anti-modernist Discourse

Turning to the anti-modernist position that features in Freeden's interpretation of the myth concept of fascism, there is some indication of a
potential overlap with the myth-making element that could be viewed
as an attribute of nationalism. There would appear to be a thin, possibly
at times indecipherable, line to be drawn between myth-making in order
to create a, supposedly positive, sense of patriotism and to colour events
in a more favourable way to your particular ethnic group or ideological
position – as could be observed in the various claims of valour and
glory that have emanated from the diverse traditions that represent all
of the protagonists who took part in an actual historical incident, such
as a sporting contest or a choral or brass band competition that crosses
ethnic or ideological boundaries, for example – and myth-making for
a more malicious invention of, or rewriting of, a sometimes true but
more possibly fictitious, or semi-fictitious, event or epoch. Although
differentiation is very difficult in these instances, it may be possible
to make a case that the former is normally attributed to nationalism or,
more specifically in Plaid Cymru's case, communityism, whereas the
latter is more likely to be found at the forefront of fascist discourse.
Nevertheless, it is important to stress a degree of caution in regard to
these interpretations because, as previously noted, there are ambiguities
and areas of distortion and overlap.

Saunders Lewis's anti-modernist approach is most clearly represented through his anti-industrialisation stance. From the 1920s
onwards, Lewis's writing and speech-making is littered with attacks
on both the process and the reality of industrialisation itself, and the
political parties, Labour especially, which, he claimed, fed off it. In
1938, Lewis, as editor of Plaid Cymru's monthly paper *Y Ddraig Goch*
(*The Red Dragon*), launched a scathing attack on Marxism. He attacked
Marxism's materialist base and 'its acceptance of capital "factoryism"
as the basis of life.'[72] Lewis had, in fact, been advocating a return to
an agrarian Wales for many years. As he remarked, 'agriculture should
be the chief industry of Wales and the basis of its civilisation.'[73] In the
Plaid Cymru pamphlet *The Ten Points of Policy*, published in 1934 and
penned by Lewis himself, the author maintained that 'for the sake of
the moral health of Wales and for the moral and physical welfare of
its population, South Wales must be de-industrialised.'[74] Other, though
by no means all, Plaid Cymru figures were to adopt this highly contentious position. Like Lewis, Plaid Cymru's parliamentary candidate in
the Rhondda throughout the inter-war years, Kitchener Davies, also
'viewed his nationalism as part of an anti-Communist tirade.'[75] It must
be remembered, however, that, while Lewis and some of his supporters

were attacking left-wing ideology at this period in time, others, such as D.J. and Noelle Davies, were advocating socialist solutions for Wales's woes.

There was, nevertheless, a belief among some in Plaid Cymru circles that Wales and the Welsh people were enduring a regressive stage in history as materialism and materialistic values, of both a capitalist and a socialist bent, were ubiquitous. In terms of decline, of equal disaster in the eyes of many of Plaid Cymru's theoreticians was the recognition that the language and value-culture of old Wales was also rapidly disappearing. For those within the party who held these views, such as Lewis and Kitchener Davies, progression, as the solution to this regressive stage, was to deindustrialise and to rediscover their Welsh identities through the Welsh language, predominantly, but also through the absorption of the available indigenous literature and culture. Hence, for Lewis, amongst others, modern, industrialised Wales was an undignified and deteriorating geographical space that required urgent, Plaid Cymru-inspired, attention if it was to reverse its seemingly terminal decline. This decline had apparently been in motion since the Victorian era, if one considers the opinion of Ieuan Gwynedd Jones. Appearing to summarise the thoughts of Saunders Lewis on this undignified period, Jones stated that 'the Welsh language was a precious and singular possession of the masses of workers at a time when the inhuman, dehumanizing and brutalizing forces of industrialism were alienating them from nature and from society.'[76] It was this dehumanising environment that Lewis sought to radically transform by showing the people of industrialised Wales that nationalistic principles and practices, embodied, as he saw them, by Plaid Cymru, could not only offer deliverance from industrial enslavement but could also help in providing a greater purpose and meaning to their lives through an appreciation of Welsh values.

Although this undoubtedly Arcadian view of Lewis, and others within Plaid Cymru – an Arcadianism that could be categorised as being a slant on the anti-modern myth concept espoused by fascism – could be labelled politically naive, when the harsh realities of everyday life all around them were taken into consideration, is it really appropriate to term the actual rhetoric and application of Lewis's, and the party's, anti-industrialisation views as fascistic in tone or ambition? Although there is no disputing the fact that some activists within Plaid Cymru did appeal to Welsh workers to abandon capitalist industries, there was no demand for them to do so; again, harking back to the rejection of totalitarian organicism mentioned earlier, this appeal could not be portrayed as totalitarian in attitude or essence. Hence, the words of Lewis, Kitchener Davies and others appear to be no more than pleas to people's better judgements by asking them to abandon the austere industrialised environment in order to seek fulfilment in a return to nature.

Where the naivety element of this appeal could be further highlighted, however, is when one considers the reality of life, and survival, in the harsh economic conditions that beset industrialised Wales in the 1920s and 1930s. At a time of high unemployment and minimal welfare relief, asking people to abandon their workplaces – assuming they were in employment – in order to start afresh in rural Wales, and asking them to subsist through the undertaking of tasks that they were not trained for, was an impractical proposition. Whilst many people had to rely on soup kitchens for a meagre daily meal, Saunders Lewis and his supporters were remarkably reticent on the ostensibly pressing matter of finding alternative employment for the destitute. So, rather than making policy announcements on measures to alleviate the severe conditions, Lewis turned his thoughts to the renewal of community harmony through spirituality and nationhood. What the people of industrial Wales should take on board, Lewis maintained, is the fact that 'nationalism is above all a fountain head of heroism and of brave resolve. It gives a beaten people hope. It gives them resourcefulness and drives away apathy and cynicism and selfishness.'[77] This rhetoric comes across as equating nationalism with salvationism and, in addition, the reference to selfishness further exemplifies Lewis's disdain for materialism; even though materialism in this context would have meant steady employment and the basic provisions which that employment could provide. In this reading, therefore, and trying to gauge how this would have played to the audience at that time, it is little wonder that, when presenting its ideology, Plaid Cymru as a whole, and not just the visions of Lewis and his allies, was seen as unworldly.

Similarly, taking into account the emerging bipolarity of activist politics across Europe in the 1930s, with fascism and communism attempting to attract the participation of the masses, the dismissive and intransigent position that Saunders Lewis and, if only through party connection if not through any deep sense of conviction, the membership of Plaid Cymru took on the ideology of communism – at the very time that communist sympathisers on the ground in the South Wales coalfield were at the forefront of providing help to impoverished communities – made them easy targets at this turbulent time in modern European political history. Foremost in their condemnation of the chimerical views of Lewis, Kitchener Davies and their followers was the Labour Party, which dismissed Plaid Cymru as merely 'profascist rabble'.[78] Although the Labour Party censure was perhaps to be expected, Richard Wyn Jones has commented on Plaid Cymru's impracticable oratory at the time. For Jones, 'the Nationalists, whilst able to incorporate community into their political philosophy, found it hard to relate to what one might term "actually existing societies".'[79]

What Lewis, and Plaid Cymru, did not succeed in doing throughout this period was taking on board what Freeden referred to as cultural constraints. Freeden comments on how 'cultural constraints on ideologies serve to anchor them firmly into the context of space and time.'[80] Arguably, Plaid Cymru positioned itself outside these cultural constraints – Saunders Lewis most certainly did – as practical considerations were ignored or sidelined. Had Saunders Lewis petitioned the people of industrial Wales when there was full employment and a buoyant economy and asked them to consider deindustrialisation and the adoption of a rustic existence, then he would not have impinged on the cultural constraints that are present whenever the mental or ideational construction and, more importantly, the implementation of political ideology occurs. It seems that Plaid Cymru, or certainly elements within the party, had not learnt the harsh lesson that, when presenting any political perspective to the general public, coping with everyday actualities must always appear to be a more pressing concern than promoting that party's political theories. Some within the party, however, were acknowledging actually existing societies, and it was these voices – those of Kate Roberts, D.J. and Noelle Davies, Gwynfor Evans and J.E. Jones for example – that challenged the pronouncements of Saunders Lewis at various times throughout this era.

Criticism of Plaid Cymru's Perceived Fascism

Perhaps not surprisingly, some critics of Plaid Cymru throughout this period tried to align the party to far right ideas, though it must be said that most, if not all, of these critics would not have been conversant with the intricate nature of political ideologies. Even as recently as 2002, the Labour MP for Caerphilly, Wayne David, shocked those around him when he launched a tirade against Saunders Lewis and Plaid Cymru in the House of Commons during a debate on racism in contemporary Wales. David claimed that

> the strong strand of racism and xenophobia in Plaid Cymru's history is well tabulated. We only have to look at some of the writings of Saunders Lewis, the founder of Plaid Cymru, to recognise the truth of that. Let me make it clear he was an anti-semite.[81]

Even allowing for embellishment on Wayne David's part, there is no doubt that some people within Plaid Cymru made the task of the critics who sought to label the party as fascist fairly straightforward. This was partly because, after Saunders Lewis, one of the leading Plaid Cymru activists and theoreticians at the time was the revolutionary-minded Ambrose Bebb. Bebb was an admirer of the tactics of Action Francaise, the French fascist movement. With people such as Bebb declaring his admiration for the visceral activism of Action Francaise it is little wonder that the opponents of Welsh nationalism sought to tarnish Plaid Cymru with the hallmark of a fascist organisation. As Gwyn Alf Williams noted, Bebb, in one outburst in 1922, had cried out 'it is a Mussolini that Wales needs.'[82] Likewise, 'in a startling speech in 1923, he called for military discipline, a training camp, five years of drill and prison martyrs.'[83] These may rightly have been viewed by Bebb's opponents as inflammatory comments but it is quite justifiable to state that, at the start of the Second World War, Plaid Cymru did open itself up to criticism through its opposition to conscription 'on the grounds that Welshmen should not be forced to fight in an English war.'[84]

Not surprisingly, given this stance and the criticism it brought with it, the early 1940s were 'a period of confusion and decline for the Welsh Nationalist Party'.[85] Perhaps the most sustained denunciation of Saunders Lewis and Plaid Cymru around this period came from the *Western Mail*. One of its columnists, angered by Lewis's call in 1943 for a negotiated peace to end the Second World War, wrote, in a seemingly heedless tone, 'week by week for years they have been preaching their doctrines of racialism and neo-Fascism in the by-ways of Wales.'[86] As a lot of this criticism can be put down to political point-scoring by other political parties, and by newspapers hostile to Plaid Cymru's message, a defence could be forwarded here that backs the argument, made by Carwyn Fowler[87] among others, that it would be wrong to consider Plaid Cymru to be in any sense of the term a fascist organisation or, indeed, one that consciously embraced fascist core or even peripheral concepts.

This whole debate raises several points when circumstances arise in which nationalist bodies are being tarnished as crypto-fascist, or even fascist sympathisers or borrowers of some elements of fascist ideology. Thus, in a wider sense, the overlap between nationalism and fascism, using Freeden's model, may well be too harsh on nationalism, and its borders; that is, however, if consideration is made of the empirical knowledge available that rightly suggests that fascism is a far more intoxicating and bellicose ideology altogether. On this point of bellicosity, Freeden observed that fascists 'exploit nationalism as the justification of offensive militarism directed at real and imagined enemies.'[88] Considering the linkage cited here by Freeden, it would appear somewhat paradoxical, however, for anyone to attempt to attribute an overtly militaristic attitude, exhibited through fascism, to Plaid Cymru as a whole. This is because two of the ideological concepts that are attributable to the party, and which some members take pride in proclaiming to this day, are pacifism and its adjacent concept of non-violent direct action. These concepts, and their relevance to the thought-practices of Plaid Cymru, will be analysed at later stage.

This is not to claim, however, that militarism as a concept and engine for transforming society is completely lacking from Plaid Cymru's reasoning. As stated above, Ambrose Bebb was militaristic in his social and political theorising and, similarly, a militarist perspective has been laid at the door of Saunders Lewis. Having experienced military life during the First World War, Lewis followed Bebb in 1923 'with his proposals that Welsh patriots should accept military-style discipline, and that Wales would benefit if someone would carry out an action on behalf of the nation resulting in a prison sentence.'[89] Without seeking to confer blanket approval of these sentiments, it is important that a few words of caution are injected here. This is because both these calls to arms were made before Plaid Cymru's formation and no doubt reflected, to some extent, the radical nationalism of the age, visible to varying degrees, it could be argued, in Ireland, the Middle East and, in an admittedly different ideological sense that was shortly to turn menacing, in Italy.

Furthermore, in the case of Lewis cited above, his comments were made at a meeting at the Eisteddfod; there is a tradition of political orators using the opportunity of speaking at a meeting on the *eisteddfod maes* (field of competition) to punctuate their addresses with a generous dose of hyperbole. Additionally, and this relates to the charge that Lewis sought to bring fascist or extremist ideas into his nationalistic outlook, Lewis countered criticism by saying that 'excess, in all movements, is an ever-present threat. I have no hesitation in saying that hot-headed and limitless nationalism is a highly dangerous thing.'[90] In a supportive note, Hywel Davies, in a similar manner to Carwyn Fowler, has dismissed claims that Saunders Lewis embraced elements of fascism or ultra-nationalism. Davies wrote that Lewis's anti-statist views were in direct contradiction to the intentions of fascist ideologues. As Davies observed of Saunders Lewis, 'rejecting the fascist emphasis on the state and the allegiance of the individual to the state, Lewis described the nation as "a community of communities".'[91] The concept of communityism within Plaid Cymru's morphology – communityism, along with the idea of the nation, being the concept that envelops the notions of allegiance and the individual's supposed affiliation to society – shall be assessed in further detail later.

Overall, therefore, it is feasible to contend that while Freeden may be generally accurate in his labelling of the core concepts of both nationalism and fascism, our general interpretation and understanding of the range and depth of each individual concept – the multifarious usages, positive and negative, of myth-making, for example – may require a far more in-depth analysis than this particular examination can allow. What must be reiterated, however, is that nationalism and fascism in general, and certainly if the relationship or similarities between the two are applied to the case of Plaid Cymru in particular, should not be regarded as natural, even symbiotic, allies or, as may specifically occur when the example of nationalism is concentrated upon, one that is seen as a gateway or stepping-stone to the other, as, for example, a Marxist would argue that socialism should be a step on the road to communism.

Green Ideology, Lewis and Plaid Cymru

In the preceding assessment of Plaid Cymru's anti-industrialisation rhetoric it was noted how a call for a return to nature must have sounded futile to those people who were in most immediate need of short-term materialistic relief. In the light of this, therefore, it would be germane to examine the extent to which these green ideological concepts feature in early Plaid Cymru thinking. Michael Freeden has identified four core concepts of green discourse. These are 'the relationship between human beings and nature; valued preservation; variants of holism; and the implementation of qualitative human lifestyles.'[92] Taking them step by step, and applying them to the pronouncements of Saunders Lewis, it is evident that the first core concept, the relationship between human beings and nature, has to enter the equation whenever talk of a return to nature is mooted. If Saunders Lewis was serious about deindustri-alisation, and its inevitable consequences, such as deurbanisation for instance, then this first core concept needs careful consideration as it may prove to be a core of early Plaid Cymru ideology. This is because 'nature becomes an overriding factor in guiding human conduct.'[93] However, whether deindustrialisation and deurbanisation would lead to policies that championed nature as a prime mover, should Lewis's vision have come to fruition, is unclear. There is little doubt that if deindustrialisation had been enacted the workings and existence of the natural world would have become a major consideration for Plaid Cymru. Nonetheless, the concept of nature becoming an overriding factor is probably too prescriptive, even for Saunders Lewis, as it puts a deep ecology commitment to the forefront.

The second concept is the valued preservation of all forms of life on earth. The acceptance of the finiteness of resources would have some relevance here, as capitalist expansion was even more unchecked then, as Plaid Cymru repeatedly indicated, than it is at present. Subse-quently, if Plaid Cymru were to seek a return to a rustic, pre-industrial society, then issues such as the ethical utilisation of animal husbandry, and the arguments for or against vegetarianism, would have to be broached. The fact that these issues do not feature among Plaid Cymru rhetoric or literature of the time undoubtedly adds to the contention that Plaid Cymru's green agenda was not meticulously fashioned. What appears to be more plausible, if these green core concepts are to be attributed to Plaid Cymru, are the adjacent concepts that attach themselves to these core concepts. Hence, the inevitability of 'imposing constraints on progress, development, and thus on history'[94] would have been looked at favourably by those within the party who saw Wales being subsumed ever further into a capitalist world that was dehumanising society.

The third concept that Freeden summons up, the promotion of variants of holism, is noticeable when the idea of the individual in tune with, but not subservient to, his or her geographical space is considered. The evolving community-based focus of Plaid Cymru thinking was also an area in which this holism could apply, as failure to operate with, and appreciate the presence of, those around you – both human and non-human – inevitably leads to a diminishing of one's own life. Depending on the circumstances, some adjacent concepts to holism, such as egalitarianism and social change, could be summoned. In the case of Plaid Cymru it is feasible that these adjacent concepts would be brought into the arena as egalitarianism could signify equality under the nation, and, subsequently, equality of opportunity and contribution, for all of those who are part of the decentralised community, could result. This would appeal to those nationalists who eschew overbearing centralisation or top-down directives. This egalitarianism is not necessarily comparable to financial equality, but it is more of an egalitarianism of belonging and inclusion. When the concept of social change is addressed, it is fair to say that this must inevitably occur, to a certain degree, whenever a fresh ideological direction is introduced. Plaid Cymru's desire for social change, however, is far-reaching and it is evident through its transformative programme. This social change would be enacted through a clear structure and direction and it ties in with green ideology in its championing of the natural world as a positive thing-in-itself, and also as a bulwark against the dehumanising effects of industrialisation, which is portrayed as a process that automatically leads to the despoiling of nature.

On the fourth concept of green ideology, the implementation of qualitative human lifestyles, Saunders Lewis invoked aestheticism. The flourishing or reawakening of the arts, literature and cultural experiences of Wales was seen as part of Plaid Cymru's holistic vision of Welsh society as interactive and interdependent. In this refined, uncluttered and spiritualistic society, the quality of life would be raised not just for those who could seek material pleasures, but for everyone. So a move away from the daily grind of work within a capitalist environment would supposedly free up the people of Wales and enable them to develop the spiritual and artistic sides to their nature. This, in theory, would lead to qualitative improvement all around.

If Plaid Cymru was attempting to conjure up an ideal scenario, in which Welsh society flourishes in a rural idyll, then it could be argued that this leaves the party open to accusations of promoting primitivism. It may be a valid argument at this stage to raise the question of whether Plaid Cymru was merely accepting primordialist assumptions, assumptions that maintain that beneath the surface of history the forms and complexities of society remain relatively unchanged.[95] If this was to be the case, and primordialism could be appended to Plaid Cymru's ideology, then it would appear to reinforce Plaid Cymru's view that Wales is, in essence, an agrarian society. What has transpired over time is that this society has been pummelled into accepting modernity and industrialisation. In this line of reasoning, all of the events in Welsh history since the death of Llywelyn in 1282, and certainly those since the Act of Union in 1536, could be seen as an unnatural detour away from what primordialists would argue is the exact condition of Welsh society. Raymond Williams's writing on nationalism, in which he commented that 'all the real processes have been cultural and historical, and all the artificial processes have been political, in one after another dominative proclamation of a state and an identity',[96] serves to show how political and, additionally, legalistic developments can be contextualised away from cultural and historical actions and processes. In this case, therefore, some within the party, at its formative stage, may have wished to argue that Plaid Cymru could align itself into the primordialist camp, as the party regards the survival of the Welsh language and culture, along with an intrinsic sense of what Welsh values and traditions entail, as more important than the political administration of the geographical space that is Wales. To use a Foucauldian analogy,[97] therefore, it would appear that there are two separate and distinctive power structures at work.

Other Thought-Practices in 'Early' Plaid Cymru

The three major statements of intent produced by the party in the years between 1925 and 1945 were *Egwyddorion Cenedlaetholdeb* (*The Principles of Nationalism*) in 1926, *Ten Points of Policy* in 1934 and

Can Wales Afford Self-Government? in 1939. The first of these, *The Principles of Nationalism*, represents Saunders Lewis's views on what the party should be all about. Focusing heavily on his contention that Wales had to reclaim her inheritance – linguistic and Christian – Lewis states that freedom is more important than independence. The degree of freedom that Lewis seeks is 'exactly that degree of freedom which is necessary in order to make civilization secure in Wales.'[98] In this evaluation of freedom, Lewis tried to clarify his view that this was not a conception of freedom that would prove challenging to those other forces who are likely to come into contact with it. As *The Principles of Nationalism* stresses, 'that freedom will not only benefit Wales but will also contribute to the welfare and security of England and all other neighbouring countries.'[99]

So what can be deduced from this rendition of the concept of freedom? Michael Freeden, in his model, cites L.T. Hobhouse's notion that freedom 'required control and limits on human action.'[100] The freedom extolled in *The Principles of Nationalism* appears to run parallel to Hobhouse's conception, as his theory maintained that certain limitations on an individual's actions – hence, not unconditional, libertarian freedom – could entail greater liberty for people overall. In theoretical terms, this is approaching utilitarian territory, although it would appear anomalous to contend that the presumption of the greatest happiness of the greatest number could sit comfortably in a nationalist setting wherein the nation and its properties are supposed to bring absolute, and not just majoritarian, happiness – unless, that is, some divisions in society (i.e. class or religious differences) were to be accepted and even propagated. However, this would appear to contradict a basic tenet of nationalism, namely the intention to create or mould a unified, if not fully homogeneous, society.

Adding further to the lack of clarity on this matter, Saunders Lewis's reading of freedom also accepted that Wales could never be totally independent, because a self-governing Wales would still have to operate within an interdependent global network. Moreover, and this was non-negotiable for Lewis, Wales would be only a component part, and not a separate entity, within a reinvigorated Christendom. With these aspects to consider, Lewis commented that he could never support 'the principle of independence ... as it is anti-Christian.'[101] Building on this remark a decade later, Lewis proclaimed that Plaid Cymru 'has sought to base itself on Christian sociology, and that Christianity is as essential to the Nationalist Party as is anti-Christian materialism to Marxism.'[102]

What Lewis was seeking for Plaid Cymru, it would appear, was a discourse and direction that rejected the scientific rationality of the Enlightenment project. This, like so much of Lewis's political philosophy, is paradoxical because Lewis was adopting an ideology, nationalism, which had emanated out of the Enlightenment, to argue for its displacement with some re-energised version of Middle Age Christian adherence. It may be fair to conclude, therefore, that this ideological pattern returns Lewis's thoughts to the field of conservatism. This type of outlook has resonances in the Burkean tradition, German conservatism and the French ultramontanism that followed the Revolution of 1789.[103] As he was a Roman Catholic, it is clear to see the appeal of ultramontanism, at least, to Lewis. Perhaps unsurprisingly, his Catholicism may account for why Lewis introduced religion into many of his political and philosophical declarations while, concurrently, others within Plaid Cymru perceived of their religious views as being strictly personal and, hence, distinct from their political pronouncements.

Religion, consequently, could be seen as an adjacent concept to Freeden's third core nationalist concept of ensuring politico-institutional expression over the first two core concepts of the nation and its positive valorisation.[104] The problem arises, however, as to where this expression is to be sited. Lewis did not advocate a Welsh base for his Christianity. Instead, he promoted a European notion of Christendom that would operate outside the normal jurisdiction of the nation-state. Alas, there are clearly difficulties in this line of reasoning for any advocate of nationalism to overcome. If sovereignty, albeit mostly a spiritual account of sovereignty as opposed to a concrete political one, rests with extraneous forces, then the role of power within the nation – power being another adjacent concept to the nation[105] – would appear to decrease. In a sense, therefore, what is being brought into play is the way in which nationalism can embrace other social, cultural, political or, in this instance, religious bodies. The argument for nationalism to adopt an internationalist stance, to a certain extent, also enters the ideological discourse at this time. What this all comes down to is Lewis's insistence that there is no real substance in the notion of independence as a panacea. This is almost certainly why Lewis stressed the term freedom time and time again. Further to this, the notion of freedom – albeit that it is a more amorphous image of freedom than Lewis envisaged – has remained a powerful and recurring theme for Plaid Cymru's members throughout its existence.

Adopting a liberal perspective, Lewis saw the enactment and extension of freedom as constituting the high point of a civilisation. If that freedom then led the Welsh people to accept a distinctly non-Welsh (i.e. European) reading of Christianity then that is perfectly acceptable. In this, and other conceivable instances, the ideal of the nation, and its positive valorisation – notwithstanding the assertion that any nation is merely an abstract concept in the first place – does not take precedence over the free thought and expression of its key component parts, namely its people. Looking at evidence such as this endorsement of individual choice and freedom, and a rejection of particularistic tendencies, it becomes apparent that Lewis's thought, and the overall aims and objectives of Plaid Cymru at that time, were running in opposite directions to the, then fashionable, centralist and statist rejection of individuality in favour of the politics and philosophy of the undifferentiated masses. It is possible to argue, therefore, that the ideologies of fascism, communism and socialism seem somewhat out of kilter with the theories springing forth from *The Principles of Nationalism.*

Plaid Cymru and *The Ten Points of Policy*

Another personal declaration by Saunders Lewis was *The Ten Points of Policy*, published in 1934. In this document Lewis confirmed 'social pluralism within national communities as being the keystone of his social vision.'[106] The extent to which this social pluralism could be realistically enacted, given the party's call for a monolingual, Welsh-toned society, is somewhat unclear. If pluralism is to be taken at face value then a diverse society must ensue. There is little evidence to suggest that this is what Plaid Cymru, or at least Saunders Lewis writing on behalf of Plaid Cymru, desired. If this terminology were offered today then interpretations regarding the creating of a multicultural or multiethnic society would abound. As there was no genuine conception of this in inter-war Wales, Lewis's appeal for social pluralism has an undefined and possibly hollow ring to it, especially given some of Plaid Cymru's earlier pronouncements on the objective of encouraging the development of a degree of conformity – linguistic and religious at least – within Welsh society.

Furthermore, given Saunders Lewis's undeniable disdain for capitalism in general, it seems highly unlikely that a capitalist industrial sector would be allowed to operate within, and add to the enhancement of, this environment of social plurality. Knowing that the party sought to distance itself from both the concepts of capitalism and industrialism, it would be fair to conclude that, should Plaid Cymru have attained political office in this period, neither would have been seen as being central to the development of Welsh society. Similarly, it would appear evident, given past pronouncements, that any movement designed to expand and encourage the use of languages and cultures, other than Welsh, would receive little sympathy in the same administration. Social pluralism, therefore, could be seen as a rhetorical, though unrealisable, feature of Plaid Cymru's ideology at that time. Social pluralism itself could be considered as only a peripheral concept within that ideology, and a very weak concept at that. Again, it would be fair to argue that in relation to this concept, and its place within Plaid Cymru's thinking, the dichotomy between thought and action appears substantial.

What is also notable, as a general point within *The Ten Points of Policy*, is how the document reflects Lewis's 'stated aim of seeking a Welsh point of view that could be applied in wider contexts.'[107] In this instance, Lewis envisaged the Welsh model becoming a guiding light for countries far and wide. Wales, it was predicted, would prove to be a progressive example of a country reclaiming her inheritance. In this example, the prioritising of the nation, combined with the conservatism and romanticism of celebrating times past, is evident. What is not on view, however, is any display of ethnic nationalism or expansionist rhetoric; indeed, the Welsh model is designed to be used as a tool for forging relationships with outside bodies as opposed to alienating them.

One area of *The Ten Points of Policy* that entered new ground was the reference to the proposed organisational structure of Welsh society, and its management of the economy, under a Plaid Cymru administration. As point five of the document noted, 'trade unions, works committees, industrial boards, economic councils and a national economic council, cooperative societies of individuals and of local and administrative authorities, should have a prominent and controlling role in the economic organisation of Welsh society.'[108] Here, for the first time in an accessible form, Plaid Cymru's economic policies were being enunciated. With the inclusion of trade unions, works committees and cooperative societies, there are clear indications of the more left-inclined policies that others within the party, such as Kate Roberts, and D.J. and Noelle Davies,[109] saw as essential to the party's ideological development. By including a range of bodies that need to be consulted and included in the management of the Welsh economy, there is undoubtedly a sense of economic pluralism in the party's reasoning, even if the social pluralism mentioned earlier is still questionable. Where there was still inconsistency, however, was in the fact that Saunders Lewis was opening up to these representative bodies – indicative of his philosophy of cooperative nationalism[110] – whilst maintaining a series of attacks on capitalism in general and the industrialisation process in particular. Trying to square the circle on this remains one of the conundrums of Lewis's legacy as Plaid Cymru's president and its chief political thinker in its early years.

The Price of Self-government

Published in 1939, the pamphlet *Can Wales Afford Self-Government?* offers a departure from the domineering political viewpoint of Saunders

Lewis. The pamphlet also took Plaid Cymru's economic reasoning into unprecedented areas. Furthermore, it could be argued that it grounds, and offers justification for, the party's socialist and cooperativist principles – areas of Plaid Cymru's ideology that will be addressed in detail later in this book. As noted above, one instantly perceptible difference about *Can Wales Afford Self-Government?* is its authorship. Unlike the hitherto examined texts, this pamphlet was written by D.J. and Noelle Davies. Commenting on their style and approach, Laura McAllister noted how 'the Davieses's was a pragmatism quite different to that of Lewis.'[111] Sidelining the romanticism of Saunders Lewis, D.J. and Noelle Davies argued for a reconstructed Wales 'based predominantly on decentralist socialist policies and including the large-scale nationalisation of key industries';[112] it is interesting to document that these demands came a decade before the implementation of Attlee's nationalisation programme. On this theme, it is worth noting that D.J. Davies and Noelle Davies had both been members of the Labour Party. This was at a time when workers' control under Clause 4 was a central principle for the Labour Party. What is most notable about the work of D.J. and Noelle Davies, however, is the way in which they cleverly weaved their radicalism, and their socialist inclinations, in with the historical positioning of Wales as a formerly well-endowed nation. Evidence of this arises when they quote the mediaeval Wales of Giraldus Cambrensis in which 'no one of this nation ever begs, for the houses of all are common to all, and they consider liberality and hospitality amongst the first virtues.'[113]

The recounting of this companionable society, according to D.J. and Noelle Davies, was in stark contrast to the situation being experienced in their Wales of the 1930s. The reason they give for Wales being poor was down to the contention that 'under an alien imperialist Government, seeking alien interests, her resources have been unused, disused and misused.'[114] Further to this abandonment and squandering of resources, D.J. and Noelle Davies also introduced the notion of power into their argument. For this purpose, Michael Freeden's assessment of power as an adjacent concept[115] can enter the discussion as power is portrayed, in this instance by the Davieses, in a hegemonic sense. Hegemonic power involves social control, and its two liberating forces, in the view of the Davieses, should be nationalism, to rid Wales of the alien imperialist government, and socialism, to act as a liberator of the Welsh economy. The hegemonic view is an interesting perspective as it allows for a redressing of grievances.

What manifests itself out of all this, according to the pamphlet, is 'the eternal distinction between the imperialists whose whole life comes to depend on dominating others and the nationalists who ask for nothing but liberty to "cultivate their own garden" without interfering with any-body else's.'[116] This is an example in which calls for the unshackling of the chains of imperialism was designed to evoke a strong sense of injus-tice among the indigenous people: freedom from extraneously imposed power being a key component of liberationist nationalist thought. Furthermore, the citing of the liberationist argument within the realm of hegemonic power invoked the work of Antonio Gramsci; Gramsci believed that the ideology of the ruling class is arranged in order to safeguard that class's interests.[117] D.J. and Noelle Davies, therefore, skilfully intertwined nationalist and socialist discourse to offer a cri-tique of imperialist capitalism and its effects on Wales, and, in so doing, began to redress the ideological balance within Plaid Cymru away from Saunders Lewis's romantic vagaries and towards a more realistic socio-economic vision of what could be achievable within Wales.

One example, from *Can Wales Afford Self-Government?*, in which the aforementioned socialist and nationalist grievances coalesced, emerged when the Davieses proclaimed that 'this catastrophic depres-sion in the Welsh coal trade was the direct result of the policy of the English Government.'[118] Apart from the nationalistic solution of self-government, one way out from this crisis in the coal industry that the Davieses proposed was that there should be a revival in Welsh agri-culture under a 'system of owner-occupiership'.[119] The Davieses, per-haps slightly quixotically, contended that the move away from heavy industry and onto an agricultural base would not entail major upheaval as 'many miners have spent their childhood on farms.'[120] Consequently, it is interesting to note how, akin to Saunders Lewis, the Davieses foresaw a restructuring of the Welsh economy, away from a centralised industrialised core and outward to the rural districts, wherein coopera-tivism would flourish. The differences between Saunders Lewis and the Davieses, however, is visible in the way that the Davieses used the language of socialism to describe their vision for an economic transfor-mation of society, whereas Lewis stuck more closely to the imagery of deindustrialisation without going into fine detail about its replacement. The intervention of D.J. and Noelle Davies, and the publication of *Can Wales Afford Self-Government?*, was important at this stage of Plaid Cymru's ideological development, as the Davieses, and the pamphlet, either introduced or enhanced concepts such as decentralisation and cooperativism, and the ideology of socialism, into the political arena. Plaid Cymru, as a whole, was then able to discuss these matters and, to varying degrees, the party became associated with these concepts and thought-practices.

Nevertheless, it is evident that what was beginning to emerge by the end of the 1930s was a sense of multiple ideological identities within

Plaid Cymru. As the party's thinking became more advanced, and as more individuals engaged in the ideational processes within the party, so adjacent and peripheral concepts arose to enhance the overall ideological make-up of Plaid Cymru. The point at which Plaid Cymru could be said to have stepped outside of its nationalism came when D.J. and Noelle Davies endorsed socialism over and above the core concepts of nationalism. Perhaps this diversion from nationalism's core concepts was inevitable as all political parties, at some stage, have to attempt to construct a programme that is comprehensive and relevant enough to justify their existence. The notion of this ideological branching out was observed by Freeden. As he pointed out, in defence of his contention that nationalism 'fails to meet the criteria of a comprehensive ideology',[121] nationalism's 'conceptual structure is incapable of providing on its own a solution to questions of social justice, distribution of resources, and conflict-management which mainstream ideologies address.'[122]

The Davieses may have presciently realised the limitations that nationalism carries and therefore they may have decided to expand the ideological underpinning of Plaid Cymru's morphology. Hence, the contribution of D.J. and Noelle Davies to Plaid Cymru's ideological development was crucial in that their 'particular brand of co-operative, decentralist socialism … merged neatly with Plaid Cymru's existing commitment to the small-scale economic unit, and its anti-state focus.'[123] Moreover, the political outlook of D.J. and Noelle Davies was also 'much needed in an organisation which, until then, had interpreted politics largely from a cultural perspective.'[124] Noelle Davies, evidently influenced by European cooperative movements, also maintained that the party should champion a heightened cooperativist approach. Furthermore, Noelle Davies thought that the emerging Danish model of social and educational cooperation was one that Wales could emulate and even augment.[125] If this line of reasoning is observed in the context of her allied campaign for the greater use of the English language within the party, then Noelle Davies could be portrayed not merely as an important figure in the gradual modernisation and evolution of Plaid Cymru as a social and political force, but also in respect of her achievements as a woman within a male-dominated political party operating within a male-dominated society.

Overall, it could be proposed that by intervening in the ideological debate, the Davieses instigated, or at least accelerated, the demise of early Plaid Cymru thought-practices and opened up the arena for what would be a perceptible ideological realignment within Plaid Cymru after the Second World War. In a sense, therefore, there occurred a distinctive ideological break from the political philosophy and thought-practices of Saunders Lewis-inspired early Plaid Cymru.

The Denouement of Early Plaid Cymru Ideology

Saunders Lewis's problem lay in terms of his ideological clarity, certainly, that is, in the eyes of the general public, which Plaid Cymru had to win over if it wanted to achieve its stated political aims and objectives. Given the evidence at hand, it is fair to assume that Saunders Lewis was clearly not an unmitigated conservative, fascist or green thinker. Although some elements and concepts are undoubtedly brought in, it is possible to contend that Lewis's form of nationalism is the host-vessel in which these concepts rest.

Interpreting Lewis's thinking, it is the nation that is the arena for cognisant change – cognisant change that should involve the nation providing both the geographical space and the intellectual environment for cerebral, as well as concrete, transformation. Putting this across in a way that was not too subliminally inclined was, and possibly still is, the problem. Lewis's predicament – ideational confusion – may prove to be Plaid Cymru's predicament. It could certainly be argued that there is a case to be made for claiming that the ideology of nationalism could be seen as Lewis's flag of convenience. If that is so, and if Lewis's beliefs were in tune with the core concepts of nationalism, then Plaid Cymru's ideology – certainly that is the ideology of post-1945 Plaid Cymru, whose beliefs and policies are less conspicuously nationalistic than those of Lewis – would be even more open to charges of using nationalism as a flag of convenience than was Lewis, and Plaid Cymru, in its early incarnation.

With the withdrawal of Saunders Lewis from frontline politics at the end of the Second World War, what Plaid Cymru had to do, particularly given the onslaught against the party for its supposed flirtation with fascism, was to dispose of those parts of its thought-practices that the party found uncomfortable or distasteful – like the linkage with the obtainment of nationalism through a militaristic channel – along with those elements that took the party's ideology into the field of cultural constraints – namely the adherence to a quixotic philosophical stance that projected the unrealistic attainment of a society in Wales that was deindustrialised and observant of a morally righteous anti-materialist position. Admittedly, some of those within the party who held different opinions and diverse political perspectives from Saunders Lewis on a series of issues had already challenged the leadership line through the processes of internal debate and the publication of articles and pamphlets. However, post-1945, and in many respects post-Lewis, the party's theoreticians had to attempt to open up Plaid Cymru's policy and philosophical arenas so that fresh, more relevant concepts could be absorbed. 1945 can be pinpointed as the year, therefore, in which the ideology of Plaid Cymru underwent an ideational or even, arguably, an epistemological break, as Lewis's rationale was to be replaced by new thought-practices and Plaid Cymru left its early stage and entered its modern one.

Notes

1. Thomas Combs, *The Party of Wales* (Ann Arbor, MI: Ann Arbor Press, 1984), p. 37.
2. *Western Mail*, 15 May 2004, p. 14.
3. Peter Beresford Ellis, *Wales: A Nation Again* (Letchworth: Garden City Press, 1968), p. 70.
4. Michael Freeden, 'Is nationalism a distinct ideology?', *Political Studies*, vol. XLVI, 1998, p. 754.
5. Ibid., p. 754.
6. Ibid., p. 754.
7. G.A. Williams, *The Search for Beulah Land* (New York: Holmes and Meier, 1980), p. 1.
8. Ibid., p. 31.
9. Ibid.
10. Ibid, p. 132.
11. Ibid., p. 132.
12. Thomas Combs, *The Party of Wales*, p. 54.
13. Gareth Miles and Rob Griffiths, *Socialism for the Welsh People* (Cardiff: Y Faner Goch, 1979).
14. Ibid, p. 10.
15. Peter Beresford Ellis, *Wales: A Nation Again*, p. 77.
16. Ibid., p. 67.
17. Ibid., p. 80.
18. Simon Thomas, *BBC Wales Today*, 4 May 2004.
19. G.A. Williams, *Peace and Power: Henry Richard, a Radical for Our Time* (Cardiff: CND Cymru, 1988), p. 7.
20. Ibid.
21. Erica Benner, 'Nationality without nationalism', *Journal of Political Ideologies*, vol. 2, no. 2, 1997, p. 189.
22. Thomas Combs, *The Party of Wales*, p. 68.
23. Michael Freeden, 'Is nationalism a distinct ideology?', p. 761.
24. Michael Freeden, *Ideology: A Very Short Introduction* (Oxford: Oxford University Press, 2003), p. 99.
25. Michael Freeden, *Ideologies and Political Theory* (Oxford: Clarendon Press, 1996), p. 588.
26. Ibid., p. 181.

27. Michael Freeden, 'Is nationalism a distinct ideology?', p. 760.

28. Ibid., p. 762.

29. Thomas Combs, *The Party of Wales*, p. 87.

30. Michael Freeden, *Ideologies and Political Theory*, pp. 425–426.

31. See Chris Sparks and Stuart Isaacs, *Political Theorists in Context* (London: Routledge, 2004), and Nancy S. Love, *Dogmas and Dreamers* (Chatham, NJ: Chatham House, 2005).

32. James Farr, 'Social capital: a conceptual history', *Political Theory*, vol. 32, no. 1, 2004, pp. 6–33.

33. Karl Marx, *The Communist Manifesto* (New York: Vanguard Press, 1926), p. 1.

34. Benedict Anderson, *Imagined Communities* (London: Verso, 1991).

35. Chris Sparks and Stuart Isaacs, *Political Theorists in Context* (London: Routledge, 2004), p. 225.

36. Gwynfor Evans, *The Fight for Welsh Freedom* (Talybont: Y Lolfa, 1992), p. 110.

37. Harri Webb, *A Militant Muse* (Bridgend: Seren, 1998), p. 74.

38. Jane Aaron, *The Welsh Survival Gene* (Cardiff: IWA, 2003), p. 7.

39. Ibid.

40. Gwynfor Evans, *The Fight for Welsh Freedom*, p. 128.

41. Carwyn Fowler, 'A durable concept: Anthony Smith's concept of national identity and the case of Wales', Political Studies Association conference paper, 2002, p. 4.

42. Gwynfor Evans, *Land of My Fathers* (Talybont: Y Lolfa, 2008), p. 442.

43. G.A. Williams, *When Was Wales?* (London: Penguin, 1985), p. 281.

44. Alun R. Jones and Gwyn Thomas, *Presenting Saunders Lewis* (Cardiff: University of Wales Press,1983), p. 4.

45. Ibid., p. 23.

46. Ibid., p. 4.

47. Gareth Miles and Rob Griffiths, *Socialism for the Welsh People*, p. 12.

48. D. Hywel Davies, *The Welsh Nationalist Party 1925–45* (New York: St Martin's Press, 1983), p. 29.

49. Michael Freeden, *Ideologies and Political Theory*, p. 337.

50. Ibid., p. 337.

51. See Bruce Haddock, 'Contingency and judgement in Oakeshott's political thought', *European Journal of Political Theory*, vol. 4, no. 1, 2005, pp. 7–21.

52. Gareth Miles and Rob Griffiths, *Socialism for the Welsh People* , p. 12.

53. Saunders Lewis, *The Principles of Nationalism* (Caerdydd: Plaid Cymru, 1926).

54. Charlotte Davies, *Welsh Nationalism in the Twentieth Century* (Connecticut: Praeger, 1989), p. 30.

55. Michael Freeden, 'Is nationalism a distinct ideology?', p. 762.

56. Michael Freeden, *Ideologies and Political Theory*, p. 333.
57. D.J. Davies, 'The way to real co-operation', *The Welsh Nationalist*, May, 1932, p. 8.
58. Ibid.
59. Michael Freeden, 'Is nationalism a distinct ideology?', p. 762.
60. Alun R. Jones and Gwyn Thomas, *Presenting Saunders Lewis*, p. 29.
61. Ibid., p. 34.
62. G.A. Williams, *When Was Wales?*, p. 279.
63. Jones and Thomas, *Presenting Saunders Lewis*, pp. 24–25.
64. Michael Freeden, 'Is nationalism a distinct ideology?', p. 763.
65. G. A. Williams, *When Was Wales?*, p. 281.
66. D.J. Davies, 'The insufficiency of cultural nationalism', *The Welsh Nationalist*, March 1932.
67. D.J. Davies, 'The way to real co-operation', *The Welsh Nationalist*, May 1932.
68. Ibid, p. 281.
69. Diego Mura and Alejandro Quiroga, 'Spanish nationalism: ethnic or civic?', *Ethnicities*, vol. 5, no. 1, 205, pp. 9–29.
70. Paul James, *Nation Formation* (London: Sage, 1996), p. 142.
71. R. Tudur Jones, *The Desire of Nations* (Llandybie: C. Davies, 1974), p. 15.
72. D. Hywel Davies, *The Welsh Nationalist Party 1925–1945*, p. 102.
73. Ibid., p. 101.
74. Ibid.
75. Chris Williams, *Democratic Rhondda: Politics and Society 1885–1951* (Cardiff: University of Wales Press, 1996), p. 168.
76. John Davies, *A History of Wales* (London: Penguin, 1993), p.392.
77. Alun R. Jones and Gwyn Thomas, *Presenting Saunders Lewis*, p. 31.
78. Chris Williams, *Democratic Rhondda*, p. 168.
79. Richard Wyn Jones, 'Care of the community', *Planet: The Welsh Internationalist*, 109, 1995, p. 18.
80. Michael Freeden, *Ideology*, p. 58.
81. Carwyn Fowler, 'Nationalism and the Labour Party in Wales', *Llafur*, vol. 8, no. 4, 2003, p. 101.
82. G. A. Williams, *When Was Wales?*, p. 280.
83. Ibid.
84. Charlotte Davies, *Welsh Nationalism in the Twentieth Century*, p. 69.
85. Ibid.
86. D. Hywel Davies, *The Welsh Nationalist Party 1925–1945*, p. 239.
87. Carwyn Fowler, 'Nationalism and the Labour Party in Wales', pp. 97–105.
88. Michael Freeden, *Ideology*, p. 99.
89. D. Hywel Davies, *The Welsh Nationalist Party 1925–1945*, p. 27.
90. Alun R. Jones and Gwyn Thomas, *Presenting Saunders Lewis*, p. 27.
91. D. Hywel Davies, *The Welsh Nationalist Party 1925–1945*, p. 28.

92. Michael Freeden, *Ideologies and Political Theory*, p. 527.
93. Ibid.
94. Ibid.
95. Paul James, *Nation Formation*, p. 18.
96. Ibid., p. 104.
97. Geoff Danaher, Tony Schirato and Jen Webb, *Understanding Foucault* (London: Sage, 2000), p. 24.
98. Alun R. Jones and Gwyn Thomas, *Presenting Saunders Lewis*, p. 29.
99. Ibid.
100. Michael Freeden, *Ideologies and Political Theory*, p. 202.
101. D. Hywel Davies, *The Welsh Nationalist Party 1925–1945*, p. 82.
102. Ibid., p. 102.
103. Michael Freeden, *Ideologies and Political Theory*, p. 364.
104. Michael Freeden, 'Is nationalism a distinct ideology?', p. 752.
105. Ibid., p. 754.
106. D. Hywel Davies, *The Welsh Nationalist Party 1925–1945*, p. 100.
107. Ibid.
108. Ibid., p. 101.
109. Laura McAllister, *Plaid Cymru: The Emergence of a Political Party* (Brigend: Seren, 2001), p. 160.
110. D. Hywel Davies, *The Welsh Nationalist Party 1925–1945*, p. 101.
111. Laura McAllister, *Plaid Cymru*, p. 27.
112. Ibid., pp. 27–8.
113. D.J. and Noelle Davies, *Can Wales Afford Self-Government?* (Caernarfon: Swyddfa'r Blaid, 1939), p. 38.
114. Ibid.
115. Michael Freeden, *Ideologies and Political Theory*, p. 77.
116. D.J. and Noelle Davies, *Can Wales Afford Self-Government?*, p. 39.
117. Michael Freeden, *Ideologies and Political Theory*, p. 19.
118. D.J. and Noelle Davies, *Can Wales Afford Self-Government?*, p. 43.
119. Ibid., p. 60.
120. Ibid.
121. Michael Freeden, 'Is nationalism a distinct ideology?', p. 751.
122. Ibid.
123. Laura McAllister, *Plaid Cymru*, p. 55.
124. Ibid.
125. D. Hywel Davies, *The Welsh Nationalist Party 1925–1945*, p. 108.

IV

MODERN PLAID CYMRU AND THE IDEOLOGY OF NATIONALISM

Having determined how different ideologies and ideological concepts played their part in the development of Plaid Cymru's thought-practices in its formative years, it is now important to trace developments after the Second World War. As previously mentioned, 1945 has been chosen as the date that marked a watershed in Plaid Cymru's thinking. This date has been arrived at because it was at this time that the party had to face up to the emergence of a new social, economic and political environment in Britain, as the arrival of the Beveridgean welfare settlement secured the bond between the individual and the state. In addition to this new individual–state relationship, the arrival of Gwynfor Evans as party president, in 1945, enabled Plaid Cymru to evolve in different ideological and structural directions. This was not altogether surprising, given that Evans's own social and political interests differed somewhat from the pre-war leadership of the party. Hence, the period from 1945 can be regarded as the era of modern Plaid Cymru. Nevertheless, it must be stressed that this is an estimated date, because an ideological evolution, and a realisation that a change of direction and emphasis was required, had actually been taking place in some quarters of Plaid Cymru during the Saunders Lewis presidency of the inter-war years – as expressed by activists such as D.J. and Noelle Davies, for example. Therefore, perhaps somewhat inevitably, there will be instances where this analysis will return to pre-1945 statements and literature as certain issues materialise, and also because there is no absolute division between what can be regarded as early or modern Plaid Cymru. Hence, in chronological terms, some modern pronouncements and thinking can be attributed to the days of early Plaid Cymru.

Four ideologies – nationalism, socialism, liberalism and feminism – will be examined in this and the subsequent chapter. The first three of these – nationalism, socialism and liberalism – are the ideologies that predominantly emerge within the language and writings of modern Plaid Cymru. Thus, it is these three ideologies that will dominate the discussion. The fourth, feminism, requires some degree of attention, nevertheless, as feminist ideas have emerged within Plaid Cymru over the years and it would, therefore, be amiss to discard the ideology of feminism in its entirety. Although these four ideologies have been highlighted, it is not the intention of this analysis to completely dismiss other ideologies, or to claim that the ideology of Plaid Cymru can be examined only in relationship to, and using the tenets of, these other competing ideologies. It is merely a case that investigations prove that the aforementioned four, but in particular the first three of nationalism, socialism and liberalism, have dominated the political rhetoric within the party in the last sixty or so years.

Another macro-ideology, conservatism, will not be addressed, as any conservative viewpoints displayed by Plaid Cymru representatives were garnered overwhelmingly in the period that can be labelled early Plaid Cymru. Though there are some traditionalists within the party – guardians of the Saunders Lewis tradition, they may be called – who would regard themselves as social or religious conservatives, their numbers within the party today are very few, and are rapidly dwindling. Whilst conservatism has its place within the thought-practices of Plaid Cymru, therefore, it can be contended that those advocating the conservative disposition are peripheral to the party's ideological motor. Hence, conservatism, though in existence within the party since 1945, will not feature as one of its major ideological strands. As a result, of the four stated ideologies, nationalism must be addressed first of all. This is because nationalism is the ideology that Plaid Cymru's thought-practices are most often measured against, attributed to and labelled as.

Nationalism

Rightly or wrongly, any survey of a hundred Welsh people with a moderate understanding of, and interest in, Welsh politics would undoubtedly conclude that Plaid Cymru is a nationalist political force. This is understandable, to a very great extent, as the party's formative name was Plaid Genedlaethol Cymru (National Party of Wales). It is also apparent when a review of party literature is undertaken. With anti-Englishness in evidence on occasions – England being the traditional enemy or other in nationalistic terms – the spectre of nationalism pervades Plaid Cymru's narrative. As far back as 1939 the opening paragraph of 'The New Wales: synopsis of the policy of the Welsh Nationalist Party' emphasised Plaid Cymru's belief in maintaining its conception of the traditional society in Wales. To demonstrate this, Wales is described

as a *teulu* (family).[1] This communitarian-style depiction appears innocent enough until the reader is informed that the English have, over
the centuries, 'completely disintegrated the "tribe", and the traditional
idea of "*bonedd*" and "*perchentyaeth*".'[2] Whereas *bonedd* equates to
bond in English, *perchentyaeth*, like *hiraeth*, has no straight translation.
It broadly means possession-of-a-house (ism) – a wide distribution of
property ownership. There are hints here of a blood and soil nationalist
position being adopted by Plaid Cymru as the bond is seen as traditional, and a steadying influence on society, and those outside the bond,
the English in this instance, are portrayed as the destructive force which
has demolished that precious connection. The idea of the bond and
attachment to things Welsh was further exemplified by D.J. and Noelle
Davies. The Davieses summoned up a Welsh term *cydweitbrediad*[3]
(working together) to project the future. According to them, the only
alternative to *cydweitbrediad* would be 'the progressive swallowing up
of Wales by England, with an inevitable further deterioration in both the
quantity and the quality of her population, and the ultimate extinction of
our nation.'[4] This is a fatalistic message that is typical of blood and soil
nationalism, as a doomsday scenario is presented with attachment and
commitment to the preservation of the nation seen as the only means of
ensuring survival for the culture under threat.

Where Plaid Cymru's views differ from those of many who encourage blood and soil nationalism, however, is that the party does not, on
the whole, advocate the blood element of blood and soil on two counts.
First, in contrast to, for instance, the Basque nationalists, who – in their
interpretation of what constitutes ethnicity – insist that true Basques
should be able to prove a timeline of eight generations,[5] Plaid Cymru
lays down no biological or ethnic qualification for either membership
of the Welsh nation or subsequent inclusion in the everyday activities
of that nation. Second, no indication of any call to arms is evident
within Plaid Cymru's literature or rhetoric. Justifying this position of
Plaid Cymru as a non-aggressive political force, Dafydd Wigley testi-
fied to the difficulties of cooperating with nationalist parties overseas
who 'take a different line on these things.'[6] Wigley went on to remark
that 'our nationalism is civic nationalism not ethnic nationalism.'[7] The
Meirionnydd Dwyfor MP, Elfyn Llwyd, concurred with this, as he
asserted that Plaid Cymru's 'civic nationalism is quite different from
the old Balkan-type nationalism.'[8] Dafydd Trystan, the party's former
Chief Executive, also offered a corresponding viewpoint. When asked
whether he regarded himself as a nationalist, his response, after admit-
ting that nationalism was a broad conceptual field, was that he defined
himself as 'a civic nationalist'.[9]

Although, sporadically, London, England, Westminster and so forth appear in Plaid Cymru literature and rhetoric as the oppressors of Welsh national fulfilment, it is never a belligerent opposition that stems from the party. Plaid Cymru's November 1974 Election Manifesto, *Power for Wales*, exemplified this rhetorical interplay in its appeal to the people of Wales. 'Why should we suffer for the Imperial illusions of a London government? Let us have our own government instead',[10] the manifesto demanded. In relation to Plaid Cymru's perspective on what brand of nationalism it espouses, it is important to note that, rather than being of a jingoistic variety, the opposite would appear to be true, with concepts such as pacifism and non-violence to the fore.

The Role of the *Gwerin*

One question that needs to be considered is whether some of the above observations expose a degree of indistinctness when it comes to Plaid Cymru's embracing of nationalist tenets. If an insistence on adopting a bellicose or imperialistic stance is seen by some nationalists as a pre-requisite for assuming a nationalist position, then Plaid Cymru does not fall within that category of confrontational or expansionist nationalism. However, the principle of a self-governing Wales is evident within the statements and language of Plaid Cymru, albeit one that is to be engendered and shaped by non-violent political action rather than any form of armed insurrection. Indeed, a Nietzschean approach can be observed if a timeline is started with Saunders Lewis's wartime declaration that the success of Plaid Cymru's programme was dependent upon 'the awakening of the nation, the *gwerin* [folk] of Wales, to "will" its own salvation.'[11] The use of the phrase 'will its own salvation' suggests that providence is an identifiable factor within Plaid Cymru's view of the nation's destiny.

Here another link can be made between nationalist rhetoric and a religious strand whose public image is the *gwerin*, the ordinary people of Wales, who are imbued with a greater, embedded, sense of time and place than other members of society, who nationalists sense lack the earthiness of the *gwerin*. In Marxist language this would provide justification for a proletariat revolution, given the assumption that the importance of the proletariat to Marxists is akin to the importance of the *gwerin* to Saunders Lewis, at least, but also, arguably, to Plaid Cymru as a whole. Interestingly, as the body of people labelled the proletariat has been adopted and romanticised by certain figures and organisations for their own stated political ends, so too, according to Dave Adamson, has the *gwerin*. For Adamson, the *gwerin* 'was an intellectual construct evident in all spheres of intellectual activity in Wales, reproduced as the image of the nation and itself reproducing that image.'[12]

Continuing on the theme of the *gwerin* and nationalism, Gwynfor Evans commented on the link between nationalism and the actions of the *gwerin* to achieve autonomy for Wales. Emphasising decolonisation in his nationalist vision, Evans noted how 'in Wales the first step is to supplant the present *diwreiddiedig ac uchelgeisiol griw* (the deracinated and ambitious crew); and to resist the unbearable arrogance of London civil servants and politicians who always know what is best for Wales.'[13] Evans continued by stating that 'with will and vision this nation can create her own environment.'[14] One of the party's finest theoreticians, Phil Williams, pointed out that that very environment – its geographical space and ontology – is in existence at present and, moreover, this environment plays a salient part in the everyday reasoning and expression of people in Wales. As Williams commented, despite everything that has occurred to break down the indigenous population's sense of Welshness, and the determination of the Welsh people to continue to exist as Welsh people, 'it is the single identity of Wales that is ascendant.'[15] As long as this holds – in the minds of the Welsh people as a whole and of Plaid Cymru supporters in particular – then nationalism will always be a viable and extant option. Furthermore, Phil Williams set this single identity theory into an encircling geographical and psychological milieu. For Williams, Wales is 'large enough to fill the horizon but small enough to recognise every human being as an individual. The point is this: Wales is small enough for us to care about every part of it.'[16] Introducing the concept of democracy into this debate, Cynog Dafis, while exploring the question of why group and national identity is important, observed that, in the case of Wales:

> identity derives from external factors such as terrain and location. It is consolidated through organisational networks and shared institutions. Crucially it is fed by shared historical and cultural experiences. It is transmitted down the generations. Thus has national identity survived in Wales ... despite the complete absence until very recently of formal political structures.[17]

Michael Freeden's view on this envisaging and actuality was evident when he stated that nationalism is an ideology that 'concentrates on the exceptional worth of a nation as a shaper of national identity.'[18] Lewis, Evans, Williams and Dafis appear to be implying that Welsh national identity is indeed in existence. What it needs is merely a reshaping and a reconditioning and, taking Gwynfor Evans's observation, a detaching of some aspects of its corpus. What needs to be established, therefore, is whether others in Plaid Cymru share these views and whether these opinions are identifiably nationalist. In nationalistic terms, what is interesting to establish is whether there is anything deeper or more substantial within Plaid Cymru's view of the nation other than the party's desire to merely recast the Welsh body politic so that it is in line with a more responsive, emotional and psychologically Welsh approach, which, it would appear at first glance, is the position generally favoured and endorsed by most, if not all, of Plaid Cymru's politicians and activists.

With the aforementioned in mind, however, all may not be as straightforward as it first appears. Laura McAllister, for instance, has noted how there have been debates within Plaid Cymru 'between those who view Welsh nationalism as a free-standing ideology and those who argue for a more explicit and detailed political location.'[19] If the free-standing ideology approach is accepted, then appeals to emotion and a sense of history and purpose will prevail. The recasting of the Welsh body politic will be achieved primarily through encouraging a deeper sense of Welsh identity and fostering practice that is identifiably Welsh via, for example, an extension of education through the medium of Welsh or encouraging people to take part in traditional Welsh societies such as Urdd Gobiath Cymru (Welsh Youth Organisation) or Merched Y Wawr (The Women's Movement).

Some nationalists may be content with this burgeoning of activity that is representative of the indigenous culture. Nevertheless, this seamless adoption may prove too narrow in its scope and practice for a party such as Plaid Cymru – seeking structural and societal transformation – to adopt. The dilemma of being a political party is important here because 'the electorate requires a set of policies which explains the precise type of government Plaid proposes.'[20] One of the key differences between a nationalist pressure group or organisation and a nationalist political party – purportedly nationalist, as this analysis is claiming, in the case of Plaid Cymru – is thus highlighted, as the political party is required to offer a comprehensive agenda to the general public that evinces clarity of thought and deed. Michael Freeden's talk of nationalism as a thin ideology is relevant in this instance because if Plaid Cymru's free-standing ideology supporters are seen to be in the majority, then nationalism's role or effect within Plaid Cymru will be severely limited. This thin nationalism is almost debilitating in the sense that by burdening the nation with symbolism, and then asking it to be the provider of moral strength, it subsequently fails to 'produce a scheme for the just distribution of scarce and vital goods – the famous "who gets what, when, how" question that is seen to be central to politics.'[21] It could be argued, therefore, that for nationalism to succeed, and for Plaid Cymru to succeed, if indeed it is nationalism that the party seeks to portray, a process of augmenting and expanding its subject matter and political philosophy is required.

Nationalism and Internationalism

The fear of being boxed in through identification with nationalism, and nationalism alone, could be one reason why Plaid Cymru members seek to accentuate their belief in internationalism as another appendage to the party's ideology. For instance, the Plaid Cymru Summer School and Conference held at Llangefni in 1959 discussed the issue of internationalism in great depth. Although the actual definition and usage of the term by Plaid Cymru could be challenged, it was decided at Llangefni that the term 'international' rather than 'foreign' policy should be used. The justification given by the party was that 'Plaid Cymru dislikes the division of the world into "us" and "foreigners", which the term "foreign policy" implies.'[22] There is evidently an identification here with, and not a rejection of, the other.

The former Plaid Cymru MEP Eurig Wyn is somebody who empathises with this holistic nationalist/internationalist view. Wyn has commented on how he joined Plaid Cymru at the age of seventeen because he was 'attracted to the idea of self-determination.'[23] Not content with this notion alone, however, Eurig Wyn explained how, as a young man, he 'wanted, and still wants, Wales to be part of a worldwide movement for self-government.'[24] So there are universalist concerns raised by Wyn with regard to worldwide self-determination, with the acknowledgement that the geopolitical order is based on the nation-state system. Alas, a problem may arise in this line of reasoning if the dichotomy of universal–particular is examined. However, Wyn was presenting his case along the lines of universal rationality (i.e. we want self-determination because it will be beneficial to us and thus we presume that you desire the same). Wyn's argument is thus compatible because, as Freeden remarked, 'ideologies are designed to be communicable and are by no means idiosyncratically subjective.'[25] What this connecting of concerns – national and international – ensures is that it also dampens any criticism of Wyn's views as being narrowly nationalistic or excessively particularistic.

By adjoining his concerns and ambitions for autonomous rule at home with a general concern for self-determination for whatever interested parties yearn for it throughout the world, Eurig Wyn and others who share his views bring the issue of internationalism and a global perspective into the general discourse of the party. To these ends, the existence and the potential for universal change that is held out by the existence of the United Nations is crucially important. As Charlotte Davies has pointed out, Plaid Cymru's desire for a self-governing Wales to seek admission to the UN has been an essential objective of the party since the UN's inception in 1949.[26] For instance, the party conference in 1968 asserted that 'a Welsh Government would immediately apply for membership of the United Nations organisation.'[27] While some people, such as former member and councillor Keith Morgan – 'if we had a seat at the UN who'll look at us, it is purely symbolism, purely ideology'[28] – and Dafydd Elis-Thomas – 'in my view membership of the United Nations is a piece of nonsense'[29]– play it down, for Eurig Wyn 'it is vital that Wales becomes a member of the UN.'[30] Dafydd Iwan also maintains that his 'vision of a new Wales is that it should be a proper part of the EU and a Member of the UN.'[31]

A utopian element enters the debate here as Plaid Cymru could be seen to be adopting the principles of world government, or a world forum at least, which would implement subsidiarity to subdivide the world into national and regional entities: many of which are already in existence, though calls for national and communal self-determination would have to be judged and then, possibly, consented to. This is not as far-reaching as it may at first appear, and utopianism is very much part of what Laura McAllister defined as 'Plaid Cymru's intellectual heritage.'[32] Transferring the three components of utopianism – association, community and cooperation[33] – from a national to an international scale would provide Plaid Cymru with a justification for its internationalism and the party's desire to pursue universal practice of national or communal self-determination. This idea is at variance from some nationalist parties, such as many of those that have recently arisen in the former Soviet Union and sub-Saharan Africa,[34] for example, who more often than not preach a sense of localism or parochialism at the expense of wider concerns.

Internationalism: Wales as a European Nation

In similar terms to Eurig Wyn's, Plaid Cymru's current MEP, Jill Evans, has also adopted an internationalist stance. Evans has linked her internationalism with an attack on the notion of independence as a concept, and independent existence as a practice. For Evans, 'independence is a meaningless concept in modern Wales. No country or state is independent or separate from its neighbours and partners in the world and I would not want Wales to be either.'[35] Elin Jones, the AM for Ceredigion, has similar views to Jill Evans on Wales's position in regard to its place in the world and also its 'constitutional aspect'.[36] For

Jones, the party's objective is 'freedom within the European Union'.[37] To her this is 'an internationalist perspective but it is also a nationalist perspective. But it is not an insular nationalist perspective. It is an outward looking nationalist perspective.'[38]

This development of Wales as a European nation, in an internationalist sense, has been conspicuous within Plaid Cymru for many years. Peter Lynch maintains that as far back as the 1930s 'Plaid was critical of British isolationism and a general reluctance to take a European perspective on a range of political questions.'[39] Three decades on, at the 1962 Summer School and Conference at Pontarddulais, Plaid Cymru's executive placed the party's onus upon 'ensuring the best possible terms for Welsh entry into the Common Market.'[40] Five years later, at the Summer School and Conference at Dolgellau, Plaid Cymru members further emphasised the demand for Welsh recognition within the European context with a nationalistic appeal. In a statement released at the time, the party claimed that it desired the establishment of a European community 'on the basis of equal respect' and that 'recognition of all the historic nations of Western Europe – *L'Europe des Patries* – would be completely compatible with the philosophy and aims of our movement.'[41] Taking this statement as a guide, it could be argued that a commitment to European involvement was being enshrined in the party's ideational construction as a core concept. If this is so, however, it could be interpreted as offering a challenge to the Freedenite core nationalist concept of positive valorisation of the Welsh nation. Although it would appear straightforward for a confederation of European nation-states to pool together, difficulties may arise on the questions of sovereignty – for example, if some areas of control were handed over from each individual nation-state to centralised European bodies – and in terms of allegiance; if, for instance, the European Community were to act as another focal point to which people would feel that they have a sense of duty, then the prioritisation of the nation would inevitably suffer to some degree, and thus nationalism's core concepts would be diminished.

Despite some concerns, the theme of Wales in Europe has continued apace within Plaid Cymru up to the present day. Phil Williams, who during his time as vice-chair of the party held responsibility for overseeing policy and research, produced the document *Towards 2000: Plaid Cymru's Programme for Wales in Europe*. Williams pleaded for the party to embrace Europeanism in its future thinking. Williams argued that 'if Wales is to survive as a vibrant and confident society we must win full national status within the Community.'[42]

This relationship, real or imagined, between Wales and other

European countries has been an area for discussion within the party since its inception. Just as Saunders Lewis talked of Wales's emotional and literary attachments with continental Europe, so a contemporary Plaid Cymru grandee, former leader Dafydd Wigley, is keen to stress the European dimension as a backdrop to Plaid Cymru's policy-making. Wigley maintains that he has 'always regarded Wales as being a European nation. In terms of our language and culture, our religion and our folklore we are mainstream European, and our place is in the common European homeland.'[43] On a practical note, also, Dafydd Wigley has been at the forefront of promoting links with, and speaking on behalf of, smaller nations that Plaid Cymru identifies and empathises with. Anthony Packer, a Plaid Cymru member who translated the autobiography of Vytautas Landsbergis, the leader who presided over Lithuania's path to independence, has claimed that during one visit to Lithuania he was told that the Lithuanian freedom movement 'respected Dafydd Wigley for having been the first MP to raise questions about Baltic independence at Westminster.'[44]

Despite the positive impact of Wigley's interventions on behalf of Lithuania, and notwithstanding the obvious successes that Plaid Cymru has helped to engender on the international front, there is, neverthe-less, a streak of emotionalism evident within Plaid Cymru's rhetoric whenever Wales's place in Europe is placed under the spotlight. As has been noted earlier, Freeden has identified emotion as a core con-cept of nationalism. The unusual aspect in this instance, however, is that this emotionalism shown by Plaid Cymru is not identifiable with Wales, and Wales alone, as observers of nationalism would expect, but, within the morphology of the party, it is spread further afield to incor-porate a larger geographical and, since the inception of the European Community (now European Union), a politico-institutional space. Although this may be unproblematic in itself, where Plaid Cymru may encounter serious problems in the years ahead is when it has to face up to the question of whether the maturing of a common European iden-tity – something advocated by Europhiles throughout many political parties across Europe – would represent the apogee of a post-nationalist age and would leave the nationalist, and the pseudo-nationalist, par-ties of Europe, which bought into the European project, clutching at ideological straws. Though this post-nationalism may appear somewhat of an anathema to a party that is purportedly nationalist, the ideological stance adopted by Dafydd Elis-Thomas, as noted later in this chapter, opens up new areas down which the Plaid Cymru ideological dialectic could travel.

Gwynfor Evans and the Concept of Internationalist Nationalism

Notwithstanding the assurance with which the aforementioned members hold their views on internationalism and the European dimension, perhaps the most prominent of all Plaid Cymru activists in declaring his internationalist convictions was Gwynfor Evans. Evans dedicated a chapter in his book *Fighting for Wales* to what he labelled 'Internationalist Nationalism'.[45] In an attempt to clarify his thoughts on these matters, Evans commenced his justification for using the term 'internationalist nationalism' with his contention that 'Plaid Cymru is an inherently internationalist and anti-imperialist party. It aims to free Wales from the shackles of British imperialism so that it can cooperate creatively with other nations in Europe and the world.'[46] Although Evans emphasised his, and what he contended to be Plaid Cymru's, disdain for the other, in the guise of British Imperialism, where Evans differed from some within his party was when he accentuated Wales's historical links westward with Ireland, and the other Celtic nations, rather than placing the onus on forging relationships with those countries in continental Europe that make up the European Union.

As a historian it was perhaps not surprising that Evans looked backward at times in his political writing, and this is evident when he cites and praises 'the Irish national struggle'.[47] He also mentions the close relationship that Plaid Cymru enjoyed with Fianna Fail in the 1940s and 1950s. Hence, Evans's internationalism, in contrast to the more contemporary internationalism of the pro-Europeans, placed Wales firmly in the Celtic brotherhood, as Celtic alliances, and Celtic allegiances, were prioritised. Here, possibly, Evans had more in common with early Plaid Cymru thinking, as the anti-Anglicisation, anti-imperialist nature of pan-Celtic nationalism is to the fore. Early Plaid Cymru members may have been critical of the British Empire, and supportive of the liberationist claims for those nations that were suppressed by imperialism, but 'it was the Irish campaign for self-government and subsequent developments in Ireland that provided its main source of political fascination.'[48] It could be contended, nevertheless, that, although Evans's internationalist views were more akin to those of Plaid Cymru before the Second World War, the evolution of the party's ideology, and the burgeoning of the European Community, would have forced Gwynfor Evans to reassess his outlook and take on board a less Celticist position in favour of a broader internationalist position. What Evans did manage to do during his term of office as party president was to act as a bridge between the old view of internationalist nationalism, centred on the

Celtic fringe, and the new internationalist nationalism – exemplified by members such as Jill Evans and Eurig Wyn – that looks to Brussels and beyond to forge links with ethnic groups such as the Kurds and the nomadic tribesmen and -women of the western Sahara.

Whether old or new visions of internationalist nationalism are presented, however, there appears little doubt that Plaid Cymru has, from its inception, presented itself as a party that is not introspective or geographically or ideationally restricted; fundamentally it has not fallen into the trap of aligning itself with narrow nationalist concerns. In conceptual terms, the leap has come from the traditional linking by Plaid Cymru of Welsh cultural and political interests with Celtic nationalism – sharing similar apprehension, in ethno-linguistic terms, with regard to English cultural and socio-political expansionism – and from the recent alignment by Plaid Cymru with peoples and organisations, outside the traditional confines of the British Isles and Brittany, who are advancing the case for self-determination in cultures that form part of the developing world. The interesting aspect here, certainly as far as nationalism is concerned, is that these developing world nationalisms appear to have little in common, in structural or historical terms, with Plaid Cymru's experience, as they have evolved in societies that have not endured mass industrialisation or have not taken the conventional political route that has been followed by Western societies since the Enlightenment. Thus, what Plaid Cymru has done by empathising with the Kurds and the people of the western Sahara is not just to recognise that national self-determination is part of a universal praxis but also 'to indicate a belief in the overriding validity of intuitions and to make assumptions about human similarity, even identity, with particular repercussions concerning political conduct and its conceptualization.'[49]

Consequently, it can be claimed that self-determination, be it on a national, ethnic or communal basis, eclipses particularistic historical, structural and political traditions. It can even eclipse entire macro-ideologies. If certain leading members of Plaid Cymru, such as Eurig Wyn, Jill Evans and Dafydd Elis-Thomas, are associating themselves with these ideological developments, which are occurring a great distance from Wales's borders, it could be advanced that this shows a maturity in Plaid Cymru's view of itself as a political organisation, its links with other bodies and campaigning groups throughout the world and, especially, its contentment with its current ideological position. Therefore, internationalism, or internationalist nationalism, as Gwynfor Evans labelled it, can be justly described as being an embryonic aspect of Plaid Cymru's morphology.

Plaid Cymru's *Weltanschauung*

The message emanating from the aforementioned elected representatives of the party, both past and present, is that Plaid Cymru has a *Weltanschauung* that is at the heart of the party's self-identification. This *Weltanschauung* reads that the geopolitical map is constituted chiefly through the interrelationships and interaction of political units administered chiefly on a national basis. It is fair to contend that Plaid Cymru would argue that, having reflected and evaluated the state of the world in its present constitution – and any political or cultural organisation seeking recognition and a degree of autonomy would undoubtedly concur – what is acknowledged to be the normal practice globally, namely varying degrees of self-government by people within their allotted geographical spaces, should be applicable to all who petition for it. This line of reasoning is evidenced in the party's 1968 conference debate on national freedom, during which delegates emphasised 'the inalienable rights of nationhood'[50] before reaching an accord that concluded that 'national freedom is the condition of national survival.'[51] There is a sense in this pronouncement, therefore, that if you are incapable of administering your own geographical–political space, or if you are prohibited from doing so by some repressive forces, then you are experiencing a sense of disembodiment from the standard geopolitical modus vivendi.

While this petitioning for national representation and national autonomy would appear to be a reasonable condition on which to proceed, what could be contended, however, is that this world-view of Plaid Cymru's is little more than an abstract universalism that lends itself to what amounts to an essentially conservative position, wherein the nation-state is seen as being set in concrete; an immovable 'natural political arrangement'.[52] This, it could be argued, is a problem appertaining to all nationalist parties, and all nationalisms, as the reliance on the entity that is the nation appears to override all other concerns. Nevertheless, is it really plausible for regional, national or even local fluctuations in composition to occur, and be taken on board, if the nation-state or the nation – in this case the Welsh nation – is being held out as the model for governance most suitable for, or most sought after by, the people of that geographical area. Thus, by arguing along these lines, it could be suggested that the nation is too rigid or too inflexible a component to attempt anything other than a parochial application of nationalism. In other words, it may be appropriate to conclude that internationalism causes more problems for nationalists, and their nationalism, than it creates solutions.

This method of calculation could lead nationalists to refrain from seeking any approval for their ideological positioning in the outside world; hence, their time and effort may be better employed by being centred solely on their nation and their brand of nationalism. Furthermore, if Plaid Cymru's position is considered, it would appear somewhat at odds to be desirous of, as Elin Jones manifestly is, the concept of freedom within the European Union at a moment in time when Wales is generally viewed as a regional component, rather than a national unit, of the European Union. Moreover, in the aforementioned instance, this identification may prove to be somewhat awkward because, as Elin Jones herself has proclaimed, 'I am always sceptical about too much talk of regionalisation because I don't see Wales as a region.'[53]

Plaid Cymru and Self-identification

Descriptive labelling, be it done internally or externally, can prove problematic to parties espousing nationalist ideas. With this in mind, it is important to note how the 'Wales is a region, Wales is a nation' debate is one that has led to the impression that the political discourse regarding Welsh identity can be somewhat opaque. Arthur Aughey commented on how D.E. Owens, writing about Plaid Cymru in 1985, described 'the division within nationalism not as romantic versus realist, but as regionalist versus nationalist.'[54] It can be contended that other ideologies and ideological concepts were dominating Plaid Cymru at the time that Owens made this observation and that nationalism during that period, in both thought and practice, was not to the fore in the party's rhetoric. What appears clear, however, is that, as Owens remarked, clarity of description, or the lack of it, can lead to difficulties when a political body is identified, rightly or wrongly, with a specific political ideology.

Adding to this debate on identification, some within Plaid Cymru, most notably Gwynfor Evans,[55] insist on calling Wales by its ancient Welsh-language title of *Cymru*, thus introducing another angle to the discussion about self-identity, national identity and nationhood. Richard Wyn Jones has commented on this aspect of evaluating national identity with his observation that the fact that the issue of nationhood – the 'central narrative'[56] – is not discussed more openly within Welsh society as a whole, and in particular on the Welsh political scene, 'reflects the complex and contested nature of national identity in Wales.'[57] However it is considered, this apparent shortage of discourse concerning identity and nationhood has to be problematic for Plaid Cymru. This is because any difficulty in inciting within Wales a debate on nationhood and identity – concepts that any nationalist party would put to the fore – cannot be seen to be beneficial to Plaid Cymru's advocacy of a distinct Welsh identity and an autonomous Welsh political system.

The noticeable failure by Plaid Cymru activists to transmit their own strong sense of identities – observable in research by Jonathan Bradbury, which showed that 85% of Plaid Cymru candidates at the 2001 National Assembly election thought of themselves as having an exclusively Welsh identity[58] – may be explained in terms of either a communication breakdown or a strategic miscalculation. The communication breakdown factor may be evident if the message about identity and self-identification, exemplified by the aforementioned candidates, was not being thoroughly disseminated throughout Welsh society. While it is feasible to adopt a cynical viewpoint on this entire debate on identity and nationhood, and to place these views into a pot entitled, to borrow from Michael Billig, 'banal nationalism',[59] it is, nevertheless, an indictment of either a weak nationalist position held by Plaid Cymru or, alternatively, poor strategic party management that these issues have not been forced onto the political agenda through a more proactive political campaign.

When issues outside of the nationalist or self-determinist arena are considered, Plaid Cymru has to be careful in the sense that it is not seen as a circulator of an 'illusory holism'.[60] This implies that the peripheral concept or concepts – in this instance internationalism, utopianism and the attainment of some form of democratic world government, possibly through a fortified United Nations – takes attention away from the core concepts. Adapting this into the scenario in which Plaid Cymru operates, an overabundance of internationalist or globalist ideology within the party would invariably weaken its appeal as a party of Wales – a party, that is, of a well-defined geographical space that contains its own distinctive sets of problems and issues. Nationalism, therefore, may have difficulties interacting with internationalism. These difficulties are further enhanced if, or when, a political or cultural dilemma arises that requires action to be taken that favours either the nationalist or the internationalist perspective. If Eurig Wyn, Jill Evans and others within Plaid Cymru who use internationalist rhetoric were faced with this conundrum then their attachments to nationalism, and Plaid Cymru's stated aim of putting Wales first, would be sorely tested. Therefore, any illusory holism could be their Achilles heel if, as Jill Evans has stated,[61] the party regards itself as nationalist.

Plaid Cymru and Post-nationalism

A former leader of Plaid Cymru, Dafydd Elis-Thomas, takes the debate on nationalism within the party, and the positioning and understanding of nationalist ideology in a Welsh context, a stage further. Elis-Thomas, responding to a question asked in an interview for this analysis, espoused the benefits of adopting a position he described as post-nationalism. The question sought an answer from Elis-Thomas as to whether he considered Plaid Cymru to be a nationalist party and whether he regarded his own views as nationalistic. His reply was very much in the negative on both counts: 'the party is post-nationalist and I am definitely post-nationalist.'[62] Elucidating his viewpoint, Elis-Thomas stated that his definition of nationalism is, he freely admits, rather limited. Rejecting what he called the 'back to the nation-state model',[63] he declared that he wants to see Plaid Cymru 'working within the island of Britain with our sister nations, and within the EU, to develop the greatest possible autonomy for Wales.'[64] This rejection of the nation-state model is telling as he maintains that 'you should have a national culture based on a reasonable politics of nationality but that is not the same thing as nationalism. I don't believe in this claim of the nation to historic national self-determination.'[65] This contradicts previous and, in many instances, current Plaid Cymru thinking on this matter as Elis-Thomas would appear to be questioning Plaid Cymru's original and, debatably, even its present *raison d'être*.

On the subject of post-nationalism, Michael Ignatieff has commented that 'post-nationalism, and its accompanying disdain for the nationalist emotions of others, may be the last refuge of the cosmopolitan.'[66] Furthermore, Ignatieff ridiculed the emotionalism that acts as a driver within nationalist ideology. For Freeden, emotionalism is imperative to the continuation of nationalist ideals. He has stated that 'nationalism institutionalizes and legitimises emotion as a motive force of political, not just private, life.'[67] But if sentiment and emotion are removed from the equation, thus denying nationalism of one of its core components, how can the post-nationalism advocated by Dafydd Elis-Thomas fit in to a nationalist ideological framework? Or is Elis-Thomas estimating that Plaid Cymru's political outlook is not rooted in nationalism; certainly, that is, not to the extent that it cannot change its thought-practices to either embrace other ideological approaches, or to make its brand of nationalism as thin as possible so that only the nation remains as a core concept?

One question that can be asked of Elis-Thomas here is 'Is he really arguing that there is no historical foundation to Plaid Cymru's nationalism?' He certainly sees the role of nationalism as personified by Plaid Cymru's ideology – if nationalism is what it really is – as being about 'building confidence, building the nation, building the economy and building the body politic. That is what the practical politics of the national question is about.'[68] Pragmatism, for Elis-Thomas, is a vital ideological component and it is something he feels that Plaid Cymru needs to develop and express. What is of interest in this application is the contrast between this account of practical ideals – virtually New Labour-style Third Way desires – and the heady romanticism so often evident in the pronouncements of Saunders Lewis and other members of Plaid Cymru during its early stage.

Following on from his longing for Plaid Cymru to adopt a more pragmatic approach to politics in Wales and beyond, the reference to the European Union in Elis-Thomas's view of Plaid Cymru's position is outlined further when he describes Plaid Cymru's ideology as 'green, left-of-centre, European regionalist,'[69] adding expressively, 'but you probably wouldn't get that answer from all members.'[70] When considering Elis-Thomas's ideology, and his depiction of the party's ideology as a whole, it is worth recognising that Dafydd Elis-Thomas has been an identifiably left-wing member of Plaid Cymru since the 1960s; Laura McAllister talked of his 'commitment to New Left ideas',[71] whereas Richard Wyn Jones referred to him as 'the marxisant Dafydd Elis'.[72] Moreover, his deviation from what would be regarded as traditionalist and nationalist issues reached its zenith during the late 1980s when, as party president, he refused to condemn in-migration into rural Wales despite a vocal, and often bitter, campaign fronted by the nationalist poet R.S. Thomas that sought, and gained, support from some sections within Plaid Cymru. Dave Adamson, in *Class, Ideology, and the Nation*,[73] recognised this period as one of major sociological and ideological shifts within Wales as a whole, and within Plaid Cymru in particular. It would be reasonable to conclude, therefore, that Elis-Thomas's ideological journey to a post-nationalist position undoubtedly fermented during this period.

Probing Elis-Thomas's Post-nationalist Concepts

If Elis-Thomas's post-nationalist position is to be assessed, using the Freeden model, then the concepts that he sees making up this post-nationalist position need to be analysed. Regionalism, pragmatism and green leftism appear to be Elis-Thomas's core concepts. As has already been established, Freeden does not classify any of these concerns in his core concepts of nationalism. Nevertheless, there could well be room for these concepts under a post-nationalist umbrella. Regionalism is certainly problematic to those who espouse nationalism. Elis-Thomas's view that Plaid Cymru 'should drive towards European federalism'[74] may appear to match the approach of people like Jill Evans and Eurig

Wyn, who wish to see the Wales in Europe message built upon, but it remains axiomatic that regionalism takes away from nationalism its notion of someone to oppose. Adopting regionalism encourages an encircling of the nation – in this instance the Welsh nation and any demands for autonomy from within – and locating it in a broader context. That process would nullify further nationalist demands, as regionalism has to conduct itself within clear, though restrictive, guidelines. Hence, nationalists view talk of regionalism with suspicion, as it can be perceived as a new form of political straitjacket, with the dominant state retaining its authority.

Political pragmatism is clearly important to Elis-Thomas. Asked in interview whether he saw contemporary Plaid Cymru basing its everyday practice and overall ideology more on pragmatism than on romanticism, his reply was a clear-cut 'yes'. He also commented that Plaid Cymru's thought and practice had to be 'based on the ability to govern.'[75] Laura McAllister believes that elements of this pragmatic approach have become evident over time. McAllister contended that 'the 1990s saw Plaid far more concerned with electoral tactics and organisational matters than with wider political and ideological questions.'[76] In her opinion, 'this tells us something of Plaid Cymru's emergence as a relatively mature political party.'[77] McAllister based her judgement on a review of party rhetoric at the time. For example, Dafydd Wigley, party leader during the 1990s, claimed in 1995 that 'we desperately need a dynamic non-doctrinaire progressive political party.'[78]

Although, to a certain extent, pragmatism undoubtedly has its place in getting a party's message across, and in delivering political success, this analysis would contend that any significant retreat from a romanticist position, however fragile or peripheral that position may be, must inevitably weaken the nationalist standpoint. If this line of reasoning is applied to Plaid Cymru, then any rejection of the romanticist position would inevitably further reduce the ideological line of transmission between the present and the past. Saunders Lewis's romanticism may seem dated to many, but his appeal to the past still resonates to a certain degree within the party. If Plaid Cymru were to adopt a position whereby some elements of the party's original social and political philosophy appeared to be outdated then it could be argued that that might be interpreted by some traditionalists within the party as being too radical a change for them to accept, as they might construe it as a departure from Plaid Cymru's formative aims and objectives. Therefore, post-nationalism, if it does indeed include this appeal to pragmatism over romanticism, could be seen by some members within Plaid Cymru as being a perspective that is simply too progressive for the party to take on board.

If nationalism, in a Westernised sense at least, is seen as a liberationist demand for a form of radical democracy, albeit within a defined geographical space, then green leftism can be seen as an adjacent concept in that it compels the practitioner down the radical, society-changing – both physically and psychologically – route. Elis-Thomas could therefore be justified in including green leftism in his vision of a society positioned on a post-nationalist ideology. Michael Freeden noted how, in comparison with other ideologies, green ideology is 'more pluralist, decentralized, and "democratic" or popular, but less intellectually coherent.'[79] What may attract a free floating left-winger such as Elis-Thomas to green thinking is the post-material element contained within. Freeden has cited the German greens – much admired by Elis-Thomas – and their 'switch away from consumerism towards alternative conceptions of the quality of life.'[80] This, for Elis-Thomas, is the future ideological direction of European politics, and it is a line that he would like to see Plaid Cymru adopt. As he remarked, 'I'm looking forward to the next "opening up of the green left." I think the European left, and especially the regional based green left, are going places.'[81] However, whether Plaid Cymru does indeed follow Dafydd Elis-Thomas down this post-nationalist road is yet to become clear.

Notes

1. Plaid Cymru, *The New Wales: Synopsis of the Policy of the Welsh Nationalist Party* (Caernarfon: Swyddfa'r Blaid, 1939), p. 1.
2. Ibid.
3. D.J. and Noelle Davies, *Wales: The Land of Our Children* (Caernarfon: Swyddfa'r Blaid, 1942), p. 28.
4. Ibid.
5. See, for instance, Antony Alcock, *A History of the Protection of Regional Cultural Minorities in Europe* (Macmillan: Basingstoke, 2000), pp. 75–76.
6. Dafydd Wigley, interview, 25 February 2002.
7. Ibid.
8. Elfyn Llwyd, interview, 21 October 2002.
9. Dafydd Trystan, interview, 8 March 2003.
10. Plaid Cymru, *Power for Wales* (General Election Manifesto, November 1974), p. 8.
11. Saunders Lewis, *Wales after the War* (Caernarfon: Swyddfa'r Blaid, 1942), p. 36.
12. Dave Adamson, 'The Intellectual and the National Movement', in Ralph Fevre and Andrew Thompson (eds), *Nation, Identity and Social Theory* (Cardiff: University of Wales Press, 1999), p. 67.
13. Gwynfor Evans, *Land of My Fathers* (Talybont: Y Lolfa, 1992), p. 450.
14. Ibid.
15. Phil Williams, *The Psychology of Distance* (Cardiff: Welsh Academic Press, 2003), p. 3.
16. Phil Williams, *Voice from the Valleys* (Bridgend: Seren, 1981), p. 20.

17. Cynog Dafis, 'Migration, Identity and Development', *Agenda*, Summer 2004, p. 5.
18. Michael Freeden, *Ideology* (Oxford: Oxford University Press, 2003), p. 98.
19. Laura McAllister, *Plaid Cymru: The Emergence of a Political Party* (Bridgend: Seren, 2001), p. 158.
20. Ibid.
21. Michael Freeden, *Ideology*, p. 98.
22. Plaid Cymru, *Summer School and Conference*, 1959, p. 63.
23. Eurig Wyn, interview, 22 October 2002.
24. Ibid.
25. Michael Freeden, *Ideologies and Political Theory* (Oxford: Clarendon Press, 1996), p. 31.
26. Charlotte Davies, *Welsh Nationalism in the Twentieth Century* (Connecticut: Praeger, 1989), p. 57.
27. Plaid Cymru, *Annual Conference 1968*.
28. Keith Morgan, interview, 19 November 2001.
29. Dafydd Elis-Thomas, interview, 12 November 2002.
30. Eurig Wyn, interview, 22 October 2002.
31. Dafydd Iwan, BBC Radio Wales, 5 July 2003.
32. Laura McAllister, *Plaid Cymru*, p. 58.
33. Ibid.
34. Robin Wilson, 'The Politics of Contemporary Ethno-Nationalist Conflicts', *Nations and Nationalism*, vol. 7, no. 3, 2001, pp. 365–384.
35. Jill Evans, interview, 18 May 2002.
36. Elin Jones, interview, 16 October 2002.
37. Ibid.
38. Ibid.
39. Peter Lynch, *Minority Nationalism and European Integration* (Cardiff: University of Wales Press), p. 56.
40. Plaid Cymru, *Summer School and Conference*, 1962, p. 23.
41. Plaid Cymru, *Summer School and Conference*, 1967, p. 17.
42. Phil Williams, *Towards 2000: Plaid Cymru's Programme for Wales in Europe*, p. 14.
43. Dafydd Wigley, interview, 25 February 2002.
44. Anthony Packer, 'Tough choices as Lithuania leads the way', *Welsh Nation*, Summer, 2004, p. 5.
45. Gwynfor Evans, *Fighting for Wales* (Talybont: Y Lolfa, 1997), pp. 154–161.
46. Ibid., p. 154.
47. Ibid., p. 158.
48. D. Hywel Davies, *The Welsh Nationalist Party 1925–45* (New York: St. Martin's Press, 1983), p. 107.
49. Michael Freeden, *Ideologies and Political Theory*, p. 33.
50. Plaid Cymru, *Annual Conference*, 1968, p. 17.
51. Ibid.
52. Michael Freeden, *Ideologies and Political Theory*, p. 173.
53. Elin Jones, interview, 16 October 2002.
54. Arthur Aughey, *Nationalism, Devolution and the Challenge to the United Kingdom State* (London: Pluto Press, 2001), p. 118.

55. Gwynfor Evans, *The Fight for Welsh Freedom* (Talybont: Y Lolfa, 1992), p. 9.
56. Richard Wyn Jones, 'On process, events and unintended consequences: national identity and the politics of Welsh revolution', *Scottish Affairs*, no. 37, Autumn 2001, p. 37.
57. Ibid.
58. Ibid., p. 40.
59. Michael Billig, *Banal Nationalism* (London: Sage, 1995).
60. Michael Freeden, 'Ideological boundaries and ideological systems', *Journal of Political Ideologies*, vol. 8, no. 1, 2003, p. 7.
61. Jill Evans, interview, 18 May 2002.
62. Dafydd Elis-Thomas, interview, 12 November 2002.
63. Ibid.
64. Ibid.
65. Ibid.
66. Paul James, *Nation Formation* (London: Sage, 1996), p. 196.
67. Michael Freeden, 'Is nationalism a distinct ideology?', *Political Studies*, vol. 46, no. 4, 1998, pp. 748–765.
68. Ibid.
69. Ibid.
70. Ibid.
71. Laura McAllister, *Plaid Cymru*, p. 169.
72. Richard Wyn Jones, 'From community socialism to quango Wales', *Planet*, 118, August/September 1996, p. 59.
73. David Adamson, *Class, Ideology and the Nation: A Theory of Welsh Nationalism* (Cardiff: University of Wales Press, 1991), p. 136.
74. Elis-Thomas, interview, 12 November 2002.
75. Ibid.
76. Laura McAllister, *Plaid Cymru*, p. 183.
77. Ibid.
78. Dafyyd Wigley, *Plaid Cymru Annual Conference*, 1995.
79. Michael Freeden, *Ideologies and Political Theory*, p. 546.
80. Ibid., p. 547.
81. Elis-Thomas, interview, 12 November 2002.

V

OTHER IDEOLOGIES ASSOCIATED WITH MODERN PLAID CYMRU

Socialism

Although nationalism is the ideology that mostly comes to mind whenever the name Plaid Cymru is mentioned, it is socialism that many within the party see as the basis for its political programme. As noted previously, it was the Davieses, D.J. and Noelle, who first introduced a level of profound socialist thinking, and a markedly socialist agenda, into the party's ideological arena. Phil Williams, commenting on D.J. Davies's role as a prominent thinker on economic affairs within Plaid Cymru, remarked that 'he had a very strong commitment to workers control and democracy and this has remained a constant theme in the party's policy.'[1] Similarly, Laura McAllister has argued that socialism is 'a current running through the development of Plaid Cymru. Its influence has ebbed and flowed, but from the party's beginnings, it has been a strong presence.'[2] Without returning in any depth to a discussion on the influence of the socialist-inclined Davieses on early Plaid Cymru ideology, McAllister is correct in her judgement that socialism has always been there or thereabouts within the thought-practices of the party. For instance, a motion to the party's annual conference in 1938 criticised Plaid Cymru's 'existing philosophy, recommending instead an economic and political system based upon socialist principles.'[3] However, it is only when an assessment of modern Plaid Cymru is considered that socialism becomes accepted as an ideology that most, if not all, of the party feel comfortable about endorsing.

Various interpretations of Plaid Cymru's socialism have been put forward over the years. In 1967, R.C. Collins, in a pamphlet entitled *Workers Control in Wales*, remarked that 'the Plaid programme appears to be socialist in the libertarian tradition, descending from Proudhon rather than Marx.'[4] The startling revelation here, if Collins is to be believed, is in the fact that Pierre-Joseph Proudhon was an anarchist who rallied against the state-centric policies of his day. If Proudhon's libertarian socialism were to be transposed onto Plaid Cymru's political programme, arguably at any point in the party's history, the case that the party could then advance for the centring of the nation as a focus for socio-political power would be highly implausible. This is because libertarianism 'obscures an ideology's foundational principles by reorganizing the core units of furniture.'[5] Thus, in the case of Plaid Cymru and Wales, one of those core units to be reorganised may well prove to be the nation itself.

The one core unit, or concept, that Plaid Cymru could not do without is the politico-institutional core of the nation, and its corresponding corridors of power, for it is those that Plaid Cymru seeks to inhabit in order to achieve the party's primary policy objectives. Although some of these theoretical issues will be addressed in the ensuing chapter on concepts, it would appear at this juncture that R.C. Collins's argument that Plaid Cymru's political programme follows the libertarian socialist line that has been extracted from Proudhon may well prove to be misguided. If, surprisingly, it does happen to turn out to be correct, then either Plaid Cymru's thinking on the role and centrality of the nation is distorted – either, that is, in the party's mind or in the minds of those political commentators and theorists who write on these matters – or there would appear to be a serious conceptual imbalance in Plaid Cymru's ideology as, using information garnered through R.C. Collins and those aforementioned writers who have commented on the party's ideological construction, Plaid Cymru would concurrently propose both an enhancing of, and a deconstruction of, Wales's central state machinery. In this instance, if accurate, Plaid Cymru would be transcending any hitherto ideological models.

In a more contemporary setting, questioned as to whether Plaid Cymru is a socialist party, the former chief executive of Plaid Cymru, Karl Davies, argued that it is 'far more complicated than that. The party's ideology could be said to be a mix of socialism and liberalism, although there has been a consistent thread of socialism since the 1940s.'[6] The use of this intersection with socialism and liberalism is noteworthy. In terms of radically altering a state's infrastructure through the implementation of social policies – something, incidentally, that Plaid Cymru has consistently proposed – Michael Freeden supplied a concrete example when he noted how the major changes in Britain in the past one hundred years or so have occurred under the ideological conditions that Karl Davies claims for the party. The birth and flowering of the welfare state was that major infrastructural change and 'most of the ideologists of the welfare state were hybrid social-liberals.'[7] Nevertheless, where the difficulty lies for Plaid Cymru, if it does exhibit both socialist and liberal tendencies, is whether the party views this socialist–liberal intersection as decontested, implying, therein, that members of the party are settled on their interpretations of what all of the ideological concepts within the party – be they labelled socialist or liberal – actually are. Thus, these various concepts, which are in use by elements within the party, should be clearly defined and understood. This analysis would contend, however, that the ideological debates within the party, and the variations in individual thought and action, suggest that the concepts and ideologies within Plaid Cymru are actually far from being decontested.

Alternatively, is it the case that Plaid Cymru is attempting to operate, and engage with people, on the 'semantic parameters of political language, even when these parameters are rejected by some of the participants.'[8] If so, it is perfectly feasible that some Plaid Cymru members could reject socialism, liberalism, or the conjunction of both, and still remain members and supporters of the party. Therefore, nationalism may be the ideology – albeit that it is a thin ideology that requires additional concepts from elsewhere on the ideological spectrum for it to be fully furnished and comprehensive – on which some non-socialist and non-liberal Plaid Cymru supporters could comfortably attach themselves.

Socialism and Nationalism: An Uneasy Mix?

Returning to Karl Davies's view of the party's ideology, it is interesting that he maintained that this thread of socialism has been identifiable for some time by people outside the party. In his view, 'from the 1960s onwards people have been attracted to Plaid Cymru not just because of our nationalist agenda.'[9] The 1960s appear to be a key decade for the intensification of socialist ideas within Plaid Cymru; as indeed the 1960s proved to be a fruitful period for socialist ideas throughout Western liberal societies. With this in mind, there is possibly a case to be made to claim that Plaid Cymru, rather than branching out into uncharted ideological territory with its espousal of a more socialistic programme, was merely reflecting, and pragmatically and vociferously embracing, the current political milieu. Possibly endorsing this line of argument, Charlotte Davies noted how one young man from Aberdare who joined Plaid Cymru during this era explained how he and his friends suspected that Labour was 'not a true socialist party … we chose nationalism as the best way to pursue socialist ideals.'[10] Supporting this statement, there were clearly signs of socialist activity within the party at this time, although these were not always elucidated. At the 1968 annual conference at Aberystwyth, the Ebbw Vale branch complained, in a motion, about the lack of explicit policy within the party. An amendment to this motion, proposed by West Monmouth Rhanbarth (District), added 'and in particular to urge the party to publish and explain its socialist policies.'[11]

This linking of socialism and nationalism requires further analysis as the ease with which many people within Plaid Cymru skip, almost inadvertently, from the language of nationalism to the language of socialism would appear to show that the party is a socialist nationalist or a nationalistic socialist political organisation, despite the fact, as has already been established earlier, that Dafydd Elis-Thomas has already introduced green ideology, and aspects of post-nationalism, into the debate and Karl Davies has highlighted the liberal aspects of the party's thinking. That these labels – socialist and nationalist – are interchangeable and so easily bandied about may prove that they are superficial in their ideological content and that they are ultimately shallow when put into application by Plaid Cymru's elected politicians (i.e. not only by the ruling coalition in the Senedd in the National Assembly but also by the party's local councillors who do, or have, administered county councils such as Gwynedd and Caerffili). It may also be evidence that one, or both, of their components, socialism and nationalism, are ultimately incompatible with the overall ideology of the party; the description overall ideology is used here as this examination is contending that there is no one set, or customary, ideology at work within Plaid Cymru. Rather, there are plural ideologies.

There is clearly some unease about the use of the term 'socialist' within the party. The following insights from Karl Davies may offer some guidance on the reluctance of certain people within Plaid Cymru to admit to their inclination towards advancing socialist policies. This is because they perceive Plaid Cymru as being in fierce competition with the Labour Party for the hearts and minds of the Welsh electorate: the Labour Party having been traditionally portrayed as being the flag bearer for socialism within Welsh politics. With this in mind, it is perhaps understandable to see why, when it came to policy formation and the writing of party literature, 'Dafydd Wigley was against including the word socialist, although Dafydd was far to the left of Labour on most things.'[12] This view of Wigley is backed up by Laura McAllister, who contended that though Wigley 'was concerned that Plaid attached too much importance to its socialist label … his own nationalism was firmly "centre-left".'[13] Similarly, 'Gwynfor Evans said that he would not classify himself as a socialist because, to him, socialism would always be associated with the Labour Party.'[14]

Inclusion or exclusion of words in any given statement, or through some third party perception or interpretation of your political opinions, does not mean that you are, or are not, an advocate of a certain ideology. The litmus test comes with the policies and how they are ordered within your total political philosophy. Nevertheless, the fact that two former party leaders, Evans and Wigley, were reluctant to openly admit that some of their, and the party's, principles could be described as socialist suggests either that they made a strategic decision not to enter the perceived ideological arena of the Labour Party, for fear of alienating some of their supporters, or, perhaps, that they did not see themselves, the policies they advocated and the party's ideological base as socialist. Talking about the ideological climate in the 1980s, Wigley, whilst falling short of describing his opinions as socialist, claimed that Plaid Cymru 'was on a fairly far left part of the political spectrum at that time. We still are. It is just that the whole pattern has moved. I find myself now regarded as a raging left-winger.'[15] As Wigley was regarded by many members and observers, certainly during the 1980s, as being to the centre-right of the party, it would appear to position the party, in its modern semblance, in a broadly leftist slot.

By seeing how far back this modern left-of-centre positioning actually goes – whether it is a constant, as McAllister believes it to be, or whether it stems from a 1940s realignment of the party ideology, as Karl Davies maintains – should enable a better understanding of how important socialism is within the party's thought-practices to emerge. If socialism does appear to have a salient role in the private and public language of the party, then the question can be proposed as to whether this implies that a kind of leftist nationalism has emerged as the foremost ideological strand within the party or whether, in actual fact, Plaid Cymru, despite all the indications towards nationalist thought, is, at the end of the day, a socialist political party.

Tracing the Socialist Line

When considering arguments over a political party's ideational development it is prudent to remember that the purpose of any party's existence is to attain power, be it through democratic or revolutionary methods. Plaid Cymru, as an avowedly democratic political party, needs to convince enough people to vote for the party's political programme through conveying a message to the electorate that it can do the best for Wales. Hence, as has been alluded to earlier in this examination, there are cultural constraints for Plaid Cymru to adhere to when formulating its political manifestos and, more crucially, when working through the ideology of the party. With this in mind, it is clear to see why one early Plaid Cymru member, Dafydd Jenkins, who 'believed that the Nationalist Party's social philosophy was "essentially social-ist",[16] argued that the party 'should make a direct approach to Welsh socialists whom he believed might respond to the case for national self-determination.'[17] In a response from the party that appears to be cyclical, if the caution shown by Dafydd Wigley and Gwynfor Evans over the term socialist is recalled, Dafydd Jenkins was 'told that his description of the party as "essentially socialist" was not correct.'[18] The line of denial appears, therefore, to parallel the thread of socialism that Karl Davies maintains has been a continuum for the last six decades.

The denial of socialist ideology by the party leadership can be accounted for on two fronts. First, any acceptance that Plaid Cymru is socialist could give the impression that the party is merely attempt-ing to replicate the Labour Party in Wales; in other words some within Plaid Cymru may be worried about being given the label of imitator. Alternatively, the refutation of socialism as part of Plaid Cymru's ideo-logical fabric could be down to the belief that socialism is an extrinsic ideology that should have little appeal to the indigenous population. This point of view is much misguided if the Welsh socialist Robert Owen is brought into the frame, as indeed he and Aneurin Bevan were when, under the leadership of Dafydd Elis-Thomas, Plaid Cymru's pro-gramme for the 1990s, *Wales in Europe: A Community of Communities*, was launched in 1989. The document claimed that '*cymhortha* rep-resents a set of values deeply rooted in our history, where the young protect the old and the strong defend the weak. These are the values that Robert Owen taught the world under the label "socialism".'[19]

Nevertheless, despite this statement of intent by Plaid Cymru in 1989, from the time of Plaid Cymru's formation – 1925 – up into the radical era of the 1960s and even as recently as the 1990s, when the collapse of the state socialism personified by the Soviet Union and its satellites finally put an end to the paranoia in some quarters about the red menace, there was a sense in society at large that the word social-ism had negative connotations. Dafydd Jenkins identified this type of paranoia as far back as 1938. Writing in Plaid Cymru's journal, *Welsh Nationalist*, Jenkins claimed that 'members of the party are far too ready to attack "socialism", usually meaning by that either the English Labour Party, or the philosophy of Karl Marx.'[20]

This fear of misinterpretation appears to be a leitmotif when an analysis of Plaid Cymru is conducted. For instance, Karl Davies's response, when he heard the term socialism applied to Plaid Cymru, was to immediately distance the party from the monolithic, old Eastern bloc representation of socialism. Citing decentralist socialism, which will be scrutinised in the next chapter, and searching for new interpreta-tions of socialist ideology within the party, Davies is adamant that he would argue against anybody trying to attach the label of state social-ism on to Plaid Cymru. What he termed '1970s socialism'[21] was, in his words, 'meaningless'.[22]

In similar vein, Lila Haines, dismissing the imperious state socialism of the past, advocated Plaid Cymru encouraging 'people-led social-ism'.[23] However, if, to the eyes of the political analyst, 1970s social-ism equates with policies such as the state control of industry through nationalisation or the advancement of an equalitarian and comprehen-sive education system, then those are widely held, and widely accepted, socialist policies. Is it the case, therefore, that some people within Plaid Cymru who use the terminology of socialism are merely paying lip service to the actual process of implementing socialism and its cor-responding aims, objectives and outcomes? Or are they attempting to forge policies that may have peripheral attachments to socialism but, when considered in minutiae, have no substantial relationship with the core concepts of socialism? To further evaluate some of these conten-tions, it is worth considering some of the political literature dissemi-nated by Plaid Cymru. A good way to examine this literature is through an analysis of the party's manifestos. Hence, three election manifestos from the modern era have been chosen to observe how the party uses ideological language in an attempt to persuade the Welsh electorate to embrace the party's position.

Plaid Cymru's Manifestos: Signs of Ideological Variations?

As the focus of this analysis is the ideological debate, and the iden-tification of ideologies, within Plaid Cymru, a scan of party election manifestos from 1974, 1984 and 2001 should prove insightful as to the content presented, and the direction indicated, by the party in these years. These manifestos were chosen as they are fairly evenly spaced, thus allowing for evolutionary policy change to occur. Furthermore, it is notable that three party leaders are covered by these dates: Gwynfor Evans in 1974, Dafydd Wigley during his first term in office in 1984 and Ieuan Wyn Jones in 2001. As all party leaders, of whatever political party, invariably leave their mark on policy pronouncements, the entire gamut of personal and party direction under three modern Plaid Cymru leaders should be in evidence. The exception to the post-war leaders under scrutiny is Dafydd Elis-Thomas, whose political philosophy has been covered in some depth and whose time in office could be presented as a parenthesis because, among all of Plaid Cymru's leaders, he was the most overt and forthright user of socialist language. As this section is paying attention to socialist ideas within Plaid Cymru's ideology, particular notice has been given to any content within the three mani-festos deemed to be of a socialist, or generally leftist, nature.

1974: Analysing Power for Wales

First up, the 1974 manifesto was written at a time when the world – the capitalist Western world in particular – was in the grip of a sig-nificant economic recession, as the OPEC oil crisis that began in 1973 was still sending out aftershocks. *Power for Wales*,[24] Plaid Cymru's election manifesto for the November 1974 general election, reflected the economic themes of the age. In terms of the document's content that could be labelled socialist, several left-of-centre themes emerge. Nationalisation, an idea associated with socialist thought and practice in Britain since the post-war settlement of the 1945 Labour government, takes pride of place with a section to itself. The section begins with the statement that Plaid Cymru 'has consistently advocated industrial democracy – co-ownership of firms in a Welsh framework – for more than 40 years.'[25] There is undoubtedly evidence that the party, or at least certain individuals within the party, had indeed proposed the concept of industrial democracy for many years prior to 1974. What is interesting is where this concept of co-ownership of firms in a Welsh framework could lead, and how it would be operated.

Plaid Cymru's policy, in the manifesto, can be generally read as an attack on the post-war Labour Party. However, on closer inspection, it may be possible to ask whether this attack on Labour is really a criticism of its policies, remembering that its policies are habitually left of centre, or whether it is a condemnation on Labour's position – geographically and psychologically – as a London-based party. If the policy aspect alone is examined, then the manifesto offers some explanation to this question in that it states that 'Nationalisation, although changing the nominal ownership of industry, has increased rather than decreased the power of existing vested interests.'[26] So who, for Plaid Cymru, could these vested interests be? Although the party's long-held disdain for capitalism and the plutocracy is well documented, the object of real abhorrence is reserved for the final passage of the section. By advocat-ing 'the decentralist control of Welsh industry by Welsh people',[27] Plaid Cymru shows that one of the real vested interests is the British state and its accepted hegemony over Welsh political and economic matters. The Welsh solution is thus offered by Plaid Cymru through ensuring that in future Welsh workers themselves 'must have much more of a say in the running of industry, leading towards a system of co-ownership.'[28]

The concepts of cooperativism and decentralisation will be addressed in the next chapter. Nevertheless, it is justifiable to record at this juncture that both are concepts that may be found on the periphery of socialist ideology. To this extent, therefore, it would be feasible to contend that *Power for Wales* has socialism in its make-up. However, the emphasis on industrial democracy is consistently referred to in the context of Wales, and Wales alone. There is no internationalist perspective to this policy and the sense of socialist solidarity, even with workers just across the border in England, is conspicuous by its absence. Indeed, Welsh workers are given priority and, moreover, they are imbued with special qualities. In a section subtitled 'Working Class Solidarity', the manifesto argued against the expansion of pan-European uninterrupted links among members of the working class. This opposition comes about because Plaid Cymru claimed that it is a fact that 'ordinary people have a bigger say in smaller communities.'[29] To substantiate this, and to add a particularistic element, *Power for Wales* contended that 'as far as Wales is concerned we are more likely to achieve social justice here than anywhere else in Britain because we are a united homogeneous society.'[30] In this statement there is a clear avenue of romanticism regarding Wales's supposed solidarity and homogeneity. Likewise, there is evidence of Plaid Cymru favouring one community within the British Isles over another. The manifesto also claimed that if socialist enactment were undertaken in Wales the eventual outcome would be that 'Wales would shame England into promoting equality.'[31] Therefore, this section of the 1974 manifesto still has nationalistic overtones. This is the case despite the fact that the social policy content of the manifesto does, in ideological terms, lean towards a socialist programme of intent.

As the above evidence attests, attacks on the notion of the other – in this instance England and the English – continued to pervade Plaid Cymru's literature at this time. Countries such as Norway and France are praised, along with West Germany for its devolved system of Länder, whilst England, and the whole edifice of the British state system, are consistently disparaged. Profligate defence spending and the development of Concorde – a prestigious project at the time – are derided as being component parts of the 'British Imperial myth'.[32] Nationalism is never far from the surface, and this may be testament to several things. First of all, Plaid Cymru was still riding high on the election victory of Gwynfor Evans at Carmarthen in 1966, albeit that this was eight years on from that moment. Second, nationalism was on the rise in both Scotland and Wales at the time as the Scottish National Party (SNP) championed the reality of Scotland's oil boom: a boom the SNP believed would act as a catalyst to persuade and inspire the Scottish people to demand the establishment of an independent Scottish state. In Wales, language issues and the backlash against the investiture of Charles Windsor at Caernarfon in 1969 had succeeded in introducing a new generation of radical activists into Plaid Cymru.

Third, and probably most important of all in the long term, Britain was coming to the end of its post-war consensus and both the major Westminster parties – Labour and the Conservatives – were beginning to flirt with new, and more radical, ideological strands. This breakdown in the ideological accord succeeded in creating windows of opportunity that, when added to the economic crisis gripping the UK, gave heart to Plaid Cymru. Ultimately, this newfound confidence helped to convince the party that it would achieve electoral gains on the road to self-government. Hence, *Power for Wales* sees Plaid Cymru displaying a rhetorical force and a feeling of self-assurance that captures the mood at that time. A certain amount of political expediency was to be expected, therefore, and that is what is delivered in *Power for Wales*.

It is true that both socialist and nationalist ideological concepts are on offer within the body of the manifesto. What is missing, somewhat surprisingly, is the distinctive tone of the New Left, whose indisputable influence helped to shape a generation of young radicals in Wales and beyond. Socialism is evident in *Power for Wales*, but Plaid Cymru's socialism is interwoven with the language of nation and national virility. Although other nations are praised in the manifesto, there is no talk of forging links. The document reads like a call for protectionism, both economic and cultural. Undeniably, after reading *Power for Wales*, there is little doubt that Gwynfor Evans's political philosophy still managed to cast its shadow over Plaid Cymru's policy development, and its thought-practices, almost three decades after he had first acquired the party presidency. The disdain for Imperialism echoes throughout the manifesto, as does Evans's belief that the Welsh are perpetually struggling to maintain their identity in light of the social, political, cultural and economic excesses perpetrated by their neighbours to the east. The battle for Wales's future is a significant part of this document and it can be concluded that its nationalistic underpinning comes across as being more significant than its socialist objectives.

Nationalism, in the manifesto, has been padded out by socialist peripheral concepts – such as industrial democracy or workers cooperativism – as nationalism alone would prove insufficient for a manifesto in which social policies have to come to the fore. Nationalism proves itself, yet again, to be a thin ideology that requires its host-vessels to broaden it. It may be more apt, therefore, to read *Power for Wales* as a manifesto that is socialistic in its ideational context but one that nevertheless uses the language of nationalism as a veneer to differentiate it. If this is so, then the work that nationalism does in this circumstance is to contextualise the thought-practices of Plaid Cymru and provide them with a signifier; namely Wales or the nation. The shallowness of this, however, is likely to prove a stumbling block whenever anybody seeks to conduct an exegetical analysis of Plaid Cymru's ideology.

1984: Protectionism and a Conservative Approach

Plaid Cymru's manifesto for the European election in 1984, *A Voice for Wales in Europe*,[33] inevitably saw the party turning its attention to matters beyond the borders of Wales. As the notions of regionalism and the region were the fashionable language within European cultural, economic and political discourse at the time, it is not surprising that regionalist rhetoric is used within the manifesto. Nowhere is this more evident than in the juxtaposition of calls for regional identification, played upon by the party in what could be identified as nationalistic rather than purely regionalistic tones, and the linking of socio-economic concerns. The document, nevertheless, emphasises what Wales could gain from the European Economic Community, as it then was, rather than clarifying in what ways Wales could contribute to Europe's political and economic development. Nowhere is this better exemplified than in a passage summed up by an attack on Thatcherite monetarist economics. In an appeal for the implementation of a degree of economic protectionism – a recurring theme, so it appears, within the economic discourse of Plaid Cymru – *A Voice for Wales in Europe* called for the abandonment of 'the principle of uncontrolled movement of capital ... so that protection can be given to disadvantaged areas.'[34]

Furthermore, this protectionism is emphasised by the party when the manifesto contended that 'if Wales had full national status in the Community then our minister would be totally justified in using the veto to defend what remains of the Welsh steel industry.'[35] In both economic and ideological terms this is a conservative measure that would seemingly go against the notion of an adherence to any form of unified, common European practice. What can be gathered from this is that the party was not really thinking of matters beyond Wales, and Welsh interests, in any proactive or inclusive sense. Despite the Welsh European element,[36] Plaid Cymru was still holding on to the notion of the nation as a core ideological concept of the party; this narrowing of the arguments back to the focus on the nation came despite all of the rhetoric at the time about regionalism and the responsibility that Wales, and Welsh people, had to act as constructive and inclusive Europeans.

All in all, little is made of socialism in the 1984 manifesto. In terms of content and description, there is only modest use of socialist language. This possibly indicates that socialism is a fluctuating fascination for the party rather than a constant ideological stance. The positioning of socialism as a core within the party could therefore be imprudent as it is played down at times within both the party's structural history and within its ideological development. Writing in 1978, Charlotte Davies remarked that while socialist pronouncements were becoming more prevalent within Plaid Cymru, 'the more doctrinaire positions are moderated and made more acceptable to conservative members.'[37] Judging by *A Voice for Wales in Europe*, it would appear that by 1984, six years after Davies's observation, the socialist tone had been modulated to such an extent that it is feasible to argue that *A Voice for Wales in Europe* has little overtly socialist content. This is surprising as the party was radicalised during this era, an era in which British politics was rapidly becoming more centralised under Margaret Thatcher and a London-based politico-economic elite. A period of sustained economic recession also focused minds towards protecting the Welsh economy and safeguarding Wales's manufacturing and industrial communities. To these ends, it is noteworthy to recall that, in 1983, Plaid Cymru had financed the launch of a journal, *Radical Wales*, to instigate debate in relation to socialist and nationalist issues.[38] However, it would appear from reading *A Voice for Wales in Europe* that, surprisingly, little of the socialist message emanating from the pages *of Radical Wales* appeared to have registered in the minds of the party's policy-makers. Consequently, it would appear accurate to contend that socialism was peripheral to Plaid Cymru's persona – its public persona at least – at this time.

With socialism seemingly put to one side, other ideological strands must have come to the fore. What 1984 did mark was the recognition of Plaid Cymru's position within the political arena as a party advocating the Welsh European perspective. *A Voice for Wales in Europe* expresses this Welsh European view in all its detail. What the Welsh European angle argues is that the locus for power in the years ahead should be seen to be the Cardiff–Brussels axis. Efforts would be made to encourage links and partnerships on a Wales–Europe level with the knowledge, or hope, that Westminster would play an increasingly diminishing role in the everyday decision-making process that affects Wales.

The problem for Plaid Cymru with this Welsh European approach is that the ideology of nationalism has to concentrate on the 'exceptional worth of a nation'.[39] If Plaid Cymru was now contending a dual approach to governance, and a dual approach to loyalty and identity, through the Welsh European system of thought and practice, then one of nationalism's core concepts is being fundamentally challenged. Unless a major transference of allegiance occurred, and a radically different structural approach was adopted, then the Welsh European option would seem an unlikely choice for Plaid Cymru to endorse. This is because any endorsement of this two-headed model would weaken the nation and place the nationalism claimed by some members of Plaid Cymru in a precarious position. It could be concluded, therefore, that ideological bilateralism – be it in a governmental or in an emotional and devotional sense – is not a viable option for adherents of nationalism.

Conversely, the Welsh European angle sits far more comfortably with socialist ideology. Socialists, be they inside or outside Plaid Cymru, could envisage the Welsh European position as acceptable and mutually compatible, as socialism's belief in the vitality of communities, and the escalation of human contentment through fraternity, are recognisable on both the Welsh and European layers. Socialism, unlike nationalism, does not ask the individual to differentiate between these layers, as socialist ideology does not grace the nation, and specifically the positive valorisation of that nation, with any preferential treatment. Socialism, therefore, allows the channels to remain open so that multilayering can take place. Nationalism, even when its adjacent concept of internationalism is brought into the reckoning, still finds great difficulty operating fully at the supra- and subnational levels, as its focus remains the core concept of the nation. Some of these difficulties will arise later when the concept of decentralisation is examined.

2001: A Comprehensive Ideological Position?

The straightforwardly titled *Manifesto 2001*[40] was Plaid Cymru's political manifesto for the 2001 UK general election. The attack on the Conservative Party that featured in the 1984 manifesto reappears in a section entitled 'The Tory Legacy'.[41] One of the major criticisms levelled at the Thatcherite revolution was its assault on the 'essentials of a civilised society, such as people's mutual dependence on their community and the welfare state.'[42] This mutualism was a growing theme in Plaid Cymru thinking, which was reflected in the way that the party advocated communityism, cooperativism, and decentralist socialism: concepts that will be addressed in the following chapter. Although it is arguable whether this mutualism places Plaid Cymru's thought in the socialist camp, the party's perpetual denigration of New Right principles proves categorically that Plaid Cymru eschews the laissez-faire capitalist individualism promoted by the likes of the former Conservative prime minister, Margaret Thatcher.

By 2001 devolution had begun to firmly embed itself in the Welsh political psyche, and the manifesto positioned devolution in the context of Wales's place in the British state system; its constitutional concerns being put under the spotlight. Though the manifesto appeals for legislative parity with Scotland – at a time, incidentally, when the SNP was unequivocally championing 'independence'[43] – it also displays the party's historical nationalist roots when it welcomes the setting up of the National Assembly for Wales, citing it as 'the first national governing body since Glyndwr's parliament.'[44]

Although the call for additional devolved powers was to be expected, when the debate moves on to Wales's place in Europe *Manifesto 2001* appears to muddy the waters. This is because the manifesto refers to Wales as a 'nation-region'.[45] The downgrading of Wales, even in its application in a European context, by a party that was vigorously and vociferously presenting itself by this time as Plaid Cymru – the Party of Wales – seems mystifying. In the most telling passage of the manifesto, the reader is informed that 'in discussing the future of Europe, it is crucial that nation-regions like Wales, Scotland, Euskadi and Catalunya will be able to play their part side-by-side with small states such as Ireland and the Scandinavian countries.'[46] Of the aforementioned countries and regions, Wales has by far the weakest form of legislative political power. Hence, it could be contended that Wales is the entity that is most likely of all those named to be considered, in the eyes of the casual observer, a region rather than a nation. If full national status is a nationalist demand – indeed the securing of 'politico-institutional expression'[47] is a core concept of nationalism – then classifying Wales in this nation-region paradigm could be counterproductive for Plaid Cymru. This is because it merely demotes Wales into a third category behind the confirmed nation-states (Denmark, for instance) and the aspiring, or impending, nation-states (such as Scotland). It also testifies that Wales is still no nearer reaching constitutional parity with the Republic of Ireland, the role model for generations of nationalists. Overall, therefore, this passage on Wales's seemingly unambitious constitutional objectives was hardly a bold statement of nationalist intent. If nationalism had been diluted over the course of the 1980s and 1990s, as *Manifesto 2001* may well indicate, the question must be asked, therefore, as to whether a socialist or even, as Dafydd Elis-Thomas would propose, a post-nationalist position had become implanted in the party by 2001.

Although the term socialism may be absent from *Manifesto 2001*, socialist themes are evident within the document. To illustrate this, one of the key recommendations highlighted in the manifesto is the introduction of 'a substantial increase in public spending to improve services and redistribute wealth.'[48] This line of reasoning can be found throughout socialist discourse. Backing this up, Rhodri Glyn Thomas, arguing in favour of the societal pooling of resources, has contended that Plaid Cymru 'is the only party that now believes in the redistribution of wealth. We are the only party that believes that you should contribute what you can afford to society and people should get what they need out of society.'[49]

Though he is not in any way involved in the policy-making process within the party, it is nevertheless interesting to note the views of Richard Williams, a former Plaid Cymru councillor and the party's Assembly candidate for the constituency of Blaenau Gwent in 1999. Williams is another party activist who persistently uses the language of socialism and who has argued for massive investment in public services to be financed through progressive taxation. Williams has spoken out against any form of privatisation and in favour of free meals for all schoolchildren in Wales. Concurrently, he has consistently referred to Plaid Cymru's socialist principles 'that are at the heart of our socialist programme.'[50] Williams's rationale for this propagation and application of socialism within Wales is to reinvigorate and, as he sees it, to save Welsh communities. Explaining the need for this process of re-invigoration through a flow of resources, Williams has contended that 'the capitalist system keeps money for itself, socialists re-invest.'[51]

Williams's language echoes the words of many grass-roots Old Labour supporters in Wales, and there are significant similarities between the ideological positions adopted by many activists in both political parties. Common cause can be found on issues of welfare, social justice and redistribution throughout society: in other words on traditional socialist grounds. Problems arise, unsurprisingly, when concepts such as political autonomy or patriotism enter the political arena. The issues of Welsh language and culture can also engender much debate as the Labour Party line on matters of identification is less particularistic, because identification on a British level tends to be fairly settled within Labour Party discourse. Presented at the National Assembly in early 2009, the Legislative Competence Order on greater public recognition for the Welsh language was one clear example of an issue that caused tensions between nationalist and socialist viewpoints on matters of language, culture and identity to rise to the surface.

Returning to the manifestos, another socialist staple, nationalisation – a centralising concept, as noted in the section on the party's 1974 manifesto – is also featured in *Manifesto 2001*, as the document pleaded for the return of Railtrack from private to public hands. Responsibility for the railways in Wales, the manifesto argued, should be placed in the hands of the National Assembly.[52] It could also be asserted that socialism featured in *Manifesto 2001* in the section entitled 'One World'.[53] Recalling the core socialist concept of 'human welfare as a desirable objective',[54] Plaid Cymru stated that 'The Party of Wales is totally committed to the principle of world citizenship.'[55] Furthermore, the manifesto contended that, using this principle, 'the eradication of poverty must be at the heart of all international policy.'[56]

Michael Freeden's contention that socialism 'cherishes an ideal of human welfare or flourishing based in the short run on the elimination of poverty'[57] would appear to match up with Plaid Cymru's objectives in the One World section of *Manifesto 2001*. The language of equality, another of Freeden's core concepts of socialism, is also featured. In an attempt to foster social justice and to create what Plaid Cymru terms a fairer world, there is a need, the manifesto claims, for equality 'between individuals, communities, countries and also generations.'[58] From a reading of *Manifesto 2001*, a global redistribution of wealth, resources and educational material – a demand incidentally that is replicated by environmentalists and green parties worldwide – would appear to be Plaid Cymru's solution to the problem of global inequalities.

The Depth of Socialism within Plaid Cymru

Although it has been established that the term 'socialism' certainly materialises at frequent intervals within Plaid Cymru's literature and rhetoric, is there sufficient evidence to claim that there is a genuine, and cogent, socialist project at work? Consideration must be given to whether the party's apparent lack of a distinctive and unified political ideology allows some within the party, such as Kate Roberts and D.J. and Noelle Davies in the early days, through the likes of Dafydd Elis-Thomas and Syd Morgan, to, more recently, people such as Jill Evans, Nerys Evans, Bethan Jenkins, Adam Price and Leanne Wood, to use the party as a vehicle for forwarding socialist ideas. One thing that has to be calculated is whether all of this talk of socialism within the party is a tacit recognition that the party requires a more comprehensive political agenda; hence, it may be a plea made by some individuals that Plaid Cymru must have a full ideology, in the Freedenite sense, for it to be seen as a creditable political party. Furthermore, the acknowledgement that socialism is an ideology, as opposed to being merely a concept or a theory, must be appreciated. Thus, if Plaid Cymru claims to be a socialist party, or at least some members of Plaid Cymru claim that they are members of a party that espouses a set of socialist principles, then why is the party selective, rather than comprehensive, in its adoption of socialist ideology? This is clearly a stumbling block for those within the party who seek to identify Plaid Cymru as a socialist party.

Socialism and the Decontested Nation

Michael Freeden has remarked that 'all socialisms assert the equality of human beings.'[59] If this is so, then the ideology of Plaid Cymru, if it has socialist concepts, should equate with this tenet of socialism. Nationalism can be presented as an ideology that seeks to divide rather

than unite groups of people through its promotion of one set of people
– be they ethnically, linguistically or geographically located or generated – over what is generically termed the other. Socialism, on the other
hand, is designed to rise above, or at least put to one side, ethnic or
national concerns; indeed, the only group concern that socialism advocates is the removal of the inequalities attached to class divisions within
society in order to promote social and racial harmony. So, although there
would be some losers under socialism – though strange bedfellows, the
affluent and the racist appear the most obvious examples – socialism is
designed to encourage social inclusion over social exclusion.

Nationalism has to have a degree of social, cultural, political or
economic exclusion, or a mix of these facets, if it is to champion one
particular cause or set of grievances, built as they invariably are on
either a national or an ethnic basis. To give an example of what this
entails, it is plausible to contend that socialists would encourage the
redistribution of wealth above, for instance, their providing any support
for the nationalist concept of the positive valorisation of the nation.
Where there is difficulty for Plaid Cymru in rationalising some of these
beliefs, knowing that many within the party still adhere to the description of themselves as nationalists, is in trying to examine whether the
decontesting of the nation places the views of the party into a position
wherein socialist concepts, core or peripheral, are totally incompatible. Plaid Cymru, therefore, has to begin to identify its ideological
standpoint in a far clearer and more decisive manner than previously
exhibited.

Decontesting can prove problematic for political parties as it requires
that they address concepts and arrive at settled interpretations. On the
other hand, it can also prove informative for those going through the
decontesting process. To show how decontesting the subject can offer
two varying conclusions, it is worth noting the following example. As
Freeden has recorded, the concept of the nation could be decontested as
'one of many identity-constituting groups'[60] that could be surrounded
by the adjacent concept of 'citizenship (decontested as the recognition
of individual membership as a complex of duties and rights).'[61] Freeden
then adds that there could be the perimeter practice of 'the accessibil-
ity and development of shared cultural artefacts.'[62] Into this potentially
open and pluralistic version of nationalism, socialist practice could
feasibly find an entry. Alternatively, however, Freeden also offers an
account that would make that entry nigh on impossible. According to
him, the other ideological position under consideration

> could decontest the nation as inherently superior to its mem-
> bers ... with the adjacent concept of community (decontested as

a homogeneous ascriptive group whose membership features are involuntary and natural) ... we could then add the perimeter practice of ... the development of rituals in which emotional ties are given priority over other bonds.[63]

This interpretation is vastly different as, even before the concepts can be individually assessed, its very tone eschews openness and plurality. The operation of socialism within this political climate would prove problematic. The coming together of the categorically nationalistic values, put out by Freeden's description, and any form of socialist ideology would appear to be unimaginable, as it seems unlikely that there could be any natural alliances or synthesis between the core or peripheral concepts. Thus, the prime theoretical challenge for Plaid Cymru, because its followers claim the party's ideology has both nationalist and socialist morphologies, is not only in identifying one specific ideology that the party can claim as its core system of beliefs, but also facing up to the fact that the party may encounter considerable difficulties in trying to fuse these two ideologies into a practicable and lucid ideological standpoint, taking on board the assumption that these two ideologies would appear to offer varying teleologies.

Liberalism

The next ideology that requires assessment in this chapter is liberalism. Notions of freedom – be they centred on an individual, a national or an international basis – are all visible within Plaid Cymru's literature and rhetoric. Although freedom, characterised by one of Freeden's core concepts of liberalism as 'an insistence on liberty of thought and, within some limits, action',[64] is an often used expression within the language of the party, it is Plaid Cymru's adaptation of the expression freedom, and its application in terms of Wales's structures of government and national identity, that requires examination. Furthermore, another of Freeden's stated core concepts of liberalism entails what he conveys as 'an appeal to the "general interest" rather than to particular loyalties.'[65] This could prove problematic to any party pushing a national agenda, as, under those circumstances, the party would appear to be duty bound to promote particularistic, as opposed to general, concerns. This could well be the case with Plaid Cymru and this could, therefore, seriously attenuate any claims the party may have to be adherents of liberal ideology.

In relation to modern Plaid Cymru, Laura McAllister has observed how, post 1945, Gwynfor Evans led the way in expressing liberal values. The phrase McAllister used in relation to Evans's reasoning on this matter, 'individual fulfilment',[66] has obvious connotations with liberty and the maximisation of one's own abilities in an unfettered society. Nevertheless, there are difficulties in the way that Evans's thinking evolved. The caveat in McAllister's appraisal comes about when she reports that Gwynfor Evans would like to see this individual fulfilment being 'conditional upon the establishment of full nationhood.'[67] The implications of this, given Evans's insistence on the attainment of full nationhood, are that any form of individual fulfilment, or any expression of human liberty, is lacking in its totality unless Plaid Cymru's objective of political autonomy has been realised. Consequently, Gwynfor Evans, and the party, may be seeking, albeit inadvertently, to put an obstacle in the way of people who wish to attain individual flourishing but who are not necessarily attracted to the notion that societal flourishing – seen by Plaid Cymru as achievable only through the implementation of self-government, and a strong sense of national awareness – is a prerequisite. Plaid Cymru, therefore, could be presented as a party that was placing a nationalistic constraint in the way of liberal enactment.

In addition, it is worth noting how Gwynfor Evans preferred the term national freedom when expounding on matters of liberty: the prefix national being an essential part of Evans's outlook. To illustrate this, it is perceptible that, in his coda to *Fighting for Wales*, Evans saw communal, rather than individual, action as the only way to progress. To these ends, he stated that 'national freedom is the condition of Welsh national survival. If we don't put an end to our servitude, our servitude will put an end to us.'[68] Taking this line of argument forward, and relating it to Plaid Cymru's stated aims and intentions, it is evident that any form of individual flourishing, and freedom of action and expression, would invariably weaken the attachment between the individual and his or her reliance on the abstract notions of community or nation. For someone striving for the liberal objective of unfettered living, allegiance to one of these abstract notions could be portrayed as a denial of individualism and a relapse into life under hegemonic control – merely a case, in the eyes of a liberal, of the suppression under English rule being replaced by suppression under Welsh rule.

So the nationalistic intentions of Plaid Cymru are seemingly at odds with liberalism's advancing of the individual's right to flourish in a society with minimal constriction. Likewise, those advocating liberalism would object to the placing of the nation, rather than the individual, at the centre of human existence and identification. Similarly, commenting on liberalism and liberal values within the party, Dafydd Trystan has observed that Plaid Cymru has to strike a balance in its views, and in the presentation of those views, that lies somewhere 'between individualism and communitarianism.'[69] Therefore, taking all of these points together, problems clearly exist if Plaid Cymru, as Karl Davies has already claimed, is attempting to conceptualise itself as a party that incorporates liberalism into its overall political ideology.

If liberalism were conspicuous in only a few isolated instances within the party then there might be a case to dismiss it as a fringe ideology, or as the personal flirtations of a few members. However, it is not only Gwynfor Evans and Karl Davies who use the language of liberalism within Plaid Cymru. Most notable, from a collective point of view, was the composite motion presented by the Rhanbarths of Bedwellty and Neath to Plaid Cymru's annual conference at Aberystwyth in 1970. Praising the continuation of *perchentyaeth* (home ownership) as an integral principle and component of the party's agenda, the motion claimed that this liberal approach to the right to individual possession equates with 'the whole idea of man and society from which Plaid Cymru's political aims derive; and recognised by Conference resolutions in 1932, 1938, 1943, 1945, 1949, and 1959.'[70] Furthermore, in language that could have been borrowed from liberationist thought, the motion added that 'we reaffirm our rejection of all systems, whether capitalistic or socialistic, which erode the rights of the individual, and we look forward to the establishment in Wales of a social, political and economic democracy which will liberate the individual from economic exploitation whilst strengthening his freedom and dignity.'[71]

Moving from group allegiances to individual opinions, it is evident that Eurig Wyn is one of several prominent members to incorporate liberal concepts into their own world-views. Wyn introduced a liberal element when he remarked how Plaid Cymru 'is a nationalist party and also a socialist party. Look at the party's commitment to human rights as an example.'[72] Leaving aside the claims that Plaid Cymru embraces both nationalist and socialist ideologies, Wyn's estimation that a commitment to human rights is a trait of both nationalism and socialism and hence, correspondingly, this commitment can be registered as an attribute of Plaid Cymru's political approach requires scrutiny. In historical terms alone, given that the human rights issue does not feature regularly in Plaid Cymru's pronouncements – though a subsection entitled 'Human Rights and Equality' with its demand for 'a comprehensive review of all equality legislation and ... a civilised attitude towards refugees'[73] did feature in *Manifesto 2001* – it may be fair to conclude that the human rights issue, as emphasised by Eurig Wyn, is a synchronic concept within Plaid Cymru's thought-practices. The synchronic argument could be said to be a diachronic feature if Plaid Cymru's internationalism, with its concern for the attainment of self-government by liberationist groups worldwide, is taken into account. However, this line of reasoning could be countered if the argument is elaborated to explain how the traditional concerns within Plaid Cymru have been with the self-development and political expression of communities and national groups as opposed to the specific issue of the welfare of individuals. Again, it would appear to be the case that within Plaid Cymru what can be accurately ascribed nationalist ideology, or certainly collectivist ideology, has taken precedence over liberal ideology. Regardless of this, the language of liberalism and interpretations of liberal concepts are scattered throughout the party's pronouncements, although the construal of these liberal concepts by members of Plaid Cymru may differ somewhat from accepted usage.

Although human rights can be dealt with through the spreading of respect for individuality by individuals themselves, acting in an individual capacity, it is when it comes to supporting the concept of a nation-state – being as it is a structure of government that has to deal with other structures of government around the world – that problems of interpretation and operation can arise. As noted throughout this examination, Plaid Cymru supports the implementation of a distinctively Welsh structure of government. If human rights issues (e.g. concerns over racial or sexual discrimination) are to be addressed within Wales – Wales being the immediate politico-geographical unit that Plaid Cymru seeks to operate within – then the issue of perfectionism, being 'the active intervention of political authorities in creating conditions that permit citizens to lead valuable lives',[74] has to enter the arena. The direction in which a society turns can therefore be manipulated by the ideology of the ruling political and judicial elite. Unless Eurig Wyn and Plaid Cymru want to keep their concerns for human rights on a purely theoretical basis, then, logically, a model of perfectionism, entailing as it does some form of governmental diktat, has to follow. If Plaid Cymru was to enact this perfectionism in law, then 'constrained power',[75] another core concept of liberalism, would be stretched. Plaid Cymru's championing of the nation, with its subsequent national characteristics in regard to governance and power structures, would appear to be incompatible with some of liberalism's core concepts. All of this would appear to militate against liberalism constituting a substantial component of Plaid Cymru's ideology.

A Coalition with the Liberals: Ideology or Practicality?

Putting aside some of the conceptual arguments for one moment, and addressing the issue in purely concrete party political terms, some congruency between Plaid Cymru and political liberalism may be evident in Phil Williams's explanation of the attempted establishing of links between Plaid Cymru and the Liberal Party in 1969. In that year, Williams, a leading member along with Dafydd Wigley of the Policy and Research Group that had been established in 1966, wrote to the Liberal Party magazine, *New Outlook*, claiming that 'there is a very substantial degree of agreement between the Liberal Party and the Nationalist Parties.'[76] Williams admitted that some prominent Plaid Cymru members, himself included, conducted clandestine meetings at that period in time with Emlyn Hooson and others within the Welsh Liberal Party. Williams's justification for these encounters hinged on the Plaid Cymru hierarchy's belief that the two parties were 'both committed to a very high degree of self-government for Wales and were also in fair agreement over quite a range of policies.'[77]

With regard to constitutional matters, what the Liberal Party had proposed at that point in time was a federal system of government for the United Kingdom. Phil Williams remarked that 'although this was short of what we would have wished, in terms of the day to day running of Wales, and tackling the problems of Wales, it would have been a massive step forward.'[78] Interestingly, according to Williams, the talks were discontinued not because Plaid Cymru saw no merit in progressing with them, but because of internal disputes among the Liberals. As Williams commented about the Liberal Party, and subsequently the Liberal Democrats, 'the leadership often have policies which I feel very close to ... the actual voters for the Liberal Democrats are very different.'[79]

Of particular interest within this is the apparent aligning and similarity, as Williams and the Policy and Research Group saw it, between Plaid Cymru's and the Liberal Party's policies and ideology. It is, nevertheless, devolution, or the attainment of some degree of self-government, which appears to be the policy that Williams highlights. Moreover, the administering of some semblance of political autonomy is probably the one area of policy, embryonic as it undoubtedly would have been in its nature, that both Liberal and Plaid Cymru members, if there were to have been a coalition of the third parties in Wales, could have reached a general consensus upon.

On the above points, Charlotte Davies's views on the historical differences between Plaid Cymru and the Liberal Party are worthy of consideration. Writing about the period of Plaid Cymru's incarnation in the 1920s, Davies commented on how Plaid Cymru 'projected a very different nationalist image: instead of the former Liberal nationalists' eagerness to secure a place for Welsh culture within the British imperial tradition, the new party sought positive valuation for a separate Welsh cultural tradition, to be supported by Welsh political institutions.'[80] So a British-centric politics, represented by the Liberals, would have to be estimated against a Welsh-centric politics, as favoured by Plaid Cymru. However, as the coalition under discussion in the 1960s did not emerge, this predicament did not have to be overcome.

Nevertheless, this contemplating of liberal values by some within Plaid Cymru appears somewhat out of kilter with the other ideological roads that the party was heading down in the late 1960s. While R.C. Collins's 1967 view of Plaid Cymru's ideology as libertarian socialist has already been addressed, Phil Williams also remarked on the party's evolving ideology in this period. Commenting on two by-elections that Plaid Cymru narrowly failed to gain – Rhondda West in 1967 and his own at Caerphilly in 1968 – Williams put the party's encouraging showing in the Rhondda down to a large protest vote against the sitting Labour government. However, as Williams was to claim, 'by 1968 we'd gone a lot further in developing our economic strategies and the 1968 by-election had far more emphasis on Wales as a self-governing country.'[81] Although it is true that the Liberal Party also shared this vision of a more autonomous Welsh political system, the more overtly nationalistic message that Plaid Cymru was disseminating throughout the Caerphilly by-election campaign, as indeed the party was throughout the latter years of the 1960s and the early 1970s, cannot go unregistered. This message, however, should also be juxtaposed, to some extent, with the ascendancy of Scottish nationalism in the guise of the SNP. It could be contended, therefore, that a fresh impetus for the absorption of nationalist ideas had come about in both Wales and Scotland in the late 1960s and early 1970s.

The Concept of Liberty: Individual or Collective?

Assessing all of these aforementioned conceptual and ideological shifts, it is feasible to conclude that liberalism has been, and remains, part of the ideational make-up of Plaid Cymru. This is evidenced in the liberal core concepts of 'the postulation of "sociability"... and "reservations about power" unless it is constrained and made accountable.'[82] For Plaid Cymru, sociability is paramount as the individual finds nourishment and meaning not as an atomistic being, but within his or her relevant community. This concept will be further examined when the notion of community is addressed later. Likewise, the central liberal principle of reservations about power is conspicuous in early Plaid Cymru's misgivings about unrestrained capitalism and industrialisation. Also, a perennial concern of Plaid Cymru's has been the substantial amount of power held outside Wales – predominantly in London – that is then administered on Wales in a top-down manner. Therefore, it is of little surprise that these various liberal ideological concepts found echoes of support from within Plaid Cymru and, ultimately, these concepts could prove to be a significant part of Plaid Cymru's morphology.

Where there are clear signs of disparity between liberalism and Plaid Cymru, however, is when the liberal assumption 'that the individual is the prime social unit'[83] comes into contention with Plaid Cymru's adherence to the nation as the supreme nucleus. While liberty is the guiding light, or at least the backdrop, for the liberal and Plaid Cymru assertions, the units that are to be imbued with this conception of freedom – the individual and the communal notion of the nation – are diametrically opposed. If it is liberalism's contention that it is the individual who must be the specific focal point for freedom of thought and action, then Plaid Cymru cannot possibly follow this interpretation because a collective praxis, in the guise of national activism, remains central to the party's thought-practices. This concept of liberalism, therefore, is at variance with Plaid Cymru's ideology. Nevertheless, this has not stopped Plaid Cymru from publishing a liberal statement on the party's website,[84] and, in so doing, it could be argued that the party is claiming liberal concepts as part of its specific political intentions.

The third aim (of five) that the party promulgates, according to the website, is to 'build a national community based on equal citizenship, respect for different traditions and cultures and the equal worth of all individuals, whatever their race, nationality, gender, colour, creed, sexuality, age, ability or social background.'[85] Liberalism shines through in this written aim of Plaid Cymru. Where nationalism enters the debate is over the first part of the statement wherein the desire to build a national community is proposed. Liberals would favour the replacement of the term 'national community' with either 'world-wide community' or, alternatively, simply 'community'. Indeed, Plaid Cymru uses both of the last two terms from time to time. Nevertheless, the fact that the party has settled on the national framework within which these liberal concepts will, hopefully, flourish brings the debate back, once more, to how members of Plaid Cymru see themselves and their party. Furthermore, it also focuses on how, whatever issue the members are taking into consideration, they primarily relate their political *Weltanschauung* in terms of a national or Welsh scale. Therefore, it appears that despite the liberal undercurrent that is clearly visible, and which even becomes embedded in one of the party's five published political aims, nationalism is never far from the surface. To these ends, nationalism appears to act as a fallback or counterbalance for the party. Hence, the envisaged effect that any ideas and policies may have on the primacy of the nation remains the benchmark for judging all of the political concepts and theories that Plaid Cymru encounters.

Feminism

The final ideology to be considered within this chapter is feminism. Even though, when a trawl of Plaid Cymru's more prominent literature and pronouncements is made, feminist thought and discourse may not immediately come into view, there is, nevertheless, sufficient evidence available to initiate an assessment of feminism's role within Plaid Cymru's ideology.

The Historical Role of Women in Plaid Cymru

When Plaid Cymru was established, in 1925, the originators were generally perceived to be a collection of men who, as mentioned previously, were active in fields such as academia and the church. As Deirdre Beddoe noted, 'it is a group of six men who are officially recognised as the party's founders.'[86] As a result, the image of Plaid Cymru as a male-dominated political party was activated. Nevertheless, it was Mai Roberts, one of the party's earliest female campaigners, who was actually the 'prime mover in arranging the 1925 meeting between the two nationalist groups whose merger created the Welsh Nationalist Party.'[87] Though seemingly airbrushed out of the picture of the party's formative process, Mai Roberts and other female members were not totally inconspicuous. Charlotte Davies has commented on how a 'formal photograph of those in attendance at the Inaugural Summer School held at Machynlleth in 1926 showed 26 per cent women of the fifty-three adults in the picture.'[88] It was not the fact that women were not in existence, or were in any way exempt from membership of the party, that was at issue, it was merely the case that the predominant thought and practice of the early years of Plaid Cymru's history centred on what were commonly seen as the mainstream, and arguably male-centric, matters of the day. Women, and any consideration of what may deemed to be a feminist position, were therefore peripheralised from the outset.

The Second World War inevitably changed some of the aforementioned perceptions; and not just because this period coincided with some ideological alterations to Plaid Cymru's thought-practices. During the war some women within Plaid Cymru objected to the transference of labour from Wales to England. In 1943, one of those women, Kathleen Foley from Swansea, refused to move across the border from Wales. In her defence she cited nationalist grounds. These were dismissed, however, and she was fined £25.[89] Nevertheless, Foley's act of defiance did reflect a growing confidence amongst some of Plaid Cymru's women members to engage more directly in political matters. Hence, though women were still relatively marginalised when it came to the public persona of Plaid Cymru, they were seemingly making their mark in other, less formal, ways.

In the 1950s and 1960s, alas, little progress was made when it came to the elevation of women into positions of real political power within the party. This was despite the fact that Plaid Cymru was engaged in a developmental move to the left of the political spectrum, in terms of its social and public policies, whilst, concurrently, making considerable efforts to adopt a more inclusive and decentralised style of politics. However, with few signs of movement with regard to women rising through the party's ranks, it was not a total shock, in 1974, to hear Plaid Cymru's President, Gwynfor Evans, affirm that 'women had not taken a leading role in the party.'[90] This apparent lack of high-level involvement by women in the party has been accounted for, by writers such as Laura McAllister and Charlotte Davies, in several ways. Without reiterating the in-depth analysis provided on this matter by the aforementioned scholars, it could be contended that over the years many male members would have felt apprehensive when it came to encouraging the advancement of women within the party. Hence, some attitudinal barriers that must have seriously inhibited the progression of female political talent within the party have undoubtedly existed. To these ends, for decades during the middle of the twentieth century the role of women within Plaid Cymru was seen as secondary to the role of men. This must inevitably have had a psychological effect on the ambitions of women within the party. This may explain why the Women's Section within Plaid Cymru, rather than pushing feminist issues and the cause of women in Wales, seemed to be confined to taking charge of auxiliary services at party conferences.[91] With these barriers in place, therefore, it is not surprising that women's issues were sidelined within the pecking order of party matters. As a consequence, it was as late as 1978 that Plaid Cymru's membership was to witness 'the first straightforwardly feminist motion to reach the conference ... when the party adopted a stance in favour of women's rights.'[92]

After the breakthrough of 1978, the early 1980s saw a variety of female-focused motions at Plaid Cymru's conferences. By this stage in its history, the Women's Section – the main driver behind the ever-increasing presence of women on party platforms, and the forum for debating women's issues in general – had moved from being the 'fundraiser and provider of support services'[93] in the 1960s and 1970s to a more hard-nosed and forward-looking political grouping. Sian Edwards has commented on how, by 1980, there was 'a bunch of energetic and committed women such as Carmel Gahan, Eirian Llwyd, and Rosanne Reeves, amongst others ... fighting to modernise and energise Plaid Cymru by rejuvenating the moribund Women's Section and forcing Plaid Cymru to take women's rights and equality issues more seriously.'[94]

By the early to mid 1980s, debates concerning gender equality and impartiality were beginning to move centre-stage within Plaid Cymru's policy arena. The case of female representation at an electoral level was a key battleground within the party, as, indeed, it proved to be within other political parties in Wales. By the time of the 1992 general election the party had selected seven women candidates and, as Charlotte Davies has observed, all seven women were given a high profile during the election campaign.[95] Though nowhere near a 50:50 male/female split, the fielding of seven women candidates was a clear improvement from the time, in the general election of February 1974, when the party put forward just one woman candidate in the thirty-six seats that Plaid Cymru was contesting. Moreover, it was during the 1990s that Plaid Cymru saw 'its first women national chairs and several women joining the party's policy cabinet.'[96] By the 1990s, therefore, more women were becoming clearly visible within the party as a whole and, importantly, women were becoming more involved within the party's policy-making arena. There is no doubt that some of these activists had had their interest in Plaid Cymru sparked by the 'more stereotypically women's concerns'[97] that would have acted as a counterweight to some of the more traditional, nationalistically inclined, concerns of the party. It was, however, the establishment of the National Assembly for Wales in 1997, and its subsequent elections, that enabled women within Plaid Cymru to gain a substantial electoral foothold at an all-Wales level. The party, by this time, was at last attempting to redress some of the iniquities of the past by offering women within Plaid Cymru adequate opportunities to attain political office, both within the party itself and, more importantly, through the ballot box. With regard to the latter, as Fiona Mackay has indicated, when it came to selecting candidates for its Assembly campaign, the party 'used the additional member lists to attempt to partially correct under-representation in constituencies by selecting a woman to head up each of the five regional lists.'[98] These movements, throughout the 1990s and in the early years of the new millennium, appear to have settled the debate about the institutionalised sidelining of women within Plaid Cymru.

By the 2007 National Assembly election it was evident that women featured more prominently on the party's list of candidates. In the South West Wales constituency, for example, four of the six candidates seeking inclusion on the regional list were women. Interestingly, however, there was no mention of what could be labelled women's issues on any of the electoral messages put out by these female candidates. Statements condemning the war in Iraq, calling for a new Welsh Language Act and emphasising, as one candidate, Sian Caiach, asserted, 'the very real human misery which generations of misgovernment have brought to many people in Wales',[99] appeared to have replaced the language of equal rights and representation, and anything perceptibly feminist in tone or content, within the election addresses. Therefore, it could be suggested that the position of women within contemporary Plaid Cymru – certainly when compared with the position of women with the party in 1925, 1955 or even 1985 – appears to be one of parity, certainly in terms of equality of opportunity and a lack of visible discrimination or overtly sexist attitudes.

Freeden and Feminism's Core Concepts

Michael Freeden has stated that there are three core concepts to the ideology of feminism.[100] He contends that these are (a) the centrality of the role of women; (b) the relationship between men and women, which is a key problematic in social organisation and practices; and (c) the male–female relationship as a power nexus in which women are dominated, exploited, or oppressed by men, a relationship that has to be transformed or integrated.

The first core concept, concerning the centrality of the role of women, is the key to understanding feminism and feminist arguments. It also provides the basis of any consideration as to where to situate the role of the female within the world of political ideologies and practical political decision-making. Although feminism holds to universal standards and principles, it is nevertheless feasible to decentralise the argument – to create a more exact, possibly less utopian, position from which to attempt an understanding of the precise position of women in any given society. For example, if Shulamith Firestone's conception of women regaining 'ownership of their own bodies'[101] – a universal feminist demand – is transposed onto a geographical tableau, it could be argued that feminists are engaged in an attempt to re-establish ownership over their own territory: whatever that particular territory happens to be. If interpreted from this angle, a link could be established between those seeking feminist values and practices as a universal goal and those who hold that autonomy, in a geopolitical sense as opposed to a broadly gender-based sense, may be acquired through adopting a feminist nationalist approach.

In opposition to this, however, and in an attempt to formulate an understanding about these positions of overlap and attachment, Graham Day and Andrew Thompson have observed how 'nationalism and feminism seem to be drawn into unavoidable opposition: claims for the emancipation of women threaten to undermine the avowed unity of the nation, whereas national differences weaken the proclaimed commonality of conditions among women across the world.'[102] Furthermore, on the matter of the general relationship between nationalism and feminism, Day and Thompson have observed how 'nationalist movements rarely, if ever, take women's situation as their point of departure. On the contrary, nationalism often suppresses women's concerns, or puts them aside until the "more important" issue of the nation's fate is decided.'[103] Although there is no reason to doubt the validity of Day and Thompson's findings, it is imperative to remember that this exploration is contending that Plaid Cymru is not a party that can be easily boxed in ideological terms – nationalist or otherwise – and hence feminism may not unduly suffer within the thought-practices of Plaid Cymru.

The second Freedenite core concept – the relationship between men and women is a key problematic in social organisation and practices – assesses the techniques used to establish equality within relationships. It could be argued that the problem of equality arises when universal feminist demands for an essentially equal world – the 'each counts as one' notion – are juxtaposed with the establishment of a nationalistic society – Wales in this case – in which positive valorisation of the nation appears to go against universalist feminist political philosophy. The dilemma remains, however, that at times equality 'intersects with the concept of difference. The result is a range of decontestations reflecting a spectrum of cultural positions within a broad logical network.'[104] This could be the circumstance that Plaid Cymru is faced with as the party attempts to reconcile both universalist (feminism) and particularistic (self-government) concerns.

Reflecting on matters of placement and identity, Cynthia Enloe[105] has contended that women engage in certain culturally or traditionally assigned roles within nationalist movements. If Enloe is correct, then women, attempting to campaign on either first-wave – political representation – or second-wave – gender representation – feminist issues, face considerable structural difficulties. If facing up to some of these challenges is not tough enough already, given that, as John Morrow has commented, 'political values and modes of behaviour ... are generally construed in male terms',[106] feminists who also embrace a position that could be seen as being nationalistic – such as Plaid Cymru's, for instance – encounter further difficulties in both conceptual and practical terms. This is because feminist nationalism, or nationalist feminism, is somewhat contradictory as feminism's foremost allegiance is to women as a whole whereas nationalism's is to a particular nation. These allegiances have to override all other concerns, therefore, in order for ideological attachment to continue. Thus, feminists within Plaid Cymru cannot opt out of their commitment to female allegiance, in a universal sense, in favour of their preference for commitment to the Welsh nation.

Michael Freeden's third core concept of feminism – the male–female relationship is a power nexus – concerns the perceived use of structures and networks of power, by men, in order to dominate women within society. This could, arguably, be seen by feminists within Plaid Cymru, who may wish to interweave feminist concepts with Plaid Cymru's principles, as being akin to the Britain–Wales relationship in terms of its power structure and its use of hegemonic values. It is feasible to proffer that both the male–female and Britain–Wales roles are socially constructed in terms of their values, duties and norms. However, it is important to acknowledge that these relationships and power structures are fluidic in their nature and, likewise, any feminist contentions that accompany them may well be reshaped and re-evaluated over time.

On this theme of reshaping and re-evaluation, it could be possible to contend that the objectives of first-wave feminism (circa 1890–1920) – namely the various campaigns for political rights for women – were, or plausibly still are, more in tune with feminist notions circulating within Plaid Cymru than were the ambitions of second-wave feminism (circa 1960 onwards). This may be because second-wave feminists peripheral-ised the state; that is they moved it 'from adjacent to marginal positions in their ideological constructs.'[107] So, from 1960 onwards, any move from feminists within Plaid Cymru to emphasise female emancipation through the attainment of state power would have run against the con-temporary feminist thinking of the time. This is because second-wave feminism, certainly in its radical feminist guise, had other agendas that needed addressing before that of state politics and the realisation of power through parliamentary and democratic means.

Debates over the nature and content of the state, in a practical political sense, would appear, therefore, not to have been of primary concern to feminists in the second-wave period. If this is so, then feminism within Plaid Cymru's thought-practices may have been faced with something of an ideational dilemma if other lines of feminist discourse – debates over reproduction, pornography, etc. – were highlighted before tradi-tional first-wave concerns, such as the advancement, in legislative and electoral terms, of women's political rights.

Feminism, in its second-wave guise at least, could be seen as being at odds with the nationalist, liberal and socialist ideologies at work in Plaid Cymru's thought-practices. This is because each of these three ideologies has firm conceptions of the state and its power structures. As Plaid Cymru is a party that desires fundamental structural change to occur on social, political and cultural levels, it would seem to be natural that any particular ideology, or any individual ideological concept, operating within the party should incorporate some clear notion of how these power structures are to be administered. Looked at in this respect, there could be difficulties in pursuing a feminist line of argument within Plaid Cymru, or at least for granting feminism too much space within the party's ideological set-up, as Plaid Cymru's overall vision of an equalitarian Wales, with an internal dialectic that seeks to re-arrange the structures of Welsh society along the aforementioned multifarious levels, may actually prove to be incompatible with feminism's wider, universal *raison d'être*.

The Feminist Tradition within Plaid Cymru

Women, as noted earlier, have always featured within the ranks of Plaid Cymru as grass-roots members, elected representatives, policy-makers and party theorists, although, admittedly, their influence on the party's ideological positioning, and their organisational involvement, has varied over the years. In the party's formative period, for instance, activists such as Kate Roberts were prominent. Roberts's position within the party is noticeable not only because she was a routine con-tributor to *Y Faner* and *Y Ddraig Goch*, the party's regular publications, but also through her championing of women's issues within the party in general. Nevertheless, although the setting up of a Women's Section was discussed and accepted at the party's inaugural summer school at Machynlleth in 1926, with Kate Roberts elected as chair, the Women's Section 'never became a prominent feature of party organisation.'[108] This may be a consequence of the perceived priorities of the party – cultural and linguistic protection and advancement – overriding other issues, such as the role of women in Welsh society. Alternatively, if seen from a wider ideological and historical perspective, it could be posited that feminism was destined to play a minor role within Plaid Cymru as the party was formed at a time that saw both the end of the first wave of feminism and the beginning of the era that saw the ideologies of mass activism (communism, fascism, etc.) rise to the fore. Furthermore, politics remained, at this time, a predominantly male-orientated arena. This would no doubt have affected the cause of feminism within Plaid Cymru because Welsh politics and society have a strong cultural and ideological identity that prioritises what are perceived to be male interests.

As Laura McAllister has observed, in a chapter from her book on Plaid Cymru entitled 'A Woman's Perspective: From the Outside Looking In', women's status within the party was 'almost consistently invisible.'[109] McAllister has maintained that whenever women within the party have displayed any radical or mould-breaking intentions, this has been construed by sections of Plaid Cymru's male membership as being akin to feminism. Moreover, in the eyes of many men within the party, any signs of feminist activity were perceived to be parallel to promoting an alien ideology, when juxtaposed with the brand of Welshness or Welsh political culture that the overwhelming majority of the male membership sought to encourage. Hence, whenever they attempted to advance feminist issues, figures ranging from Mai Roberts and Mallt Williams in the early days to more contemporary figures such as Pauline Jarman and Helen Mary Jones[110] were, within the party as a whole, largely either sidelined or submerged within the dominant ideologies such as socialism and nationalism. To this extent it would appear that, in general terms, women within Plaid Cymru, be they either committed feminists or simply active members of the party, have been faced with an arduous task in their attempt to achieve full recognition.

When assessing the arduousness of this task, one matter that cannot go unstated, and one that undoubtedly impinges on the discussion about feminism within Plaid Cymru, is the fact that Plaid Cymru is neither a female-only party nor a party that focuses its attention on equality matters alone. Hence, it is not clear-cut that feminism would be influential or vital to the ideational set-up of Plaid Cymru, as it almost certainly would be, for example, if an organisation such as the Northern Ireland Women's Coalition were under the analytical spotlight.

Feminism, Symbolism and Plaid Cymru

Symbolism plays a part within all social, cultural and political movements, as well as within all of the societies that they feed off and contribute to. Symbols evident, over the years, within Plaid Cymru include the triban (the party's emblem with a representation of the mountains of Wales in the background) and the Welsh national flag (*Y Ddraig Goch*). It is the imagery associated with Wales as a whole, however, that provides for greater interest when any assessment of feminism is considered. Despite folklore in Wales featuring the allegorical symbol of the Welsh Mam, which will be considered shortly, it is the more perceivably masculine imagery of coal, slate, steel, rugby and male voice choirs that people, both inside and outside the country, routinely associate with Wales. Added to this, the dragon symbol itself, along with the Gorsedd of Bards and the poetic tradition, is steeped in male-orientated institutional practice, although a process of feminisation in some of these domains is slowly but surely transpiring.

Whilst acknowledging that male symbolism in Wales is a potent force, one facet of Welsh symbolism whose importance is often downplayed is the concept within Welsh society of the Welsh Mam. Whilst portrayed in popular culture and mythology as a stabilising role within a strictly domestic setting, it should be noted that the values and ideals of Welsh Mam(ism) have also permeated life in Wales outside the family home. Therefore, the Welsh Mam image could be portrayed as a strong and vibrant image and, consequentially, could be used as a model for feminists within Plaid Cymru to follow.

The Welsh Mam could be venerated by feminists in terms of the power wielded, within certain locations, by the mother or grandmother figures. Two aspects of the Welsh Mam that are notable are the notions of *parch* (respect) and being *duwiol* (pious, or God-fearing). *Parch* signifies the respect shown by all members of the family to the senior female figure. This respect can also have a communal meaning as the Mam is recognised and respected by others outside her immediate family domain. *Duwiol* refers to the Welsh Mam's unstinting support for religious practice and religious values, which are inferred as being essential in order for *parch* to flourish. The Welsh Mam, though based on the real-life examples of our own mothers and grandmothers, and the love and respect evident within family units, is nevertheless an allegorical, and indeed a reified, figure within Welsh social and culture history, and Welsh identity. For feminists within Plaid Cymru, therefore, the question remains as to how they interpret the significance of the Welsh Mam in a political sense.

On the subject of interpretation and usage, writers such as Nira Yuval-Davis draw attention to the link between allegorical and political representation. This is because 'it is women who reproduce nations, biologically, culturally and symbolically.'[111] Though Yuval-Davis's remark is an intriguing one and, debatably, a prescient one, the fact nevertheless remains that the predominant symbols that are apparent within everyday Welsh society are seen as being more conventionally masculine in origin and content. Similarly, and to exemplify the fact that this is not a Welsh predicament alone, Begona Echeverria has also highlighted similar difficulties in the Basque country, wherein feminist attempts to dismantle male symbolism have met with little success. This is down to the fact that 'Basque nationalist pedagogy foregrounds male contributions to Basque language and culture by erasing the efforts of their female counterparts.'[112] Hence, it would appear that feminist efforts to alter these embedded signs of particularism, be they Welsh or otherwise, face an uphill struggle.

Feminism and the Universalism–Particularism Debate

Comparing and contrasting debates on feminism in Wales, and within Plaid Cymru in particular, with other examples of feminist conduct elsewhere is apposite. This is because it must always be remembered that feminism is a universal ideology. Its universalism is apparent in the sense that its conception of female emancipation is not spatially limited. Nationalism advocates particularism, with a geographically or ethnically confined agenda under consideration. Therefore, the question for those wishing to label themselves nationalist feminist or feminist nationalist must be what is the ultimate aim of their endeavours? Is it sisterhood – in a universal sense – or nationhood – in a geographical and political sense? If sisterhood is the ideal ending then the particularistic claims of the nation – a nation that may not pursue the objective of sisterhood as rigorously as feminists would like – would appear to be somewhat at odds with universalist female demands. Similarly, if nationhood were to take precedence, then feminists might encounter occasions on which they were asked to drop their universalist desires for female emancipation and amelioration in order that national, or nationalistic, requirements be pursued.

Another consideration in this line of reasoning is the role of host-vessels. If nationalism, or any of nationalism's concepts, are allowed to enter the host-vessel of feminism then particularistic statements and values could soon dominate and play down the feminist core concepts – concepts that are non-particularistic in a national or ethnical sense.

Left-Liberalism and Plaid Cymru's Feminism

One of the questions of interest, at this juncture, is whether feminists within Plaid Cymru subscribe to what Michael Freeden has termed the 'left-liberalism'[113] within feminism's thought-practices? This left-liberalism employs 'a perimeter concept to flesh out equality: affirmative action, not as a transformation of human relationships, but as a compensation for the disadvantages suffered by women within existing political systems.'[114] If the feminists within Plaid Cymru adopted this notion of left-liberalism, with its commitment to redressing the balance in regard to small-scale or localised, as opposed to universal, structural disadvantage, then the universal–particularistic dilemma might be partly avoided. Nevertheless, the main argument remains: that feminism attempts to liberate women from the oppression that has been engendered through sexual classification and characterisation, whereas nationalism is designed to unshackle a certain geographically or ethnically based group of people from unwanted hegemonic political or cultural systems.

Plaid Cymru and Feminism: Ideological and Historical Context

Although the role that the perimeter concept of left-liberalism could play in forwarding an equality agenda continues to be an interesting avenue for theoretical discussion, real political events often force the hand in terms of how supporters of feminism approach rapidly changing political situations. This has occurred within Plaid Cymru on several occasions throughout its history; the onset of war in the late 1930s is one example, and the party's re-evaluation of itself in the 1960s is another. However, one of the most fascinating and relevant, in terms of the feminist response, was during the end of consensus/end of Butskellism period of British politics, from around 1975 onwards. The radicalisation of Plaid Cymru in the early 1980s had been facilitated by a series of concurrent events: the disappointment of the 1979 devolution referendum result, the perceived anti-Welshness and laissez-faire doctrine of Margaret Thatcher's Conservative administration and the coming to power within Plaid Cymru of the left-leaning Dafydd Elis-Thomas, an advocate of fringe ideological positions. Laura McAllister has acknowledged that throughout this period there was, within Plaid Cymru, some 'overlap between the discussions on ideology and the pressure for increased representation for women.'[115] Accepting McAllister's observation, it is useful to contemplate how substantial a role feminism actually played within the party's ideological reassessment in this era. Also of interest is whether the drive for equality within Plaid Cymru was really feminist inspired alone, or whether it was part of a more conspicuous left-wing politics that the party was forging in response to the events of the time.

Looking at these questions in an historical context it is interesting to assess whether feminist arguments were to the fore not only in the radicalising years of the 1960s and 1980s but also at key formative times within the party's history, such as the time of the publication of the major pre-war political pamphlets and the time of the conferences in the late 1950s, when the party's ideology moved leftwards with talk of equality and cooperation to the fore. Although feminism undeniably has a tradition within the party, it could be argued that its part in the thought-practices of the party at the aforementioned periods of time would have been more as a background pressure than as a main driver. Feminism's achievement was to create a framework for discussing issues of gender equality and female advancement within the internal dialectic. This then allowed certain avenues to be explored in far greater ideological depth than ever before. For example, feminism, and the emancipatory discussion as a whole, would have been instrumental in influencing the development of socialist thought within the party; certainly, that is, in the post-1950s era. The extensive New Left agenda, forwarded within Plaid Cymru by, for example, Dafydd Elis-Thomas and Aled Eurig, would have been open to, and supportive of, feminist ideas. It must be remembered, however, that followers of the New Left, owing to their support for adversarial politics, would have been receptive to any ideas of a dissenting or transformative nature, and not just those from a feminist perspective.

One alternative aspect of the developing feminist ideological debate becomes apparent if there are signs of eco-feminism within Plaid Cymru's thought-practices. Eco-feminism would be representative of a different ideological battle line, the human versus nature counterbalance argument, which has been evolving throughout the last few decades. This eco-feminism would also tie in with Plaid Cymru's greening as a political party. This has taken place, specifically, from the 1980s onwards, although environmentalist and back to the land themes have been conspicuous throughout the party's history. For women within Plaid Cymru, one possible link with this eco-feminist position is visible through female involvement in the anti-nuclear and peace movements, which reached their zenith in the 1980s.[116] Here the issue of counterbalance would have been placed under the spotlight, and an ideological climate arose in which socialist, feminist, green and nationalist ideologies fermented and interspersed. Nevertheless, at that time, and it remains so today, this occurred within a restricted socio-cultural and political arena within Plaid Cymru, and within Welsh politics in general. This restricted arena marginalised feminist ideology either through subsuming issues of sexual politics within other dominant ideologies or by dismissing it through anti-feminist rhetoric and practice. Thus, almost inevitably, any signs of a developing eco-feminist position within Plaid Cymru's thought-practices were destined to inhabit the party's ideological peripheries.

Plaid Cymru and Feminism: Conclusion

Despite a relatively strong case for the inclusion of feminism as an understated motivating factor within Plaid Cymru, and one that has been deliberately marginalised by a male-dominated party machinery, it would be reasonable to conclude that the role of feminism within Plaid Cymru is no more imperative than the role of pacifism and non-violence. As a fully fledged ideology, rather than a specific ideological concept, feminism's grip should be far more powerful than it actually is – if it were to be a core ideology of the party's morphology – because as an ideology it should, by its very nature, be more comprehensive and pervading than an individual ideological concept such as non-violence, for example. The fact that feminism has not dominated, or radically reshaped, the party's ideology shows that it does not play that significant a role within Plaid Cymru's ideational make-up.

Whilst acknowledging that there have undoubtedly been feminists within the party from its inception, it can be concluded that, taken as a whole, it is the three major ideologies of nationalism, socialism and liberalism, and not the ideology of feminism, whose concepts have most permeated Plaid Cymru's thought-practices. Therefore, feminism must be viewed as a peripheral conceptual driver within Plaid Cymru's morphology.

Summary and Evaluation of Modern Plaid Cymru's Ideologies

The four ideologies that have been under consideration in this and the previous chapter are not the only ideologies that feature within Plaid Cymru's thought-practices. However, of the four covered – nationalism, socialism, liberalism and feminism – the first three could each stake a claim to be representative of mainstream Plaid Cymru thinking. The same cannot be said for other ideologies although, as mentioned earlier, there are remnants of conservatism on view and, if the net is spread wide enough, there are instances, albeit very few and far between, of both extremes of the political spectrum, communism and fascism, making an appearance within the opinions of Plaid Cymru's membership.

Of the two poles of political opinion, it is the far left members who are the most conspicuous and who have contributed the most to the party's thought-practices over the years. This mode of thinking is exemplified by, to take just two examples, Dafydd Elis-Thomas's penchant for Marxist rhetoric and Dafydd Trystan's admission that he was a member of the Young Communist League until he decided to join Plaid Cymru because he 'thought Plaid Cymru was a better bet for moving forward a left wing agenda in Wales than fringe left wing politics.'[117] It must be stressed, however, that, in an assessment of the history and evolution of the party's thought-practices, these are primarily fringe elements and the views of the policy-making elite within the party have tended overwhelmingly to fall within three of the four ideologies – nationalism, socialism and liberalism – that have been covered at some length. This is not to claim, however, that some or all of the concepts that will be examined in the following chapter fit neatly within, and are constitutive of, these three ideologies.

Nevertheless, what nationalism, socialism and liberalism represent are the major ideologies whose concepts and general ideas find daily usage within Plaid Cymru, certainly since 1945 in Plaid Cymru's modern guise and, it would be reasonable to claim, since the party's inception in 1925. Although nationalism has been the principal ideology, as its Freedenite core concept of the positive valorisation of the nation has been a constant and, it could be argued, a major component of the party's *raison d'être* since the first meeting of Plaid Cymru eight decades ago, the language and values represented by socialism and liberalism both feature in the everyday thought-practices of Plaid Cymru.

Therefore, nationalism, socialism and liberalism are the major ideological schools out of which Plaid Cymru's ideology has evolved. As to the exact composition and face of that ideology, a clearer picture should emerge after some of the ideological concepts that are attributed to Plaid Cymru are evaluated. Eventually, in the concluding chapter of this book, it should be possible to construct a model of Plaid Cymru's ideology. Whether that model can then slot into one of the three ideologies outlined here remains to be seen. Alternatively, a hybrid ideology may emerge. Before that stage, however, an assessment of the concepts arising in Plaid Cymru's rhetoric and literature needs to be undertaken.

Notes

1. Phil Williams, interview, 25 September 2001.
2. Laura McAllister, *Plaid Cymru: The Emergence of a Political Party* (Bridgend: Seren, 2001), p. 160.
3. Laura McAllister, 'The perils of community as a construct for the political ideology of Welsh nationalism', *Government and Opposition*, vol. 33, no. 4, 1988, p. 512.
4. R.C. Collins, *Workers Control in Wales* (Caernarfon: Plaid Cymru), p. 9.
5. Michael Freeden, *Ideology: A Very Short Introduction* (Oxford: Oxford University Press, 2003), p. 95.
6. Karl Davies, interview, 9 October 2001.
7. Michael Freeden, *Ideology*, p. 86.
8. Michael Freeden, 'Ideologies as communal resources', *Journal of Political Ideologies*, vol. 4, no. 3, p. 413.
9. Ibid.
10. Charlotte Davies, 'Ethnic Nationalism in Wales', PhD dissertation, Duke University, Durham, NC, 1988, p. 207.
11. Plaid Cymru, *Annual Conference*, 1968, p. 55.
12. Karl Davies, interview, 9 October 2001.
13. Laura McAllister, *Plaid Cymru*, p. 169.
14. Karl Davies, interview, 9 October 2001.
15. Dafydd Wigley, interview, 25 February 2002.

16. D. Hywel Davies, *The Welsh Nationalist Party 1925–1945* (New York: St Martin's Press, 1983), p. 104.
17. Ibid., p. 105.
18. Ibid.
19. Plaid Cymru, *Wales in Europe: A Community of Communities* (Cardiff: Paid Cymru, 1989), p. 3.
20. D. Hywel Davies, *The Welsh Nationalist Party 1925–1945*, p. 105.
21. Karl Davies, interview, 9 October 2001.
22. Ibid.
23. Lila Haines, interview, 4 March 2003.
24. Plaid Cymru, *Power for Wales* (Caernarfon: Plaid Cymru, 1974).
25. Ibid., p. 5.
26. Ibid.
27. Ibid.
28. Ibid.
29. Ibid., p. 13.
30. Ibid.
31. Ibid.
32. Ibid., p.12.
33. Plaid Cymru, *A Voice for Wales in Europe* (Cardiff: Plaid Cymru, 1984).
34. Ibid., p. 10.
35. Ibid., p. 14.
36. Laura McAllister, *Plaid Cymru*, p. 18.
37. Charlotte Davies, 'Ethnic Nationalism in Wales', PhD dissertation, Duke University, Durham, NC, 1988, p. 217.
38. Laura McAllister, *Plaid Cymru*, p. 78.
39. Michael Freeden, *Ideology*, p. 98.
40. Plaid Cymru, *Manifesto 2001* (Caernarfon: Plaid Cymru, 2001).
41. Ibid., pp. 5–6.
42. Ibid., p. 6.
43. Marcus Hoppe, 'Nationalist parties and Europeanisation', University of Budapest, ECPR conference paper, 2005, pp.13–16.
44. Plaid Cymru, *Manifesto 2001*, p. 9.
45. Ibid., p. 11.
46. Ibid., p. 11.
47. Michael Freeden, 'Is nationalism a distinct ideology?', *Political Studies*, vol. XLVI, 1998, p. 752.
48. Plaid Cymru, *Manifesto 2001*, p. 20.
49. Rhodri Glyn Thomas, interview, 14 May 2001.
50. Richard Williams, hustings meeting, 26 October 2002.
51. Ibid.
52. Plaid Cymru, *Manifesto 2001*, p. 18.
53. Ibid., p. 34.
54. Michael Freeden, *Ideologies and Political Theory* (Oxford: Clarendon Press, 1996), p. 425.
55. Plaid Cymru, *Manifesto, 2001*, p. 35.
56. Ibid., p. 35.
57. Michael Freeden, *Ideology*, pp. 83–84.
58. Plaid Cymru, *Manifesto 2001*, p. 35.
59. Michael Freeden, *Ideologies and Political Theory*, p. 430.
60. Michael Freeden, 'Is nationalism a distinct ideology?', p. 755.

61. Ibid.
62. Ibid.
63. Ibid.
64. Michael Freeden, *Ideology*, p. 81.
65. Ibid.
66. Laura McAllister, *Plaid Cymru*, p. 65.
67. Ibid.
68. Gwynfor Evans, *Fighting for Wales* (Talybont: Y Lolfa, 1997), p. 221.
69. Dafydd Trystan, interview, 8 March 2003.
70. Plaid Cymru, *Annual Conference*, 1970, p. 23.
71. Ibid.
72. Eurig Wyn, interview, 22 October 2002.
73. Plaid Cymru, *Manifesto 2001*, p. 29.
74. Michael Freeden, 'Understanding liberalism: between ideology and philosophy', Manchester, Political Studies Association conference, April 2001, p. 21.
75. Ibid., p. 23.
76. Liberal Party, *New Outlook*, Spring 1969, p. 7.
77. Phil Williams, interview, 25 September 2001.
78. Ibid.
79. Ibid.
80. Charlotte Davies, *Welsh Nationalism in the Twentieth Century* (Connecticut: Praeger, 1989), p. 83.
81. Phil Williams, interview, 25 September 2001.
82. Michael Freeden, *Ideology*, p. 81.
83. Ibid.
84. Plaid Cymru: www.plaidcymru.org.uk.
85. Ibid.
86. Deirdre Beddoe, *Out of the Shadows: A History of Women in Twentieth Century Wales* (Cardiff: University of Wales Press, 2000), p.193.
87. Charlotte Davies, 'Women, nationalism and feminism', in Jane Aaron, Teresa Rees, Sandra Betts and Moira Vincentelli (eds), *Our Sister's Land* (Cardiff: University of Wales Press, 1994), p. 243.
88. Ibid., p. 245.
89. Deirdre Beddoe, *Out of the Shadows*, pp. 116–117.
90. Charlotte Davies, 'Women, nationalism and feminism', p. 243.
91. Ibid., p. 246.
92. Ibid., p. 247.
93. Ibid., p. 249.
94. Sian Edwards, 'Danger – revolution in progress', in Deirdre Beddoe (ed.), *Changing Times: Welsh Women Writing in the 1950s and 1960s* (Dinas Powys: Honno, 2003), p. 273.
95. Charlotte Davies, 'Women, nationalism and feminism', p. 250.
96. Laura McAllister, *Plaid Cymru*, p.186.
97. Charlotte Davies, 'Women, nationalism and feminism', p. 249.
98. Fiona Mackay, *Love and Politics: Women, Politicians and the Ethics of Care* (London: Continuum, 2001), p. 42.
99. Plaid Cymru, South West Wales Election Package, April 2006.
100. Michael Freeden, *Ideologies and Political Theory*, p. 491.
101. Shulamith Firestone, *The Dialectic of Sex: The Case for Feminist Revolution* (London: Women's Press, 1979), p. 19.

102. Graham Day and Andrew Thompson, *Theorizing Nationalism* (London: Palgrave, 2004), p. 115.
103. Ibid., p. 108.
104. Michael Freeden, *Ideologies and Political Theory*, p. 492.
105. Cynthia Enloe, *Bananas, Beaches and Bases: Making Feminist Sense of International Politics* (Berkeley: University of California Press, 2000).
106. John Morrow, *History of Western Political Thought: A Thematic Introduction*, 2nd edition (Basingstoke: Palgrave Macmillan, 2005), p. 375.
107. Michael Freeden, *Ideologies and Political Theory*, p. 495.
108. D. Hywel Davies, *The Welsh Nationalist Party 1925–1945*, p. 70.
109. Laura McAllister, *Plaid Cymru*, p. 187.
110. Ibid., p. 186.
111. Graham Day and Andrew Thompson, *Theorizing Nationalism*, p. 115.
112. Begona Echeverria, 'Privileging masculinity in the social construction of Basque identity', *Nations and Nationalism*, vol. 7, no. 3, 2001, p. 349.
113. Michael Freeden, *Ideologies and Political Theory*, p. 510.
115. Ibid., p. 511.
115. Laura McAllister, *Plaid Cymru*, p. 192.
116. Ibid., p. 189.
117. Dafydd Trystan, interview, 8 March 2003.

VI

CONCEPTS WITHIN PLAID CYMRU'S IDEOLOGY

Introduction

This chapter will concentrate on evaluating some of the most prominent ideological concepts that have arisen within Plaid Cymru's literature and within the pronouncements of the party's members. It is not intended to be a comprehensive list of each and every concept and idea that has emanated from within the party's ranks since 1925 – not least because space would not allow an assessment of the entire breadth of concepts that have emerged over time to be discussed. Moreover, some concepts have been raised by only one or a handful of people, who may not be in any real positions of importance within the party, and are therefore so marginal to the policy-making processes within Plaid Cymru and, subsequently, to the ideology of the party as a whole that they do not require any extensive assessment. Nonetheless, these minority views are not unimportant or irrelevant. It is simply a fact that lone voices, unless they are able to garner a substantial degree of support for their points of view, are, in any significantly sized organisation, bound to remain tangential to the overall thinking of that organisation.

The major conceptual themes to be explored are essential components and motivators within the party's ideology. They are crucial to any understanding of the party's modus vivendi and some are, incontrovertibly, perennial features. Through scrutinising these core and peripheral concepts, a clearer picture of the party's true ideological constitution should ensue. Initially, therefore, the concept of religion, or metaphysical concerns in general, will be analysed because, in chronological terms, it has proven to be evident within the language of Plaid Cymru since the party's inception.

Religion

If Charlotte Davies's citing of religion as an important building block for Plaid Cymru is true – and it is evident that there is a stream of religious opinion on record – then it should be seen as a synchronic, as opposed to a diachronic, construction. It is worth remembering that Plaid Cymru was formed a mere two decades after the great religious revival of 1904–5. Many early Plaid Cymru members were active participants in this resurgence of faith, and this was an episode that had an enormous influence not only on religious matters in Wales but also on Welsh political and social life in general. As noted earlier by Rhodri Glyn Thomas, Plaid Cymru, in its formative stage, attracted a great deal of support from clerics across Wales, and the cross-fertilisation of ideas across professions was conspicuous. Elfyn Llwyd agrees with Thomas on these points and, furthermore, has commented that:

> in the early days of Plaid Cymru you could rely on two individuals in every village being a member of Plaid Cymru: the Schoolmaster and the Minister. Maybe it did play a major role – look at the Reverend Lewis Valentine for example – after all we had pledges to God and so forth.[1]

This politico-religious synthesis, however, seems to have faded with time. So much so, it would appear, that when Elin Jones was asked about the part religion plays in the thought-practices of the party today her response was unequivocal. Jones commented, 'not as far as I'm concerned. As a Plaid Cymru member for many years … it has no play whatsoever.'[2] To prove that there may well be some generational disparity, which would account for the synchronic nature of religious adherence within Plaid Cymru, Jones then added, 'perhaps older members would be more influenced by religion.'[3] Religious underpinning has not completely vanished from the mindsets of younger members, however. Darren Price, a former chair of Plaid Cymru's Student Federation, tied his religious values in with his nationalist convictions. In Price's opinion, 'people should be proud of where they come from and they should have Christian beliefs to help those around them.'[4] Before going down the route towards a particularist perspective, however, Price contended that these views were personal and that Plaid Cymru 'is no more influenced by religious ideals than any other party',[5] adding that 'there is a range of religious views within the party, some non-Christian.'[6] As an example, the Muslim faith of former party member and Assembly Member Mohammed Ashgar would certainly testify to this.

So is there a culture of religious ideas within Plaid Cymru that occasionally emerge within party policy? Laura McAllister, amongst others, would appear affirmative on this point. McAllister has claimed of party members that 'from Saunders Lewis to Gwynfor Evans, and even Dafydd Elis-Thomas, religion has strongly influenced their political vision for Wales.'[7] McAllister may be correct in her analysis of the religious convictions of these individuals, but personal belief systems, even if held by party leaders, do not necessarily infuse the political ideology of that leader's party. With this in mind, therefore, this analysis would contend that support for a variety of religious beliefs, as opposed to a singular belief system, is evident amongst Plaid Cymru's membership. Furthermore, Plaid Cymru's ideology in its collective guise, as opposed to any individual or factional ideology that may emerge from party members, remains, first and foremost, a political, rather than a politico-religious, ideology.

It is interesting, nevertheless, to compare the arrangement of religion within Plaid Cymru's thought-practices with Michael Freeden's description of one of the core concepts of conservatism. By Freeden's reckoning, 'over time, and as explanatory paradigms of order have altered, different "extra-human origins of a permanent social order" have been invoked.'[8] Applying this interpretation to Plaid Cymru could prove somewhat problematic as extra-human origins could, for example, be summoned by some within the party as justification for the party's social and moral philosophy. Where the awkward component of this concept arises, though, is in the reliance on adherence to a permanent social order. If this were an order to be created – leading to some futuristic ideal state, maybe – then the championing of its permanency would be understandable. However, as Plaid Cymru is a political party whose ambition it is to radically alter all of the layers of the existing order – social, political, economic and cultural – then a campaign in favour of perpetuating the existing social structures, sustained by an appeal to some metaphysical body, would appear nonsensical.

Religious practice, therefore, as traditionally experienced in Wales through the Christian churches, and viewed by critics and practitioners alike as the upholder of a particular set of values, could be interpreted as being at variance with Plaid Cymru's stated aims: those stated aims being a change in the socio-political and cultural dynamic within Wales. Obviously, new paradigms offering religion as a core concept can be presented within ideologies; the most notable cases of this are the emergence of fundamentalist political parties for whom politics and religion materialise in dualistic fashion. As for Plaid Cymru, however, if religion is to be considered as a core concept then further clarification and enunciation is required. What the party does not offer in any of its pronouncements to date is some strategic reasoning why religion should be a core concept of the party's ideology. Furthermore, what religious convictions do exist within the party cannot be identified and classified as a coherent, unified system of beliefs. Therefore, religion loses credibility if cited by members of Plaid Cymru as one of the primary stimuli driving the party's thought-practices. This conclusion has been arrived at because religion has no explicit impact on the party's social policy and, within Plaid Cymru, religion does not 'attempt to influence the social arrangements of the entire political community.'[9]

Various Faiths and Directions

Although there is evidence that religion – chiefly in the guise of non-conformism – did influence some within the party, others, notably Saunders Lewis, the party's prime theoretician in its early phase, advocated Catholicism. Such was the apparent association between Lewis's political outlook and his religious beliefs that, in a scathing attack on the political and religious thought-practices of the party as a whole, Gwilym Davies, writing in the quarterly magazine *Y Traethodydd* in 1942, claimed that Plaid Cymru was a 'crypto-Catholic party, indebted for its social programme solely to the Papal Encyclicals.'[10] Furthermore, attempting to cast Plaid Cymru as a right-wing organisation, Davies went on to argue that, in political terms alone, Plaid Cymru was 'the child of Action Francaise.'[11] In the pamphlet *The Party for Wales*, co-authored by Saunders Lewis and J.E. Daniel, Lewis responded to Gwilym Davies's condemnation of the party by stating that 'his "Christian Nationalism" is not the same as the "nationalism integral" of the atheist Maurras.'[12]

In addition, Saunders Lewis contended that both Plaid Cymru as a party and the Welsh people as a whole have a lot to learn from Catholicism and its correlation with political and social enhancement. From Catholic social reformers, Lewis affirmed, comes

> the certainty that our development – our emphasis on the family, the neighbourhood and locality, co-operation and trade unions, and agriculture as the foundation, opposition to the rule of finance in the life of society, opposition to the oppressive state, opposition to one-sided profiteering industrialism – was all consistent with the general principles of the Christian Faith.[13]

The interweaving of religious, social and political principles is certainly conspicuous in this adaptation of the party's political philosophy and, by taking into account the authority and presence of Saunders Lewis as leader and chief theoretician at that specific point in time, a case could be presented for religion to be attributed as one of the core concepts within the ideology of early Plaid Cymru.

It would be wrong, however, to concentrate too much on this period in which religion was undoubtedly a major source of inspiration for many within the party. Likewise, it would be inaccurate to view Plaid Cymru's theological direction as emanating just from Catholic social and religious teachings. To highlight this, in a discussion regarding the influence of religion on the party, Derek Hearne has pointed out the differing nature of religious convictions among Plaid Cymru members.[14] Hearne has commented, for instance, on how Gwynfor Evans's religious opinions were 'nonconformist, pragmatic, teetotal, egalitarian and pacifist. Saunders Lewis's convictions, on the other hand, led him down a pathway to Catholicism, dogmatism, oenophilia and traditionalism.'[15] Hence, despite what Saunders Lewis may have written about Plaid Cymru's debt to Catholicism, there is no one religious line that could be said to supply the party with a firm politico-religious basis. To these ends, there is no stringent or fundamentalist religious configuration operating within the party as a whole. although that is not to dismiss the possibility that certain individuals may hold fundamental views and may, secretively at least, desire the introduction of more religiously based content within the party's thought-practices.

Plaid Cymru: Religion as a Core Concept?

In summing up, therefore, Charlotte Davies's argument that religion provides Plaid Cymru with one of its core concepts – a concept that gives the party a vital spiritual constituent – can be refuted, if the entire timeline of the party rather than a specific era is taken into account. Additionally, if religion had been a core concept throughout Plaid Cymru's existence, and if it was still a prime source of inspiration for the party today, this could have led Plaid Cymru on the pathway to a theocratic style of presentation and, ultimately, a politico-religious style of governance. In this instance, the role of religion within Welsh politics, and within Plaid Cymru's morphology, would be akin to an Althusserian 'ideological state apparatus'.[16] As far as this analysis is aware, no single Plaid Cymru member has ever publicly advocated that the religious convictions held by people within Wales should be manipulated into an uncompromising politico-religious option. Hence, although religious faith is visible, and although a sense of spirituality that could be translated as a theory of concern is conceivable – not only as an individual belief but also as a collective political aim – there is no irresistible justification for placing religion, as a generic principle, as a core concept within Plaid Cymru's ideology. There is a case, nevertheless, as will be argued later, for placing the notion of spirituality, and the adoption of a non-materialistic view of what Welsh society is and what it could become, at the centre of the party's thought-practices.

On a practical note, apart from the justification required for mixing religion and politics in a political setting any appeals to metaphysical phenomena, as opposed to corporeal bodies, may also appear to be a sign of weakness in a predominantly secular society, and in an almost totally secular polity. Criticism could be forwarded that appeals to higher beings to help solve earthly problems are tantamount to antediluvian attitudes; neither, it may be suggested, offers a great deal towards the solving of contemporary socio-economic and political dilemmas. Therefore, religion, when looked at in the realm of mainland British politics as a whole, tends to be kept out of the public domain, with politicians and political activists conducting their religious adherences within the private rather the public sphere.

Given these circumstances, religion could prove an uncomfortable concept for Plaid Cymru to proclaim as a core belief, should it so wish, on two important counts: namely that there is no one resolute religious line within the party with which the overwhelming majority of Plaid Cymru's membership would feel comfortable, and also because the pragmatism, and the acknowledgement of reality, evident within contemporary politics in the Welsh, British and European settings does not sit comfortably with the dedication required by any political grouping intent on maintaining an overtly religious political stance. Hence, the conclusion to be arrived at is that, certainly in terms of the party's everyday public persona and pronouncements, religion is not a core concept as far as Plaid Cymru is concerned. However, it may be accurate to register it as a peripheral, but waning, concept within the party's ideology.

Pacifism/Non-violence

The two individual concepts of pacifism and non-violence have been placed together not because they are tautological but because people within Plaid Cymru frequently address their convictions regarding non-belligerence by interweaving the two concepts into their general ideological language. When it comes to scrutinising these two concepts, however, it may become evident that whereas the notion of non-violence – and the accompanying preference to resolve disputes through negotiated settlements – can be seen as a peripheral concept within Plaid Cymru, the absorption of pacifist ideals appears to have been confined to the consciences of certain individuals rather than being a core concept within the party.

Pacifism and the Pacifist Spirit

It may be true to claim that pacifism and non-violence are attributes that are not normally associated with the morphology of nationalism. A specific example such as Gandhian nationalism in India, however, may be seen as the exception to this rule. Nonetheless, it could well be an exception that may be relevant to any understanding of Plaid Cymru's ideology. Indeed, Hywel Davies has commented on how, in the run up to the Second World War, and at the same time that Plaid Cymru was objecting to the locating of an RAF base at Penyberth on the Llyn Peninsula through, amongst other ways, the use of non-violent direct action by three of the party's leading figures, Saunders Lewis, D.J. Williams and Lewis Valentine,[17] the party had 'an increasingly pacifist spirit.'[18] This was a brand of pacifism that was 'often couched in nationalist phraseology.'[19] Pacifism and a representation of Welsh nationalism appear to have coalesced in this era as Plaid Cymru's staunch opposition to the Second World War was steeped in rhetoric that was deliberately poignant. In a section of the pamphlet *Wales and the War* – emotively entitled 'Welsh Mothers and Children Sacrificed' – Plaid Cymru blamed the British state machinery for bringing war to Wales's doorstep. In an arguably xenophobic and uncompassionate paragraph, the party contended that 'without any consideration for the welfare of the Welsh nation, its language, culture and health, the Government moved scores of thousands of English evacuees into Wales.'[20]

Though never openly declaring himself a pacifist, Saunders Lewis also voiced his concerned over wartime activities in what amounted to an often emotionally charged, and sometimes incautious, manner. Commenting on the extension of the Cadet Movement to include boys of fourteen, Lewis claimed that there was 'a strong tendency towards the Nazification of the State.'[21] Furthermore, bringing nationalistic concerns into his area of thought, Lewis argued that 'these measures are killing loyalty to Welsh habits and traditions.'[22] Hence, an assessment could be made that any non-violent sentiments expressed by Lewis, and the party as a whole, throughout the period of the Second World War tended to be encircled by rhetoric that was both anti-state and anti-Westminster, while concurrently favouring anything of an indigenous nature. From the viewpoint of the overall ideological position of the party, therefore, it is evident that some of the traits of nationalism are conspicuous in Plaid Cymru's ideology during this epoch.

Whatever shades of opinion may have entered Plaid Cymru's thought-practices at this period in time, the ironic thing about the pacifist spirit mentioned above is that it shone through during an era in which Plaid Cymru was being attacked from several quarters for allegedly succouring fascism. Although the imagery of English evacuees, cited above, may appear objectionable to many, the contrast between the doctrine of fascist expansionism and the type of pacifist defiance proffered by Plaid Cymru is immense. Hence, it appears incalculable that these two opposing concepts – one a visceral approach to increasing power, the other a cerebral approach designed to dampen excessive power – could be interlinked within the ideology of Plaid Cymru. It is overwhelmingly the latter, pacifism and its appendage of non-violence, that is the approach that forms part of, and provides an accurate précis of, Plaid Cymru's political identity.

Pacifism and Green Issues

Despite the above reference to Gandhian nationalism, and the implication that Plaid Cymru was, and still is to a certain extent, linking pacifist concerns and non-violence in with a nationalistic agenda, it is evident that pacifism does not feature as a core concept within nationalism. Then again, this does not exclude this analysis from placing pacifism as a concept – core, peripheral or adjacent – within Plaid Cymru's ideology. This is because, as is being discovered, Plaid Cymru's ideology may not be wholly reflective of nationalist ideology. Having stated that, the role that pacifism plays, within the realm of political ideas, is generally that of a perimeter concern that rises to the surface whenever there is 'the outburst or threat of war'.[23] In historical terms, it also has a rebellious tinge, as pacifism has 'united many greens with other dissenting or radical ideologies.'[24]

A fairly recent example of this green link with other radical or dissenting ideologies was the 1992 parliamentary by-election victory of Cynog Dafis at Ceredigion, on a Plaid Cymru/Green Party ticket. What was striking about this achievement was that it was remarkable that the two parties worked together because 'in some ways there are quite fundamental differences.'[25] Summing up their different ideologies, Jane Aaron asserted that

> … independence, that's not going to appeal to the Green people … If you don't have someone who feels strongly about green ideas in the Plaid, the political connection isn't obvious … but it was totally sincere because the Green ideas were important to Cynog and to some of the people working with him. But it's not important to everyone in the Plaid.[26]

Although Aaron claimed that green ideas, including pacifism, did not have universal approval from Plaid Cymru in 1992, overall it would appear to be reasonable to accept that linking pacifism, as a component of green ideology, with other progressive ideologies could prove insightful. This is because many within Plaid Cymru would see themselves as part of that radical, dissenting tradition that encapsulated an anti-war stance without necessarily being attracted to pacifism as a first option, or core concept, in their own individual ideologies. Hence, pacifism and non-violence may be concepts that can be seen as having permeability; that is they feature as concepts in different ideologies. If this is the case, then Plaid Cymru's link with the Green Party becomes even more relevant, in ideological rather than simply expedient electoral terms, if the concepts of pacifism and non-violence appear as components of green ideology as well as being part of the ideological formation of Plaid Cymru.

Some Perceptions within Plaid Cymru on Pacifism and Non-violence

On broaching the subject of pacifism and pacifist identification within the party, Elin Jones has contended that most members of Plaid Cymru were not, in her words, 'strict pacifist'.[27] Nevertheless, Jones qualified this by stating that Plaid Cymru's opposition to recent conflicts in the Middle East proved that 'the idea of war is not an idea that is attractive to members of Plaid Cymru.'[28] Jones then made a bold statement of what she sees as her party's political philosophy. She claimed, 'because we don't subscribe to a lot of the hypocrisy of politics we are more detached from the state and we see things from the point of view of minorities and from the innocents' perspective.'[29] That hands-off attitude to state matters has clearly been subsumed by the events of time and the fact that Elin Jones herself is now a minister of state in the third Assembly government. Nevertheless, Jones's claim remains of interest on two levels. First, she seemed, in 2002 at least, to want to break away from a state-centric position. Second, she appeared to be claiming that, when considered against other political parties, Plaid Cymru is more in touch with the feelings and sentiments of people who may be described as being socially excluded, be they in Wales, Zimbabwe or Afghanistan. Both positions, however, may prove to be contrary to the political aims and intentions of Plaid Cymru.

If Plaid Cymru envisages Cardiff, as the capital of Wales, as being the prime location for political power and political decision-making for matters relating to Wales, then the mission for any autonomous Welsh government would seemingly be to build upon, and strengthen, the existing state machinery. In simple terms, the Welsh nation, and the existing institutions and organisations therein, would be transformed under a Plaid Cymru government into the Welsh nation-state. Jones, at a later stage, called for Wales to become 'a full member state of the European Union.'[30] Thus, a certain degree of confusion appears to have arisen in Jones's linking of pacifism with a state sceptical agenda, given that she advocates a national future for Wales. Again, it must be confirmed that these are purely Elin Jones's opinions at a certain point in time and, hence, they do not necessarily reflect any lack of coherence within Plaid Cymru's policy agenda in regard to these matters.

The second point made by Jones is her view that Plaid Cymru's attachment to the notion of grass-roots activism and identification enables the party to empathise with minorities and the innocent. As the concept of minority rights is not embedded within Plaid Cymru's manifesto declarations, it is difficult to present a case, as someone like Elin Jones may wish to do, for the party having a prominent minority rights component to its ideological basis. On the matter of representation on behalf of, and sympathy for the plights of, innocent people caught up in war and turmoil, Jones's views are estimable, and would probably strike a chord with many people. However, it should be acknowledged that the concept of humanitarian concern has permeability, in that it is a concept that, fascism aside, pervades virtually every ideology. Thus, no one party or ideological tradition can claim sole possession of humanitarian concern. Nevertheless, if Plaid Cymru is on the same theoretical wavelength as the dispossessed and the innocent victims throughout the world, as well as the minority liberationist organisations and ethno-cultural groupings, then ideological concepts such as emotionalism and altruism must feature in the party's morphology; indeed, in these circumstances, Plaid Cymru's *Weltanschauung* comes back into focus as attention passes from matters confined to Wales, in a purely geographical sense, to a view of an interconnected world system. Plaid Cymru's *Weltanschauung* is thus extending the spatial boundaries beyond the scope of conventional nationalist opinion. Again, this could be cited as an example of Plaid Cymru's disaffiliation from the straitjacket of restrictive nationalist ideology.

Pacifism within the party can be separated from the debate over the role of the state if the position of the most prominent pacifist within Plaid Cymru, Gwynfor Evans, is assessed. Evans's pacifism should be viewed in a reflective moral and philosophical context, rather than in the sense of it being part of a natural human aversion to aggressive confrontation. While most people would support the idea that it is better to live in a peaceful world rather than a violent one, Evans took the idea of repudiating acts of violence one stage further. Evans's view of living in a non-violent society – a non-violent Welsh society primarily but also one that is inextricably linked to the rest of the world   is a decontested concept. His pacifism was comprehensive in its scope and it constituted a great part of Evans's personal moral conduct; in an ideal scenario, and in his measured reasoning on behalf of Plaid Cymru, Evans, indubitably, would have longed to have pacifism regarded as being a collective and not just a personal moral position. Despite his ardent desire for Wales to attain political autonomy as soon as it is feasible, Evans totally refused to countenance any armed insurrection in Wales or civil war on mainland Britain. Hence, in attempting to create a collective moral position for Plaid Cymru through pacifism, he is on record as stating: 'as a party we completely reject war as a means of achieving self-government.'[31]

Plaid Cymru's Employment of Non-violent Direct Action

Although pacifism is a philosophical statement of intent against any promotion of, or adherence to, bellicose tactics, the concept of non-violent direct action is a more practical political manoeuvre that is often designed to alter a political position through steadfast, though firmly passive, opposition. The concept of non-violent direct action has been an instrument of political activism for centuries. From the martyrs who refused to change their religious or political views in the face of Hobbesian-style autocracy through to the suffragettes and up to the civil rights rhetoric and deeds adopted by leaders such as Martin Luther King, non-violent direct action has been an effective tool against repressive regimes. For Plaid Cymru, it has proved to be a useful form of obstructionism and has been used with varying effect since the party's inception. Acts as straightforward as painting the word *rhyddid* (freedom) on public buildings and in open spaces was one early example of defiance that implicated no physical damage to individuals or any loss of life.

Notably, the party's campaign against the drowning of Cwm Tryweryn, in order to create a reservoir to serve the people of Liverpool in the late 1950s, involved sit-down protests and mass rallies. Although some protests against the drowning did involve a degree of confrontation, these, generally, did not occur during the events that were organised and staged by the party. On the occasions that they did transpire, the Plaid Cymru leadership was quick to distance itself from these isolated actions. This distancing was important because Plaid Cymru had to preserve an air of respectability as it attempted to build an electoral base in the 1950s and 1960s. Dave Adamson has maintained that, with regard to this era, 'the dichotomy between Plaid Cymru's quest for electoral respectability and the direct action of other nationalist organizations characterized nationalist politics in Wales throughout the post-war period.'[32]

Despite the trepidation that may have been shown by some members of the party's upper echelons towards non-violent direct action – in contradistinction to many grass-roots activists who viewed it as a useful tool for political campaigning – acts of civil disobedience continued, albeit on a less frequent basis after the acme of Tryweryn and the altercations across Wales with regard to the status of the Welsh language in the 1960s. As far as the party's more recent history is concerned, however, the landmark example of non-violent direct action was Gwynfor Evans's planned hunger strike in 1980. This was premeditated after the refusal by Prime Minister Margaret Thatcher to allow a Welsh-language television channel, Sianel Pedwar Cymru (S4C), to come into being. Evans announced that he would commence his hunger strike on 6 October 1980 unless the Conservatives rescinded their decision. However, on 17 September 1980 Willie Whitelaw, deputy leader of the Conservative Party, said that the government had changed its mind on this issue. Evans, Plaid Cymru and many ordinary people across Wales saw this as a critical victory in the long-running battle for recognition of the Welsh language.

The pacifist position places love over war, in both theory and practice. However, for a political party, in this instance Plaid Cymru, that advocates the existence and continuation of a nation – the Welsh nation – and seeks to advance the quality of life for those within that geographical and political space, the refusal, be it on philosophical or practical grounds, to eschew the realist position – recognition that we exist in a habitually violent world wherein the need to defend oneself, and one's homeland, is a practical consideration for everyone – would appear to be an aberrant stance to adopt. If a position is adopted that contends that Gwynfor Evans was unreal in his views and leadership, and this is then taken to its logical conclusion, then Plaid Cymru's ideology for the thirty-six years of Evans's stewardship could also be viewed in this light. This conclusion could be arrived at because of the undeniable fact that pacifism was a core concept within Gwynfor Evans's ideology.

Hegemony and Cultural Constraints

Allied to pacifism, the concept of hegemony must also be addressed because, if Plaid Cymru has the intention of replacing one form of hegemony with another – assuming that some semblance of a unified ideological posture would emerge in an autonomous Wales – then the question to be asked is whether this hegemonic position could be achieved under a pacifist philosophical position. Michael Freeden has pointed out that the Gramscian notion of hegemony, and in particular the establishing of that hegemony, involved 'the co-ordination of different interests and their ideological expressions, so that an all-embracing group, possibly society as a whole, would be engaged.'[33] If hegemony is to be established under a society influenced by the ideology of Plaid

Cymru, then pacifism has to fit into the all-embracing group. The problem for pacifism is likely to arise in the general field of 'cultural constraints'.[34] As pacifism falls outside accepted, or at least standardised,
notions of defence, as practised by nation-states, the pressure on Plaid
Cymru's pacifist stance to adapt and reconstitute itself would be enormous. Hence, any condemnation of Gwynfor Evans's position as unreal
may be not merely hollow criticism from an anti-pacifist perspective
but more a case of being a realistic assessment of the operations of
contemporary societies.

In contrast, non-violent direct action does not face the same degree of
cultural constraint as pacifism because it is generally portrayed within
the political arena as a pragmatic tactic of last resort, as opposed to a
trenchant ideological or philosophical position. Moreover, a series of
celebrated cases have proven the efficacy of non-violent direct action,
and the concept is now embedded in mainstream culture. For Plaid
Cymru, therefore, the advocating of non-violent direct action necessitates less of a negative response, and is undoubtedly less problematic
when contrasted with the concept of pacifism. This could account for
the mixed responses of party activists to the question of whether Plaid
Cymru should favour pacifism. However, when non-violent direct
action is considered,[35] party members appear more willing to accept the
liberal description and they then tend to envisage this form of protest as
a constituent part of every person's individual, and collective, human
right to freedom of expression and protest.

Further to this ease of acceptance for non-violent direct action over
pacifism, some contemporary Plaid Cymru leaders have acknowledged
their debt to influential figures who have promoted the non-violent route
to national or ethnic self-determination. Ieuan Wyn Jones, for example,
in an interview for the party's on-line discussion forum tribancoch.com,
cited Mahatma Gandhi, Martin Luther King and Nelson Mandela as his
personal political heroes. Jones claimed that he admired Gandhi's per-
severance that led to the securing of independence for India and added
that this was achieved 'without compromising his moral position.'[36]
Jones continued by stating that he thought that Gandhi 'had even more
than pacifism; he had great moral and personal courage to bring a nation
forward.'[37]

Despite these acknowledgements, one self-confessed pacifist within
the party, Rhodri Glyn Thomas, has stated, 'I don't think Ieuan describes
himself as a pacifist but certainly he is anti-war, and in that sense most
of the party is anti-war.'[38] Although anti-war can be a flexible expression in the sense that anti-war can cut across the left–right political
spectrum, as it is generally considered that most people despise the idea
of conflict and, in Plaid Cymru's case, the use of the phrase 'anti-war'

certainly does not tie individuals or the party into a rigidly pacifist position, Rhodri Glyn Thomas also accredits Plaid Cymru's historical association with the concept of pacifism. Explaining how the concept has come to the fore at different periods in the past, and how it has acted against the party on a few occasions, Thomas noted how 'that line was very clear in Gwynfor Evans's day, and he suffered hugely by being a conscientious objector during World War Two.'[39]

Leanne Wood, an acknowledged radical voice within the party, goes even further than Ieuan Wyn Jones in her opposition to the entire concept of militarism. Wood has been a severe critic of Britain's close relationship with the United States, particularly in recent years, and has commented that Plaid Cymru, and other forces on the left whom she seeks to ally Plaid Cymru with, 'must oppose further military spending and the insidious arms trade that wields so much influence.'[40] Enunciating some of these concerns in its 2002 alternative budget, *A Billion Ways to Build a New Wales*,[41] Plaid Cymru announced two measures in relation to defence. These were total nuclear disarmament, which, across the UK, the party equated with a saving of £650 million, and the ending of arms export subsidies, which the party calculated would save £800 million. When the raising of additional taxation, using socialistic measures to hit the wealthiest the hardest, is taken into account, Wales's share of the peace dividend, according to Plaid Cymru, would be £1 billion.

Pacifism and Non-violent Direct Action: Core or Peripheral?

While all of these sentiments help to distance Plaid Cymru from the perceived pro-militarist stances of other political parties, it is interesting to note that any total abandonment of Britain's or Wales's defence forces and defence procurement has not been tabled by Plaid Cymru. Hence, pacifism appears to have been rejected as a practical solution for creating a more peaceful environment. Certain members within Plaid Cymru may, over the years, have envisaged pacifism as a core concept within the party's ideology. But this impression has thinness to it, as pacifism, not just in theory but also in practice, is all-embracing in its condemnation of aggressive attitudes in society. By summoning up the figures of Gandhi, Luther King and others, it could be argued that Plaid Cymru is presenting its political ambitions vicariously through these heroes of a non-violent or pacifist approach. It could be analysed as being the case that, in a purely idealistic sense, Plaid Cymru desires pacifism, and a sharing of non-violent methodologies, as a core concept but is realistic enough to accept that pacifism is not a viable option within contemporary global politics. Hence, pacifism is at best a peripheral concept that influences, but does not exist as a main driver for, the ideology of Plaid Cymru.

The same can be said of non-violent direct action. To place this as a core concept within Plaid Cymru's ideology would be inaccurate as non-violent direct action is an occasional tactical option for the party, as opposed to a constant theme or form of expression. Despite the success of Gwynfor Evans's aforementioned act of defiance, non-violent direct action is on the margin of discussion whenever the party debates policy or philosophical matters. Unlike the tactics of certain Green or anarchist movements where non-violent direct action is a core concept, Plaid Cymru's more established parliamentary approach to politics – gradually evolving since the 1960s but burgeoning in the last decade or so – tends to favour conventional political discourse over direct action. Hence, non-violent direct action, like pacifism and religion, is an existing but slowly diminishing concept within the party's ideology.

Decentralisation

In his book *Summer Meditations*,[42] during a discussion on how different layers of power, and their distances from a central system, affect people's lives, Vaclav Havel talked of concentric circles that were diffuse in nature but, in an holistic sense, amalgamated to make up the whole. Plaid Cymru's linking of the party's conception of what constitutes the local community to the nation, and further beyond to global outlooks via Europeanism, could be viewed as corresponding to Havel's notion. As far as Plaid Cymru is concerned, it clearly shows that when the party addresses these various concentric circles the last thing that it could be accused of is isolationism or absconding from any engagement in dialogue at the multifarious layers of political administration. Where decentralisation equates with this notion is in the way that it offers plural identification and deliberation on many levels. Decentralisation can be adapted to suit plural concerns. For a party that puts great emphasis on people engaging in decision-making in their localities, decentralisation could prove an invaluable concept. Gwynfor Evans favoured this decentralist approach as he maintained that centralisation 'tends to lead to totalitarianism and the erosion of decision-making by individual persons and by communities.'[43] This theoretical, anti-totalitarian approach of Evans was to connect with his practical assessment that proper government, or at least the most effective form of government, could be conducted only on a small scale and at a local level.

Initiating Decentralisation

Removing the perceived shackles of central authority was also a theme pondered on by other theoreticians within Plaid Cymru. In wording reminiscent of the Enlightenment thought of Jean-Jacques Rousseau, D.J. and Noelle Davies proffered the idea that Welsh society needed to be re-evaluated and liberated. In their view, 'man is an organic being. He cannot move forward freely in education and culture while economically and politically he is in bondage.'[44] This is a rational liberal approach that views the general interest of society as a whole in non-aggregative terms.[45] This freeing up, therefore, could be achieved through decentralisation and an acceptance of a non-authoritarian, decentred 'spirit of self-help and co-operation.'[46] This, it was envisaged by D.J. and Noelle Davies, would be the total opposite to the Keynesian prescription of 'increased centralisation and bureaucratic control, increased concentration of industry and increased sacrifices by the people.'[47]

Here, in its clearest form, is the difference between centralised state-managed social democracy and the decentralised, community-based socialist alternatives proffered by Plaid Cymru. Tying in the administration over these forms of decentralisation with the aforementioned concentric circles theory, it is evident that what is of importance to the party as a whole is the fact that the theory diminishes any notions of an us and them syndrome, wherein various factors compete over resources and argue over authority. Discourse within concentric circles, therefore, is positive and inclusive and it would appear that decentralisation – especially Plaid Cymru's version of it – is ultimately designed to foster the all-encompassing ideals that give strength to community and, correspondingly, national life.

With this linkage between the centre and the apparently decontested concept of decentralisation, as Plaid Cymru envisages it, in mind, what must be addressed is whether there is likely to be any difficulty in portraying a decentralisation message if it is nationalism – with the idea of the nation to the fore – that your party is supposedly representative of. Cynics could argue that the language of decentralisation is used by Plaid Cymru merely as a descriptive slogan to entice supporters who are, or were, disillusioned with state-centred politics and economics, or with the idea that globalisation will ultimately bring total conformity: the Starbucks-land theory. Furthermore, if decentralisation is not a core concept within nationalism, which according to Freeden's model it is not, then why does Plaid Cymru attach such importance to it? This attachment could back up the contention that Plaid Cymru is not an adherent to nationalism in its strictest form, or it could act as an example of how nationalism, not being a full ideology, does not furnish Plaid Cymru with a comprehensive enough agenda; hence, Plaid Cymru has to look outside nationalism for concepts that appeal to the ideological viewpoints of both its membership and its prospective supporters.

It is probably accurate to contend that what Plaid Cymru is attempting to do through the use of decentralisation is seeking to apply a method of diversifying the debate on politico-economic expression away from, and what for some members may be in contradiction to, the centralised nationalist viewpoint. Nevertheless, for decentralisation to mean anything, and to possibly justify this decentralist approach, given the fairly settled composition of the current British state system, it must have a higher context to decentralise from. Ultimately, as Plaid Cymru visualises that higher context as being Wales rather than Britain, there has to be some notion of self-government for Wales underpinning this decentralisation.

The higher context out of which decentralisation would ensue must be the political and geographical entity that is Wales, as nobody within Plaid Cymru would testify to the radical forms of decentralisation proposed by the party being attainable under the current UK governmental or socio-economic systems. In these circumstances, therefore, before decentralisation can occur in Wales, further decentralisation from London must come about, be that decentralisation in the form of bolstering the method of devolution currently in existence, as an absolute minimum, or, as is the preferred option for Plaid Cymru, through the establishment of a government in Wales that would be entirely autonomous from the British state system. Theoretically, at least, Plaid Cymru could begin to activate a decentralised structure if, under the present conditions set by the devolutionary settlement, it attained overall power in the National Assembly not, it must be noted, as junior members of the present coalition, but as stand-alone or majority partners. However, to be realistic about the effectiveness of any extensive decentralisation for Wales, and for that system to be thoroughly operational, substantial self-government for Wales would be required.

Decentralisation Policy in Practice

In policy terms, one aspect of decentralisation that Plaid Cymru highlights is economic diffusion. In an article entitled 'Spreading the wealth', Dai Lloyd described Plaid Cymru's economic policy proposals of 'regional targeting' as 'a way of spreading the wealth. The economic needs of rural Wales are different from Swansea's. We are the only party to recognise these different priorities.'[48] Similarly, Elin Jones has argued the case for economic decentralisation from the capital outwards.

Responding to an announcement about job creation in south-east Wales, Jones, whilst welcoming more employment in general, noted that 'creating 1000 jobs for Cardiff is no use to rural Meirionnydd where they are struggling to keep their young people in Wales and their economy thriving.'[49]

It is clear, therefore, that economic concerns, as much as communal identification and cultural and linguistic matters, affect the debate on centralisation within the party. Hence, the state of the economy has had a noticeable effect on how the decentralisation concept has been handled and how it has progressed, recalling within this context that the Welsh economy, on the whole, has long been in desperate need of rejuvenation, having suffered to a great extent, in the last thirty years or so, from the demise of heavy industry and agriculture. It must be noted, however, that this message of social amelioration through economic decentralisation is not unique to Plaid Cymru's ideology, as the emergence of a decentralised socio-economic agenda – often wrapped up in the concept known as subsidiarity – throughout the European Union, and indeed throughout the global trading arena in its entirety, has had a huge impact on regionalised and localised practice. In a sense, therefore, it would be accurate to support the argument that decentralisation is now accepted as customary, rather than innovative, practice. Thus, Plaid Cymru's championing of its policies on decentralisation as radical and inimitable may well be slightly fanciful.

Decentralisation: Locating Outwards from Cardiff

Looking at decentralisation on another front, some Plaid Cymru activists were contending, in the build-up to the advent of the National Assembly, that the Assembly should actually be a peripatetic institution. If it became one, this line of argument developed, the Assembly would be more accountable to the people of Wales as it would not be seen as a centralised, Cardiff-based institution. John Ball, a former Plaid Cymru councillor and prospective Assembly and Parliamentary candidate, was one of those who proposed a radical decentralist solution. Ball contended at the time that Plaid Cymru should 'dump the Regional Committees, and the Assembly should meet in Caernarfon at some stage of the year, meet in Wrexham at another stage, and meet in Aberystwyth at another stage.'[50] Ball's suggestion would seemingly offer a challenge to those within the party who side with nationalism as a centre-led political ideology, as this decentralisation would throw up locations of power. Nationalists within Plaid Cymru may see this as a challenge to the siting of Cardiff as the locus of power. Cardiff, as Wales's capital, also stands as a beacon for the representation of

Wales at international level. In nationalistic terms certainly, but also within nation-states generally, capital cities, which are customarily the seats of government, also offer a focus for unification. The type of decentralisation envisaged by Ball would invariably challenge that sense of unification as people are asked to display some allegiance to a fresh set of geographical entities. What should, however, be taken into consideration by those who advocate establishing new centres of political power is the fact that many people already identify with an assortment of community, regional, national, UK-wide, European and global entities.

Another apparent problem, in the case of decentralisation within Wales itself, is that, although John Ball cited Caernarfon, Wrexham and Aberystwyth as his centres out of which a new peripatetic Welsh government could function, Phil Williams observed how it is actually towards Liverpool that many people in the north of Wales, and in particular those in the north-east of Wales, turn their attention.[51] This is because, as Williams noted, people in the north of Wales regard Liverpool as a large urban area that can provide for all of their economic, cultural, consumer and leisure needs. This is highly problematic for Plaid Cymru as Liverpool never has been, and never will be, within the ambit of any Welsh political administration. Hence, decentralisation in practice would not necessarily facilitate a more Welsh Wales, should that be what some people within Plaid Cymru are ultimately seeking from any implementation of a programme of decentralisation. Indeed, competition for resources and disputes over the locations for the seats of decentralised power may actually induce a more diverse and fractious, as opposed to harmonious and pluralistic, body politic.

Rurbanisation and Green Ideology

Phil Williams gave words of caution about how Plaid Cymru should proceed with decentralisation. Williams said that the party has to clarify its intentions and it has to be regularly reminded that 'the ultimate decentralisers are the New Right in America.'[52] Although Williams's observations may be true, there is also a more common, and more appropriate, tendency to associate decentralisation with green ideology. For Michael Freeden, decentralisation 'may invoke simplicity, bioregionalism, and "back to the land", but it can be put to work in complex technological urban settings.'[53] It is intriguing to note how the green values that Freeden is addressing could be translated into the thought-practices of Plaid Cymru. Simplicity, for example, could be seen as an appeal for a less dehumanised and more face-to-face society in which social interaction is centred primarily on an individual's immediate environs.

Bioregionalism and 'back to the land', meanwhile, are evident within Plaid Cymru's appeal for sustainable development at a local level. The party has advocated 'redirecting support into agri-environmental programmes, integrated rural development, with special attention to the family farm and new entrants to the industry.'[54] If Plaid Cymru were to implement these policies – and Elin Jones, Welsh Assembly Government Rural Affairs Minister, has certainly attempted to do so – it would undoubtedly foster a more localised economy in which family-run farms, and other small-scale businesses, would become centres of production within a multitude of decentralised zones.

Furthermore, it is worth remembering that the back to the land call was a feature of early Plaid Cymru and, in particular, it served to occupy much of the time given over by Saunders Lewis to his political thought. Hence, the notion of decentralisation could be adapted to update Saunders Lewis's romantic, anti-industrial rhetoric. In this context, Plaid Cymru's desire to achieve rurbanisation requires some attention. Championing rurbanisation as part of a campaign to transfer land from the gentry to the peasantry, D.J. and Noelle Davies contended that rurbanisation meant 'the diffusing through the countryside of the best amenities … enjoyed by the town while ensuring that, instead of a slowly urban cosmopolitanism, a living Welsh culture informs the life of town and country alike.'[55] Rurbanisation, in the thinking of D.J. and Noelle Davies, would be a natural path for Wales to proceed upon, and it would be the correct choice for Plaid Cymru's social philosophy; indeed it is contended that this rurbanisation is actually rooted in a chain of values that exist in Wales and, therefore, it merely requires augmentation. This is because, D.J. and Noelle Davies claimed, throughout history Wales has stood for 'individual liberty and initiative combined with co-operation, decentralisation as opposed to bureaucracy, and a genuinely democratic culture rooted in the homes and daily life of the whole people.'[56]

With this in mind, and in order to visualise the role played by the concept of decentralisation within Plaid Cymru's ideology, the question to be asked of modern Plaid Cymru is whether the party's understanding of decentralisation as a concept owes its principles to the early Plaid Cymru vision, or whether decentralisation has taken on a new guise. The answer would appear to lie somewhere in between. There is little doubt that there is still a degree of romanticism in the party's celebration of the notion of association that is, purportedly, evident within small-scale communities; communities and communityism being a concept that will be explored later in this chapter. Moreover, although anti-industrialisation does not feature in Plaid Cymru's contemporary pronouncements, there is, nevertheless, a sense of post-Fordism in the way that the party champions its vision of the localised production of goods and services and the primacy of communal transactions.

Breaking Down Power: The Polyarchic Approach

Another area where there may be problems for Plaid Cymru in favouring the language of decentralisation is in assessing how far down this decentralisation should go. Unless a cogent and unambiguous policy of subsidiarity is introduced, and it is taken right down to the level of each and every individual, then cases will inevitably arise where individuals will still be subservient to layers of socio-economic and political power; in other words, some form of polyarchic system of governance would undoubtedly have to be developed for decentralisation to be true to its name. In considering this polyarchic approach, Phil Williams claimed that he found a strong commitment within Plaid Cymru to the principles of direct democracy. Plaid Cymru has a record of decentralist rhetoric, and around about the time that Phil Williams was contemplating joining the party, in the early 1960s, Plaid Cymru was confirming its opposition to 'the evils of centralised authority, which regards doctrines and the maintenance of its centralised power as more important than alleviating human and social distress.'[57]

Williams was clearly influenced by this talk – so much so indeed that he proposed a system of subsidiarity for Wales as far back as 1970[58] – and, in an apparent commitment to an anti-statist position, Williams once declared that 'one of the things that attracted me to Plaid Cymru was its commitment to the breakdown of concentrations of power and it seemed that it applied as much to the industrial sector as to the political sector.'[59] Should these theoretical dissections come to fruition, however, what may ultimately transpire is a scenario in which, unless this breakdown of the concentrations of power is provided for through legislation, this polyarchic system may occur de facto. If it does arise through de facto causes then the decentralisation may be uncontrollable as far as the central, or national, system of administration is concerned. This is because any decentralised pattern of governance may go against the edicts of the national government, irrespective of whatever party happened to be in control at the national level at the time. In the case of Plaid Cymru, if a decentralised body went against Plaid Cymru policy – in rejecting bilingualism for instance – then Plaid Cymru may have created, in decentralisation, a monster over which it would have limited control. Unless, that is, it decided in those circumstances to use recourse to a centralised system and diktat from above, which would merely be defeating the objective of decentralisation.

Giving the state of affairs mentioned above, therefore, rather than expanding a sense of freedom and bringing simplicity to the Welsh political system, decentralisation could rebound on Plaid Cymru if the new decentralised layers were seen to be petty bureaucratic or flamboyantly free-thinking institutions or, most alarmingly, if they were to become fractious and overly independent and thus disrupt governance within the overall political entity of Wales. In her ethnographic study of Welsh identity, Alison Griffiths observed that 'postmodern accounts of subjectivity suggest "Welshness" as fractured and multi-determined.'[60] Decentralisation, it could be argued, would only strengthen this fractured and multidetermined environment.

It may be feasible to contend that for a perfect decentralised system of government and society to emerge a *tabula rasa* would be required. This is because any attempt to alter an existing system would be competing against norms, conventions and age-old prejudices and, hence, any cultural change could prove awkward to administer. If Plaid Cymru truly seeks decentralisation, then the party must face up to these inherent weaknesses as opposed to embellishing the supposed strengths. Also, it would appear that there has to be an acknowledgement from within the party that the implications of overseeing a policy of decentralisation would prove to be a far more radical option for the structure and governance of society in Wales than previously envisaged.

Further to this, and connecting the concept of decentralisation with the concept of freedom, Plaid Cymru has to evaluate whether decentralisation broadens its conception of freedom and vice versa. Michael Freeden has observed that all forms of freedom 'contain the notion of non-constraint.'[61] If this is so, then Plaid Cymru, if it accepts and endorses the concept of freedom, and the non-constraint notion that is a constituent part of that freedom, cannot feasibly prohibit the expression of political views that are antithetical to those of the party if, when the time arises, the party sanctions the system of decentralisation in which these oppositional voices are allowed articulation. Any deviation from this acceptance of the non-constraint principle would put into question the concept of liberty and its use within Plaid Cymru. Consequently, a conflict of concepts within Plaid Cymru's ideology may be evident, as the above variances demonstrate. If this discrepancy is accentuated, it would then be up to the party's theoreticians and policy-makers to adapt the party's ideology to create an equilibrium of opinion.

Nevertheless, despite some reservations about the extent to which the party has decontested the concept of decentralisation, and whether the application of the concept has been thoroughly and coherently reasoned, it would be reasonable to support the idea that decentralisation is a core concept within Plaid Cymru's ideology. The contention that Wales needs a system of government that is not totalitarian, to paraphrase both

Saunders Lewis and Gwynfor Evans, appears to be a leitmotif in the party's thought-practices. The concept of decentralisation also engages in an overlapping consensus with the concepts of decentralist socialism and communityism. Similarly, decentralisation also acts as an enveloper for the theories of rurbanisation and subsidiarity. Thus, the volume of evidence appears overwhelmingly to place decentralisation as a core concept within the party's ideology.

Without decentralisation as a core, or even if decentralisation was relegated to a peripheral status, many of Plaid Cymru's policy statements about the role and vibrancy of local communities and their distinctiveness in the holistic vision of Wales and Welshness would appear too fragile to comprehend. Meanwhile, this insertion of decentralisation as a core concept leaves the perception of Plaid Cymru as a political party whose ideology is identifiable as nationalist in serious doubt. By positioning decentralisation at the heart of the party's thought-practices Plaid Cymru's theoreticians may well have, albeit unwittingly, negated its nationalism.

Decentralist Socialism

The concept of decentralist socialism within Plaid Cymru's ideology can be seen in relation to the concept of decentralisation. But, significantly, it is also a concept that Plaid Cymru likes to maintain that it is developing as an alternative to state socialism. Hence, the message that emanates from Plaid Cymru circles is that decentralist socialism is not another manifestation of established state socialism – a state socialism that many in the party would equate with an oppressive politico-economic system that is akin to Big Brotherism. For Plaid Cymru, therefore, decentralist socialism represents the advocating of lively, small-scale communities with a green ethos.

When asked to define decentralist socialism, Rhodri Glyn Thomas, introducing a liberal line of reasoning into the debate, affirmed that the rejection by Plaid Cymru of centralised socialism had come about because that particular strand of top-down socialism 'clearly had an effect on an individual's freedom within society.'[62] Thomas also perceived Plaid Cymru's version of decentralist socialism as developing organically. As he commented, 'the idea of devolved or community socialism is that it comes out of the roots, it comes out of people's lives and it is based on social justice.'[63] Furthermore, Thomas also added a moral angle to this decentralist socialism as he believes that it would incorporate a 'responsibility to share things with other people who are not as privileged as us. But it is not something that is forced from the top. It is something that grows out of people's everyday lives.'[64]

The Evolution of Decentralist Socialism

The concept of decentralist socialism has been forwarded by certain individuals within the party who have championed its worth as a radical alternative to the status quo. However, its clarity as an ideological concept within the party remains unclear. One of the prime movers for decentralist socialism within the party, Phil Williams, admitted that he had been working on the theory of decentralist socialism since the 1960s. Nevertheless, Williams is on record as candidly stating that he remained uncertain as to its actual definition and he was unsure regarding decentralist socialism's viability as a political and economic concept.[65] However, these uncertainties did not prevent decentralist socialist themes and pronouncements appearing intermittently within Plaid Cymru's thought-practices. These were often contentious, and they did not go uncontested, as the party's records show. An example from the late 1960s proves this point. A document from 1967, *How Much Policy?*, argued that decentralist socialism was a side issue. It pleaded with the party, 'Why lose support over workers control in industry when there are already too few prepared to support self-government?'[66]

Alternatively, a year later, at the party conference in 1968, the Conway Rhanbarth accentuated the definite application of the concept of decentralist socialism as it 'called upon the National Council of Plaid Cymru to establish a committee to work out a detailed policy on worker control in industry.'[67] Whatever the level of debate over the perceived prominence of this matter within the party's set of principles, and whatever outcomes derived from the attempts to delineate the conceptual content of decentralist socialism, by the time of Dafydd Elis-Thomas's presidency in the 1980s the pursuance of decentralist socialist objectives 'had been placed on party membership cards.'[68]

Yet again, it could be proposed that this championing of concepts such as decentralist socialism by a few key individuals and policy-makers within the party implies that individual voices within the party were attempting to explore avenues that the party could travel down. Even though the second aim of the party, as enunciated on Plaid Cymru's website, is 'to ensure economic prosperity, social justice and the health of the natural environment based on decentralist socialism',[69] there is a line of argument that certain key players are driving the party's thought-practices and that, subsequently, the ideas stemming from these theoreticians find their way into party manifestos and appear in pronouncements on party websites. It could be viewed that as long as these innovative concepts and theoretical avenues are not too far removed from the general social philosophy shared by members of Plaid Cymru, then these conjectural explorations all add to the party's overall ideological position; although to what extent these concepts are put into practice by Plaid Cymru when it has a degree of power at community council, local authority and, since 2007, national level remains questionable.

Decentralist Socialism: A Non-Nationalist Concept

Whatever the genealogy of this particular ideological concept may be, what is of interest is the fact that decentralist socialism is one of several 'non-nationalist issues of concern to Plaid Cymru.'[70] It may be accurate to contend that this emphasis on decentralist socialism as a non-nationalist issue further strengthens the claim that what is under consideration is a set of political ideas and principles that may well have Wales as their focal point but, barring the element of location, is ultimately an ideology that does not fit comfortably into conventional nationalist frameworks. Moreover, as seen by the earlier examination of decentralisation, many of the concepts found within the party's thought-practices actually counter any association with the ideology of nationalism. To these ends, decentralist socialism should be seen as the infusion of socialist economic principles onto subnational geographic units. In Plaid Cymru's eyes this would not have to be a revolutionary act, as the party maintains that these socialistic principles are actually an innate feature in what is already, in many respects, a pluralistic and localised social order. What Plaid Cymru would like to see implemented, therefore, is a decentralised Welsh polity that is fine-tuned and able to augment the already existing social, cultural and linguistic framework.

In Freedenite terms, decentralist socialism is an ideological concept that is at the heart of Plaid Cymru's social philosophy. The fact that it is a developing concept within the party, as opposed to a stagnant or waning concept, suggests that decentralist socialism should be labelled as a core concept within the party's ideology. Added to the existence of decentralisation within the party's core concepts, the overarching ideological figure of socialism begins to play a greater part in the morphology of Plaid Cymru. Moreover, the next ideological concept under consideration may further enhance the claim that it is in fact socialism, as opposed to nationalism or liberalism, that is the predominant ideology at work within the thought-practices of Plaid Cymru.

Cooperativism

Cooperativism is, arguably, a perfect system of decentralist socialism. An excellent example of cooperativism in action in a Welsh context can be seen through the workings of Tower colliery at Hirwaun, which continued to function until 2008 as a result of a workers buy-out in the 1990s. Plaid Cymru, although very supportive of the miners at Tower, cannot claim any direct influence on their decision to move into a cooperative scheme. However, Plaid Cymru has a record of championing cooperativism in the coalfield, as well as being supportive of co-ownership within the general economy of Wales. Back in 1959, Gwynfor Evans led a Plaid Cymru delegation that held a meeting with mineworkers at a condemned pit at Cwmllynfell. Plaid Cymru proposed a scheme for cooperative working at the pit that was unanimously backed by the miners themselves. With considerable support from the party, the miners found a market for their coal in the Netherlands. Regardless of this action plan, however, the Conservative government, the National Coal Board, with the backing of the National Union of Mineworkers, and the Labour Party all opposed the cooperative scheme. Cwmllynfell pit closed shortly afterwards.[71]

Despite the failure to secure a cooperativist future for Cwmllynfell colliery, Plaid Cymru was not put off from advocating the cooperativist line, and the party committed itself to 'abolishing stringent state control in favour of more real co-operative ownership and control',[72] while enunciating that 'the principles of a co-operative society should be taught at all schools.'[73] Even before the saga of Cwmllynfell, cooperativism featured in Plaid Cymru's thought-practices. Back in 1937, J.E. Daniel saw the attraction of cooperativism and envisaged its amalgamation with nationalist principles. Daniel adopted the perspective that this 'co-operative nationalism is at the opposite pole from the state-idolatry of both Fascism and socialism.'[74] A couple of years after J.E. Daniel's proposals, the party attempted to broaden out the concept of cooperativism and give it a more functional appearance. Citing Belgium as an example of a country wherein forms of cooperativism were in operation, Plaid Cymru argued in favour of the introduction of cooperative boards in order to stimulate 'co-operative control without government monopoly.'[75]

Further to this, Wynne Samuel, in a tract concerning the debilitating effects of the Second World War on Wales, and in a search for an economic panacea to remodel Wales in the years ahead, commented on how 'the principle of co-operative democracy is the basis for economic reconstruction in Wales'.[76] Although democracy and nationalism are advanced by Samuel and J.E. Daniel alike, it is the fact that both view cooperativism as an integral part of the party's thinking at the time that is important.

The Cooperativist Alternative

On an operational front, it would be very difficult for Plaid Cymru to implement a comprehensive cooperativist arrangement in a society that has a culture of functioning – both politically and economically – through hierarchical systems. Any cooperativist arrangement would require horizontal linkages to be used to the maximum. The present capitalist mode of production, within Wales and elsewhere, operates through a hierarchical socio-economic system in which vertical linkages are imperative. The introduction of horizontal linkages on a nationwide scale would appear to be an impossible task without the creation of a more equalitarian society and without a diminution, if not a total obliteration, of the existing capitalist system. So, for Plaid Cymru's cooperativism to succeed, it would appear that the adjacent concept of equalitarianism must come into play while the concept of capitalism would have to be seen by party strategists as an incompatible concept. Whatever rhetoric Plaid Cymru adopts over these matters, it seems certain that wholesale cooperativism could not possibly come to fruition unless the networks and conditions for social and economic interaction on an egalitarian economic basis are met.

The problem in all of this for Plaid Cymru is that it has seemingly failed to decontest the concept of cooperativism. Although, as Charlotte Davies has observed,[77] debates over the nature of industrial democracy did take place within the party in the 1970s, motions to party conferences on this subject tended to attract counteracting motions that sought compromise and invariably used language that was constructed in order to depoliticise rather than clarify the ideological content of these socialistic motions. If Plaid Cymru thinks that a cooperative system can come about whilst a capitalist mode of production remains in operation, then there are 'logical inconsistencies'[78] to this line of thought. Plaid Cymru's cooperativism, therefore, needs reassessment and clarification as it is not, in terms of its capacity to instigate major structural changes, and as presented by party members to date, a logical concept. As to its place within the party's ideology, it can be registered only as a peripheral concept as cooperativism may influence Plaid Cymru's economic reasoning, but it certainly does not act as a prime motor or an integral feature of the party's thought-practices.

Cymdeithasiaeth/**Communityism**

Michael Freeden has noted how the element of attachment encapsulated in the term community acts to situate individuals 'within anthropological-cultural and ideational contexts, thus meeting part of the desiderata of ideological analysis.'[79] There is a contraposition between community activity and endorsement, and liberal, or libertarian, individualism. It is a debate on structure and positioning. Where Plaid Cymru stands on this is important as it feeds into other ideological concepts and ideologies. One example of this perspective is related by Geraint H. Jenkins, who, when looking at political ideologies in the 1980s, has contrasted the differences between Plaid Cymru's ideological approaches to that of the prevailing thought-practices of the New Right. Bringing together some of the concepts assessed so far, Jenkins wrote of how 'Plaid Cymru's sophisticated drive on behalf of *cymdeithasiaeth* and decentralised socialism was a robust counterweight to the cult of Britishness and free market values.'[80]

Cymdeithasiaeth *and Communitarianism*

Within Welsh political and literary circles the term *cymdeithasiaeth* is an old expression whose meaning broadly equates with the concept of communityism. It was used, in a tangible sense, by the socialist essayist R.J. Derfel to express the genuine, inherent bond that exists within a community, and the desire of the people within that community to assist one another. Another Welsh writer, the Marxist Raymond Williams, viewed *cymdeithasiaeth* as the 'socialism of place',[81] meaning that socialism on a personal level – in a place – is comprehensible, whereas large-scale socialism is unfeasible. Whatever definition of this communityism is accepted, it remains clear that the social aspects of community – its sense of cooperation and bonding – are being encouraged.

Plaid Cymru's use of the expression *cymdeithasiaeth*, and the party's general support for community-based politics and activities, would appear, therefore, to position the party in the community socialist bracket, which has arisen from the concept of communityism. Whether or not this is a fair reflection, there remains little doubt that the adjacent concept of localism shines through as a positive socio-economic and political belief. The negative side of this for Plaid Cymru, however, may arise in the manner in which localism can breed parochialism, and what can then emerge, if this is applied onto a geo-social map of Wales, is the concept that is pejoratively referred to as villageism. As this villageism – particularly when it meets up with other villageisms, or other competing thought-practices – is generally reckoned to be divisive and the producer of social discord, the problem again arises for Plaid Cymru in that its desire – its *raison d'être* – to promote the notion of a united and harmonious geographical and political space known as Wales would undoubtedly be harmed if each locality were engaged in internecine exchanges with its neighbouring locality. Once more, therefore, a concept such as localism may appear contradictory if it is established that Plaid Cymru has certain core and peripheral concepts that are part of the nationalist morphology.

When considering the above, one area that needs to be explored is whether the emphasis on the concept of community can be seen as anything other than an attempt to foster a type of organic, predominantly rural, or at least non-urbanised, conservatism. If this promotion of organic conservatism does indeed prove to be the driving force behind the conceptualisation of community values and solidarity, then this line of reasoning could be used to evaluate, and probably lay bare, the credibility of the socialist self-prescriptions that are forwarded by people within Plaid Cymru. Whether or not this is so, it is nevertheless evident that the idea of highlighting and nurturing community values is something that does appeal to Plaid Cymru.

Although the label communitarianism is one that Plaid Cymru has, perhaps somewhat surprisingly, distanced itself from, there are signs of an overlapping consensus between some aspects of communitarian thought and Plaid Cymru's ideology. As Laura McAllister's article 'The perils of community as a construct for the political ideology of Welsh nationalism' pointed out, 'communitarianism criticizes the lack of a community focus in other political ideologies.'[82] If McAllister's analysis is accepted, then Plaid Cymru's community focus places it more comfortably within a communitarian-style ideological category than one that may be found elsewhere along the political spectrum. Furthermore, the language of communitarianism, especially the commitment, as proclaimed by Amitai Etzioni, to the 'rebuilding of moral communities',[83] would undoubtedly find support today, and would have found support in the past, from the Plaid Cymru leadership, in particular from Saunders Lewis and Gwynfor Evans. This is because Plaid Cymru's leadership and policy-making elite have consistently advocated a rejuvenated Welsh community-based society that would be established not only on political lines that encompassed the symbols of nationhood but also, and quite significantly, on spiritual and philosophical foundations that would lay the basis for these moral communities to emerge.

Freedom and Polyarchic Systems

For Gwynfor Evans, the concepts of freedom and power are interlinked with the notion of community. In an attack on what he portrayed as the totalitarianism that is endured by the Welsh people, as they cope with life under conditions of alienation, Evans noted that 'freedom has no meaning for Welsh workers unless it means being free in their home and family, amongst their friends, in the choir and the chapel in which they were reared, in the countryside which they loved as part of themselves.'[84] This is not just a political observation, according to Evans, but a reflection of a psychological bond in evidence among what he deemed to be certain innate Welsh characteristics. As he affirmed, in what could certainly be construed as a communitarian interpretation, 'so intimately bound is their personality with these things, that to sever them from them is the most cruel and damaging blow which could be dealt. These are the very things which give meaning and richness to their lives.'[85]

Gwynfor Evans's vision of community – the space evolving from the family home outward – is that it acts as the source for the nature of freedom that Plaid Cymru sees evident in localised circumstances. However, the party finds these favourable conditions for nurturing freedom lacking when it comes to observing centralised or state-centric formations. The argument evolves, therefore, that, given these circumstances, politics is more likely to be democratic and inclusive on a smaller scale than it would be in a larger, more impersonal arena. Thus, by allowing for the growth and extension of political activism within a community setting, there is the potential to forge a non-hierarchical system of politics. Along these lines, Michael Freeden, using a Gramscian analogy, has noted how grass-roots-engendered, or polyarchic, political systems allow for fragmentation, that is the process through which intellectual elites are replaced by a mass democratisation that is brought about by 'a change in the social distribution of ideological producers.'[86] Plaid Cymru's championing of the ideological concept of community, therefore, could be construed as an extension of democracy away from elitist conceptions and limited practice.

Also, in the wake of this democratic diffusion, there would undoubtedly be a burgeoning of the layers through which the ideational process could flourish. Through the involvement of the masses a more potent political dialectic may emerge, and this would inevitably offer up challenges to both the current socio-political structures and the ways in which people perceive political power within their communities. While this may prove useful for encouraging political debate among the populace, it would appear that there cannot be any way of guaranteeing that this synthesis of political thought would ultimately favour, or even broadly concur with, the ideology and political ambitions of Plaid Cymru. Given this line of debate, therefore, Laura McAllister's warning to Plaid Cymru of the perils of community may yet prove to be an accurate supposition.

Similarly, the onus on community, like decentralisation before it, to provide a set of answers to the multiplicity of problems encountered by

people within Wales could also be interpreted as reactionary in the face
of the onset of globalisation. Within contemporary society there appears
to be a growing realisation that isolationism – in the sense of parochialism or villageism – cannot operate within what is rapidly becoming
a more socially interactive and multicultural world. So a case may
be constructed, by party members seeking an alternative ideological
direction, to oppose any plans to increase particularism, or small group
identity, within Wales, if that indeed is what communityism could lead
to, or be representative of.

Community and Identification

When community is under the spotlight, the idea of who belongs within
a community, and who is perceived to be outside that community, could
also be linked in with who is absorbed and who is the other within
a nation. There would appear to be an obvious connection between
the notions of community and nationhood in that both offer a home to
certain convictions and dispositions, and both provide people with a
sense of protection against outside interests. Community can be seen
as a staging post for the individual's commitment to his or her society
– that society generally being regarded, certainly in global terms, as
the nation or nation-state. Back in 1962, Meic Stephens wrote that the
community is the location through which the individual can experience
'self-identification with a group and a place.'[87] So, for some time now,
Plaid Cymru has viewed the communal milieu as a more natural and
instinctive setting for political action and solidarity than the more centralised and rigid authority of the nation or nation-state.

Given this expression, it would be easy to link Plaid Cymru's attachment to the concept of decentralisation to this attraction towards communityism. However, one question that must be asked of a political
grouping purporting to be nationalist, or at least being identifiable with
nationalism, is: why not self-identification through the nation alone?
Why does a party that has a high level of regard for the construct of
the nation, as Plaid Cymru clearly does, require a subdivision, or rather
what would amount to a multitude of subdivisions, through which
values and political ambitions are channelled?

One line of argument on all of this could hold that Plaid Cymru is
very loose in its use of terminology and its accompanying descriptions:
in other words the party has failed to decontest these concepts to the
extent that it should have. This may be observable, for instance, when
the expression 'community' is used and assessed. Laura McAllister has
commented that the concept of community, or communityism, appears
at regular intervals throughout Plaid Cymru's history. However, 'there is

little consistency within the party in its understanding or application.'[88] Nevertheless, some within the party have attempted to elucidate the concept of communityism. Ioan Bowen Rees, for example, proposed a scheme of 'government by community' whereby government was organised on the basis of local units which could ensure the identity of the community'.[89] Similarly, a composite motion by Cardiganshire and West Denbigh Rhanbarths, presented to the 1970 Plaid Cymru conference, sought to 're-iterate Plaid Cymru's belief in the value of the small town and the rural village as social units.'[90]

What arises for Plaid Cymru out of these thought-practices is the conviction that the advocating of community, as a unit from which a certain degree of socio-economic and political power can evolve, would amount to the proliferation of diversity as a value-in-itself. Concurrently, if the augmentation of communityism was to be made a priority under a Plaid Cymru administration, Wales would inevitably experience a radical movement towards a more localised and accountable network of government. The centralised state, on the other hand, would appear to offer little apart from uniformity and inaccessibility. If the party followed this line of reasoning to its logical conclusion then the national, or nation-state, structures would appear surplus to requirement. As the party has yet to decontest what it understands communityism to mean, or even what it fully perceives decentralisation to be, then an assessment of whether or not Plaid Cymru positions these concepts above the concept of the nation or national frameworks is difficult to measure.

Community Socialism and Serving the Community

To complicate matters further, Plaid Cymru has on occasions brought the notion of community socialism into its discourse on communityism. Community socialism was actually adopted into the formal aims of the party at the 1981 conference,[91] during a period, interestingly, of intense ideological struggle within the party, which will be discussed later. Over time, however, the references to community socialism have faded, as a metamorphosis to decentralist socialism seems to have occurred. One simple, but useful, example of community socialism was forwarded by Dafydd Wigley, who called for a re-opening of railway lines to service small communities and 'an increase in community taxis.'[92] Here is an example of localism in action as a community's transport needs are met, in short-distance terms, by taxis and, when it comes to long-distance travel, by the introduction of a frequent train service. Noticeable in this context is the fact that the party does not see community as an environment in which individualist activity or a spirit of entrepreneurship arises – what would be perceived as a right-wing view of community. Rather, community is all about creating situations in which people can help others and within which democratic authorities act as overseers to ensure societal stability. Emphasis, therefore, in Plaid Cymru's rhetoric, is always on servicing the community – what may be perceived as being a left-of-centre, welfarist assessment.

When it comes to production and resources within a communal setting, Plaid Cymru has placed an onus on employing, wherever possible, 'local craftsmen',[93] though this may be interpreted by critics of the party as a submission to a discriminatory, particularist position. To pay for the improvements that the party envisages occurring in localised services, Plaid Cymru has long been an advocate of widening the powers of local authorities to finance their own projects. Proposals along these lines featured prominently in Plaid Cymru's 1969 report, which, given the party's commitment to non-violent methods, was fittingly entitled *The Peaceful Road to Self-Government*.[94] Therein, it was projected that a local income tax would be introduced for the purpose of funding community initiatives. However, in chronological terms, even earlier precedents of decentralisation can be witnessed in the 1939 document *The New Wales*. In this, Plaid Cymru emphasised its belief that the Welsh economy should be built on the principle of a 'local market for local products'[95] in a Wales in which authority and responsibility would be subdivided.[96]

One contemporary advocate of this channel of thought is Jill Evans. In her manifesto for the election of president of Plaid Cymru, published in 2000, Evans incorporated subsections entitled 'Rebuilding our communities' and 'Community empowerment'.[97] Evans's proposals included plans for banks to 'reinvest a percentage of their profits in the local community.'[98] Added to this, Evans called for 'the creation of new mini-economies on housing estates based around repair, maintenance and energy efficiency schemes.'[99] These policy measures had a radical edge about them and the focus of attention hung upon the community. According to Jill Evans, the spatial concept known as community, although playing a constructive role today, would increasingly become the source and the location for political action in the future.

Darren Price takes a similar approach to Evans, with regard to the concept of community, with his statement that 'politics is all about getting the best possible deal for your community.'[100] This is a universal truth, according to Price, but it is also a particularistic identification. In the manner in which some members of Plaid Cymru use the expression community it would appear to have no prescribed boundaries. However, the general supposition is that community represents a limited geographical, and possibly linguistic or cultural, space. Ultimately, the concept of community within Plaid Cymru's thought-practices suffers from a lack of decontestation and, therefore, further intensive scrutiny and clarification would undoubtedly benefit party members and observers alike.

Communityism: Oppression or Solidarity?

Although, indisputably, there are some positive everyday aspects to having links with people in the vicinity of where you live or work, it could be claimed that communityism can be oppressive. The political philosopher Will Kymlicka has proffered that groups or communities have sets of innate or constitutional rights.[101] If this group rights argument were to be applied to Plaid Cymru's thinking, then a possible weakness in any assessment of the party's adaptation of communityism is that the individual within a community, being a specific unit rather than being merely one of the collective, could be under-represented. Then again, individuals may possibly even be in a position whereby their opinions and actions could be repressed unless they are willing to see themselves as part of the community and, correspondingly, to give their consent to that community's norms, standards and regulations.

If Plaid Cymru champions communityism, therefore, it could be contended that the party would be going against one of the key principles of liberalism, namely the rights of the individual. If the lifestyle or viewpoint of that individual does not match up to notions of the common good, as indicated by the collective stance of the community, then the individual is likely to drift into alienation. If communityism allows this to take place, then elitist standards are being adopted wherein the person or persons outside the collective have a substandard quality of life compared with those absorbed within the collective. If communityism appears to be following these conventions then it is a majoritarian, as opposed to an all-inclusive, concept. In terms of Plaid Cymru's ideology, this selected inclusivism cannot, by its nature, embrace all national concerns. Therefore, it is unrepresentative if it is being presented as a concept within a party for whom the idea of the nation plays a substantial part.

Communityism, thus, further exemplifies some of the inherent contradictions within Plaid Cymru's thought-practices. Michael Freeden has talked of ideologies that 'when carried to their logical extremes, could lead to serious contradictions and to substantive absurdities.'[102] If this line of argument is developed for ideological concepts and not just ideologies, then it could be contended that this may apply to the concept of communityism. Whether or not there are serious contradictions, there are clearly areas within Plaid Cymru's thinking that require greater clarity of definition and purpose.

Regardless of this, however, the concept of community or communityism should be included amongst the core concepts of Plaid Cymru's ideology. This is because small-scale, community-centred ideals have inspired the party's theoreticians, and the philosophy of community as a form of natural good is embedded within the party's thought-practices. Without this concept of communityism, Plaid Cymru's ideological base would be substantially weakened. This does again throw into question the alleged nationalist attachment, however, as the social, cultural, economic and linguistic replenishment that the members of Plaid Cymru seek appears to come from communal as opposed to national outlets. Likewise, in another blow to the identification of nationalism with Plaid Cymru's ideology, these communal outlets appear to offer broader scope for ideational development than does the rather narrowly defined theoretical and policy arena in which nationalist thought-practices occur.

Language

It could be contended, in some respects, that language is tied in with the aforementioned concept of communityism. This is because 'language makes sense only as a group activity',[103] and communityism, as noted previously, is very much centred on group, as opposed to individual, activity and affiliation. Plaid Cymru's entry into this debate on community and language can be seen by the proclamation on the party's website. Therein, a statement reads that the fourth aim of the party is 'to create a bilingual society by promoting the revival of the Welsh language.'[104] Therefore, in the case of Plaid Cymru's ideology, it could be noted that communal bonding and communal advancement are being portrayed through the promotion and utilisation of the indigenous language. What must be asked at this juncture, however, is why something like language – that is attributable to all human beings, and is something that would certainly not merit political campaigning in most instances – should feature as a concept within a political party's ideology?

A possible answer may emerge from analysing Michael Freeden's writings in this area. Freeden has noted that language is a 'social product';[105] indeed, it is a product that has a great deal of power – political and cultural – attached to it and therefore is not just a medium through which social interaction can proceed. If Plaid Cymru seeks linguistic enhancement, with regard to the Welsh language, then the power structures within Welsh society will inevitably be affected as the minority language rises in political importance and is granted official status as the lingua franca of the entire geographical space of Wales. Language, therefore, is not in this instance, and arguably never is, value-neutral.

This is especially so in the case of Wales as language has played a major role in defining Welsh history, and because socio-cultural and political discourse and identity go hand in hand within Wales.

The identification of someone as a first-language Welsh speaker from, for example, Llanddarog has stronger resonance in terms of identity, and what may follow in ideological terms, than the identification of someone as a monolingual English speaker from Chepstow, for instance. There is no debate about the fact that both are Welsh in terms of the geographical space in which they were born. However, the linguistic, cultural, social and, possibly, political environments in which these two people would have been raised, and in which they would operate as adults, are very different. Although, as rational human beings, both are free to choose their particular paths in life, the social, cultural and subregional geographical constraints levied on them are enormous. In terms of language, therefore, Welsh speakers function differently, and have to react in a different way in the many culturally diverse parts of Wales, whereas English speakers, being the majority, have virtually absolute spatial and linguistic freedom.

Language and Development

Plaid Cymru's reaction to the matter of the Welsh language has played a prominent role within the party's history. However, it is not a stagnant view of a language in aspic but more a case of an interpretation of the value and vibrancy of the language that has evolved over time. Plaid Cymru, in its modern guise in particular, has recognised the positive features of the Welsh language and the enhanced standing of bilingualism within Welsh and European society. To these ends, the party has accepted that 'the division of Wales geographically on the basis of language alone would undermine the objective of Plaid Cymru to create a bilingual Wales';[106] hence the rejection by the party of the establishment of what would amount to a very distinctive language zone. Referring to the setting up of a Bro Gymraeg on the lines of the Irish Gaeltacht, Plaid Cymru has acknowledged that 'one of the dangers of a Gaeltacht style designation would be a reduction in the momentum of extending the borders of the territory of the Welsh language and the creation of a preservationist–protectionist rather than dynamic mindset.'[107] Here, the differences between the ideologies of early Plaid Cymru and modern Plaid Cymru are most noticeable. It is also worth noting how this debate on the Welsh language affects Plaid Cymru's thought-practices to a vastly greater extent than the Gaelic language debate in Scotland interposes itself into the policies and pronouncements of the SNP.

The Evolution of the Language Debate

For early Plaid Cymru the language was sacrosanct and it was, without doubt, a core concept that went unchallenged, as linguistic and cultural concerns dominated the party's ideology. Perhaps this is evidenced most clearly when the case of the attack on the RAF bombing school at Penyberth is assessed. As Geraint H Jenkins's essay on the Welsh language has noted,[108] when the trial of the three arsonists involved – Saunders Lewis, the Reverend Lewis Valentine and D.J. Williams – was transferred to the Old Bailey, the defendants steadfastly refused to speak English. In the minds not only of the British Establishment, whom the Penyberth Three had challenged, but also of the general public, this act further highlighted the contention that Plaid Cymru was inextricably linked with the promotion and use of the Welsh language, and it could be forwarded that advancing the Welsh language was seen as the responsibility of Plaid Cymru.

As Carwyn Fowler and Rhys Jones have observed of this period in time, 'Plaid Cymru, during its early years, was far more concerned with securing the linguistic and moral future of the Welsh nation than it was with electoral success or political independence for Wales.'[109] Thus, language played a particularistic role in these thought-practices and could, therefore, be viewed as being very much in the preservationist–protectionist style. The 1939 synopsis of party policy, *The New Wales*, exemplified this approach. In this document the party proclaimed that 'the keystone of the Welsh Nationalist Party's policy is that the Welsh language should have precedence over all other languages on its soil.'[110]

Modern Plaid Cymru embraced bilingualism in the 1950s as the realisation that the Welsh language cannot be enforced as the lingua franca, even in its perceived heartlands, became apparent to progressive thinkers within the party. Acknowledging the ever-changing nature of global transactions and migratory patterns, contemporary Plaid Cymru reasoning on this matter has concluded that forging the aforementioned language zones would be impracticable as 'the inhabitants of the proposed Bro Gymraeg might feel themselves to be living in a kind of "open prison" or museum.'[111] Dafydd Iwan has reiterated this opposition to sectioning Wales off into linguistic sectors by stating that reviving the Welsh language is 'important to me, the party and everyone in Wales, not only Welsh speakers … But it is not by building ramparts that we achieve our goal, but by facing the challenge with confidence and creativity.'[112]

If Plaid Cymru considers the idea of a language zone to be unworkable, then the party's commitment to the advancement of the Welsh language, and its subsequent position within the party's ideology, needs to be reconsidered. If these actions amount to an abandonment of the Welsh language as a prime motivator for the party's political ambitions then the notion that language can be calculated as a core concept within Plaid Cymru's ideology would appear to be contentious.

Plaid Cymru's Language Dilemma

Although language may not be the dominant theme in the party's rhetoric of late, it nevertheless still commands a position within Plaid Cymru's thinking that can be described as both practical and emotional. One example of this came from former party leader Dafydd Wigley. Commenting on the language in general, whilst being acutely aware that there are funding shortages within both the public and private sector finances in Wales, Wigley, in a speech at Bangor in 1999, argued that resources for the bolstering and advancement of the Welsh language had to go to areas in which that money would have the greatest effect. To these ends, Wigley stated that he longed to see 'a shift in the emphasis of language policy to very young ages.'[113] This call for a concerted set of policies to educate children, and the younger generation generally, through the medium of Welsh was, however, nothing new. Chris Rees, the party's then director of research, noted in the Plaid Cymru annual report of 1967/68 that a development plan for the Welsh language was needed that incorporated primary education and which would be 'responsible and practical enough to fire the imagination and gain support at the same time.'[114]

The realisation that a pragmatic approach and agenda was required was foremost in the party's thinking, therefore, as far back as 1968. Nevertheless, in ideological terms, what Plaid Cymru would wish to see develop within Wales is what amounts to a Burkean – and hence, arguably, a somewhat conservative – line of linguistic transmission, wherein the Welsh language, and its corresponding socio-cultural attributes such as the Eisteddfod, are passed from generation to generation and, ultimately, are decisively secured as component parts of the Welsh national identity. Although few people in present-day Wales would argue against the continuation of the Welsh language as an everyday means of verbal and written communication, the desire to maintain the language could, and often does, leave the party open to those critics who view Plaid Cymru as an essentially conservative, possibly even reactionary, party in its espousal of linguistic concerns. Although it may be found that language is not a core concept of the party's ideology, certainly in the case of modern Plaid Cymru's thought-practices, it nevertheless remains the case that the perception of outsiders who assess Plaid Cymru's policies and objectives view what they claim to be the party's placing of the language at the centre of Welsh social and political life as an integral facet of the party's make-up. Good or bad, rightly or wrongly, this perception persists within political circles.

Regardless of how accurate or fair some of these criticisms may be, what cannot be denied is the conviction that the Welsh language is inextricably bound with Plaid Cymru's conception of the Welsh nation, although Rhodri Glyn Thomas has admitted that 'it is no longer Plaid's sole property.'[115] Nevertheless, to appreciate how much of a key it is to the morphology of the party, Hywel Davies, in a section of his book entitled 'Language Dilemma', has commented on how 'the radical feature of the Welsh Nationalist Party at its inception was not its association with the objective of some degree of Welsh home rule, but its use of the Welsh language.'[116] Davies talked of a dilemma within Plaid Cymru's ranks and he has illustrated how, in its formative years, uncompromising attitudes angled towards the preservation of the Welsh language, and against the use of English within party circles, emerged. The outcome of this period of internecine language warfare managed only to confirm, as Davies has noted, 'the dominance of the Welsh language in the upper echelons of the Nationalist Party organisation.'[117]

Language as an Internationalist Concern

On intermittent occasions over the years, but more frequently in recent years, the party has also taken an internationalist line on the language by seeing it as an identifier with liberationist struggles and nationalist causes worldwide. In a press release that pledged Plaid Cymru's solidarity with the plight of the Kurdish minority in Turkey, Eurig Wyn, a member of the European Parliament at the time, considered the similarities between the suppression of the Kurds by the Turkish state and the suppression of the Welsh by the British state. Highlighting the relevant indigenous languages, Eurig Wyn contended that 'there are clear similarities between the Kurdish cultural situation and our own in Wales. The Welsh language was effectively banned early in the last century, and the same is now true for the Kurdish language that is prohibited from the school curriculum.'[118]

When used in this context, language is a political instrument as it acts as a signifier of what is essentially Welsh or, in this instance, essentially Kurdish. It also differentiates against other languages as markers of national or regional characteristics. The concept of the other, a noted feature of nationalist thinking, is thus summoned by the politicisation of language; this politicisation, incidentally, being undertaken by both sides in the argument: the oppressors and the liberationists. If Plaid Cymru is following this line of reasoning, then the party is straying down the path of particularism that can be identified with a nationalist political position.

When Freeden's model is held against the relevance and use of language as an ideological concept within Plaid Cymru thought-practices, a change in the primacy of the concept is observed. Early Plaid Cymru clearly evolved its political thinking around the evolution of a distinctly Welsh Wales. For this to come about the indigenous language had to be centred; in actual fact, cultural and linguistic preservation, as opposed to the desire to forge an overtly political or public policy agenda, was the original driver and motivational force for the party's founders. If this examination was merely assessing Plaid Cymru's ideology up until the 1950s then the promotion of the Welsh language would be classified as a core concept within that ideological framework. However, modern Plaid Cymru's attitude towards the Welsh language is far less fundamentalist, and the favouring of bilingualism as the party's linguistic goal has altered the conceptual patterns of the party's morphology.

To some extent, the formation in the 1960s of Cymdeithas yr Iaith Gymraeg (the Welsh Language Society) released the debate over the Welsh language's future prospects away from the preserve of Plaid Cymru and propelled it into the social and political arena of Wales as a whole. Today, therefore, although the Welsh language is still very important to the party's views on what constitutes Wales and Welshness, the pressure valve on Plaid Cymru has been discharged, and positive messages about the survival and growth of the language can now be heard emanating from other political parties, and from within the general realm of civil society in Wales. The identification of Plaid Cymru with the issue of language preservation has thus been broken. The Welsh language, therefore, can be viewed as a peripheral, as opposed to a core, concept within Plaid Cymru's thought-practices.

Social Justice

The theme of social justice has appeared in Plaid Cymru literature and pronouncements in recent years, corresponding, arguably, with the Labour Party's conversion to the concept of social justice. What needs to be addressed, therefore, is whether it is a case of Plaid Cymru merely mirroring New Labour in its promotion of this concept. This may not be as trivial an observation as it may first appear. This is because, when dealing with concepts within a political ideology, it is important to remember that ideologies are representative of the prevailing discourses of the time; Freeden's assessment that concepts are 'idea-artefacts that serve human convenience as ways of coming with the world'[119] would appear to be applicable in this instance. Whether or not these prevailing discourses have succeeded in putting pressure on Plaid Cymru to use the language of social justice and, by its association with Third Way thinking, the language of New Labour, social justice has certainly featured in Plaid Cymru's rhetoric and pronouncements to a greater degree since New Labour started using the term on a regular basis.

Recent cases in point, wherein incidentally the concept of self-government is juxtaposed with the concept of social justice, include the example of Cynog Dafis, who, in an acclamation of Ieuan Wyn Jones's leadership qualities, noted that 'there is fire burning in his breast and it has to do with two things in particular: social justice and the need to create a national future for Wales.'[120] Likewise, in a declaration of her personal beliefs, which appear to parallel those of Ieuan Wyn Jones, Helen Mary Jones holds the concept of social justice in high regard. Jones has commented on how she approaches National Assembly for Wales business. She has claimed, 'before I attend a single meeting or draft a single amendment I ask myself how does this move us towards full self-government, and how does this contribute to social justice?'[121]

The Socialist Aspects of Plaid Cymru's Social Justice

Although there is clear evidence of the concept's use within Plaid Cymru, that still does not pin down what Plaid Cymru's interpretation of social justice actually is. In other words, generalised comments by figures within the party would be fine if, and only if, the concept is decontested in the patterns of thought of those who seek to use it. As this ideological exploration is searching for decontestation and clarity on several fronts, any explanation of the concept by party members is deemed valuable. To these ends, somebody who gives the impression of having a relatively lucid notion of the adaptation and implications of social justice as a concept within the party's ideology is Rhodri Glyn Thomas. If his view of this concept is taken into consideration, then it would appear to be the case that, in the party's ideational structure, social justice is interconnected with socialist ideas and practice.

For Thomas, redistribution of wealth is a key factor in ensuring social justice. Praising Plaid Cymru's policy of incremental taxation and increased welfare spending, Thomas stated that 'if you are a low taxation party then you don't believe in redistribution of wealth and you don't believe in social justice.'[122] How far Rhodri Glyn Thomas's interpretation can be taken as indicative of party reasoning on this matter is debatable as Thomas is not currently a key player in terms of Plaid Cymru's policy-making team. Nevertheless, the proposal that the implementation of social justice should be linked in to a commitment to welfarism, through a greater extension, and a more systematic application, of publicly funded social and economic provision, is an interesting vision.

This explanation of Rhodri Glyn Thomas's falls in line to a certain extent with an account of social justice presented by Michael Freeden. Freeden has commented that the term social justice, as used by advocates of welfarism, can be equated as 'the equal treatment of all, spelt out as the distribution of fundamental scarce goods on the basis of need.'[123] Meanwhile, Plaid Cymru's angle on social justice, according to the party's literature, is that it is a concept that encapsulates, and connects together, the elements of cultural vitality and democratic renewal.[124] For the notion of social justice to have any veracity, therefore, Plaid Cymru maintains that it must feed off a reinvigorated awareness of indigenous cultural concerns and, assumedly, a reinvigorated sense of national identity, together with a fresh culture of democratic activism. Hence, social justice is not a stagnant theoretical viewpoint but a means through which social, cultural, economic, and, possibly, political amelioration can be achieved.

Attempting to position Plaid Cymru's social justice along the ideological spectrum involves relating adjacent concepts – brought into the arena, as they have been, by party members – such as welfarism, the redistribution of wealth and the revitalisation of cultural and democratic factors to the concept of social justice itself. If, as Rhodri Glyn Thomas has contended, social justice operates on a basis whereby the redistribution of wealth is seen as the primary component within the rhetorical theme of social justice, then a socialistic perception is visible to those inside and outside the party. Alternatively, the linking of social justice to national self-determination, by prominent party members such as Helen Mary Jones and Plaid Cymru's leader in the National Assembly, Ieuan Wyn Jones, could be viewed as promoting a nationalist agenda through the façade of the concept of social justice. On the other hand, and if Freeden's contention that nationalism is not a full ideology is accepted, this parallel approach to social justice and national enhancement may also be viewed as putting added flesh on the bone of Plaid Cymru's nationalist ideology.

It must be restated that because social justice has not been adequately decontested within Plaid Cymru's thought-practices, a definitive statement on the party's employment and understanding of the concept of social justice is hard to arrive at. Nevertheless, in its growing use by the party as a concept that amounts to securing a better deal for the people of Wales in social, economic and cultural terms, social justice has come to the fore in the party's morphology. In a sense it may be calculated that its rise as a concept has been counterbalanced by the demise of language and religion as core concepts within the party's ideological framework. To this extent, therefore, social justice, though not still fully decontested, is now a core concept within Plaid Cymru's thought-practices. Whether it remains so, however, could depend to what degree the concept of social justice remains part of the prevailing discourse; its recent ascendancy, for instance, can be gauged by the fact that the concept of social justice was not part of the prevailing discourse during the Thatcher years.

Moreover, the concept may be at the forefront of Plaid Cymru's ideology at this moment in time but it still requires clarification in order for it to be fully decontested and understood. Once achieved, the agreed understanding of what the party accepts as being the concept of social justice will require extensive dissemination. This is vital in order that – depending on the decontested version in existence – people can relate it either to the party's nationalistic commitment to an autonomous Wales or to the party's socialistic commitment to the creation of a more egalitarian society through the application of schemes designed to redistribute wealth and resources. If this latter interpretation were to be adopted, it might be proposed that the concept of decentralisation could be attached as an adjoining concept. At present, however, as far as Plaid Cymru's options for achieving transparency and precision in its presentation of its political beliefs is concerned, the concept of social justice, though a core concept, remains a concept that can be too easily misconstrued or appropriated. This elucidation, it would appear, is an assignment that lies ahead for Plaid Cymru.

Capitalism

At first glance, this may appear to be an unusual concept to cover in this section as most observers, bar those on the far left, would not immediately pick up on the point that Plaid Cymru is a political party that, throughout the course of its existence, has advocated capitalism as a concept within its ideology. Nevertheless, while alternative social and economic strategies appear throughout Plaid Cymru's history, there is a minimal amount of serious discourse regarding the abandonment of capitalism as the financial system of a self-governing Wales. Although Saunders Lewis talked of his despair at the Industrial Revolution and what it produced – namely the modern capitalist mode of production – there are very few practical references to deconstructing, or simply abandoning, capitalism within Wales; although J.E. Daniel did launch a broadside against laissez-faire and classical liberalism and, somewhat presciently given the expansion in these fields, Daniel did maintain that Plaid Cymru should mount a campaign of opposition against 'urbanisation and its inevitable proletarianisation, to chain stores and multiple shops.'[125] Thus, the theme of rurbanisation, cited earlier, is again evident in some of these pronouncements.

But, these few instances aside, is it so surprising to find limited proposals to counteract capitalism throughout the party's history? If it is the case that Plaid Cymru, or certainly some individuals within the party, really believe that capitalism breeds factoryism and, subsequently, generation after generation become dehumanised as they are servile to machines, and, furthermore, if Plaid Cymru genuinely wants to create a decentralised, socialist Wales, then it may be reasonable to contend that there is an element of contradiction conducted by the party in that Plaid Cymru is not facing up to, and honestly engaging in, a dialogue with the political and structural realities of what the continuation of an economic system such as capitalism would mean for the party's attempts to radically realign Welsh society. If Plaid Cymru is putting capitalism to one side, and regarding it as an economic rather than a political or a politico-economic concept, then what does this convey about, amongst other things, the party's commitment to societal change, the general naivety of the party membership as to the ubiquitous nature of capitalism and the party's views about whether, in the interest of the freedom of the individual, it is better for people to be allowed to participate in acts of economic spontaneity in contrast to having to endure the strictures of a planned economy; albeit one that may, in a Plaid Cymru-controlled Wales, be planned on a small, decentralised scale?

Capitalism and its Interpreters

As in the earlier discussion on the ideology of liberalism, the amount and type of freedom that Plaid Cymru seeks to cultivate is back under the spotlight. This is an imperative argument as the concepts of capitalism and freedom either clash or complement each other depending on which side of the political spectrum the observer is coming from. For J.E. Daniel, for example, industrial capitalism 'ignores all the things that make of man something more than an animated tool, the things that make him a person, family, nation, religion.'[126] Capitalism, in this interpretation, goes against the forms of communal bonding favoured by Plaid Cymru – to clarify further, that is those forms that were favoured, most vociferously, by Plaid Cymru in its early manifestation. If the colonisation and market forces theses, presented by Michael Hechter[127] among others, were taken as an accurate assessment, then Wales, as a peripheral player in the great scheme of the British Empire and the markets of the West, would inevitably suffer appreciably in any period in which an economic downturn occurred. Charlotte Davies,[128] commenting on the harsh realities of life in Wales between the wars, has contended that the responses of Plaid Cymru to the series of crises faced by capitalism at this time was variable to say the least and, taken as a whole, these responses were hardly the passionate anti-capitalist lines of attack that might have won the party a sizeable number of converts.

While the party has, from time to time, proposed a fresh modus operandi out of which Welsh society could progress, these innovative proposals invariably fell short of seeking an implosion for capitalism. Like Saunders Lewis, Michael Freeden has observed how 'the origins of socialism are closely linked to the emergence of the capitalist mode of production and to the development of urban industrial societies.'[129] Although Plaid Cymru has argued for spatial transference away from the cities to the much romanticised rural idyll, in order to advance the cultural, social, spiritual and philosophical tendencies of the Welsh people, the economic transference issue remains problematic, and arguably somewhat decontested, within Plaid Cymru's thought-practices. This is down to the fact that, even though economic transactions would still occur under rurbanisation, albeit on a more humane and decentralised level, with the mode of production being cooperativist, the method of financial exchange both within this decentralised Welsh society and with the rest of the world would remain the capitalist system. Plaid Cymru has no plans, seemingly, to induce a Stalin-like 'socialism in one country' scenario that would quixotically seek to abandon capitalism in the hope that others may view Wales as a role model and adopt this cooperativist rurbanisation and thus lead to a collapse of capitalism on a global stage. It would appear that capitalism, even under a Plaid Cymru-led Wales, is therefore likely to remain a constant. Plausibly, this could hinder any attempt by Plaid Cymru to introduce the party's radical ideas for restructuring Wales's internal configuration of socio-economic and cultural relations.

The question remains as to the extent to which the concept of capitalism overhangs other social and economic concepts within Plaid Cymru's ideology. This examination of the party's thought-practices has uncovered the fact that the ideology of socialism, or at least the overall notion of creating a socialist society, acts as a driver for the ideas fermenting and circulating within Plaid Cymru. The depth of that socialist commitment is being challenged here, however, as socialism's *raison d'être* is to confront the capitalist system, and subsequently overcome it, in order to ensure that the socialist core concept of 'the constitutive nature of the human relationship'[130] is favourably altered so that the social and economic inequalities that are observable in human relationships under capitalism no longer exist in any future societal arrangement. Unless Plaid Cymru faces up to the consequences that this major realignment of the economic system would bring about – provided, that is, that this is what the party actually desires – then its vitriol towards capitalism will remain purely rhetorical, and its support for the continuation of the capitalist system in its current form will remain in place.

The concept of capitalism within Plaid Cymru's thought-practices should, therefore, be seen as a peripheral, as opposed to a core, concept. It should also be noted that it is a concept which dares not speak its name. Very few members of the party discuss the concept of capitalism as a part of Plaid Cymru's morphology. This is because those members generally regard capitalism as a necessary evil, and, in conjunction, they would assert that the restructuring of the social and cultural aspects of life in Wales is more important than transforming the economic base. Furthermore, the estimation of these members on this issue is one of assuming that this restructuring could be realised without having to confront the entire capitalist edifice head on, which is what an organisation such as the Socialist Workers Party, for example, unambiguously seeks to do. Capitalism is, thus, a peripheral concept that the party would rather do without. Nevertheless, it is a concept that Plaid Cymru is unwilling, or unable, to present a coherent ideological case against, regardless of the seeming disdain for its existence being tendered at regular intervals over the years by key strategists, theoreticians and radicals within the party such as Saunders Lewis, Gwynfor Evans, Phil Williams and Leanne Wood.

Notes

1. Elfyn Llwyd, interview, 21 October 2002.
2. Elin Jones, interview, 16 October 2002.
3. Ibid.
4. Darren Price, interview, 11 June 2002.
5. Ibid.
6. Ibid.
7. Laura McAllister, *Plaid Cymru: The Emergence of a Political Party* (Bridgend: Seren, 2001), p. 44.
8. Michael Freeden, *Ideology: A Very Short Introduction* (Oxford: Oxford University Press, 2003), p. 88.
9. Ibid., p. 101.
10. Saunders Lewis and J.E. Daniel, *The Party for Wales* (Caernarfon: National Office, 1942), p. 2.
11. Ibid.
12. Ibid., p. 5.
13. Ibid., p. 10.
14. Derrick Hearne, *The Rise of the Welsh Republic* (Talybont: Y Lolfa, 1975), p. 51.
15. Ibid.
16. Michael Freeden, *Ideology*, p. 25.
17. Laura McAllister, *Plaid Cymru*, pp. 28–29.

18. D. Hywel Davies, *The Welsh Nationalist Party 1925–1945* (New York: St. Martin's Press, 1983), p. 167.
19. Ibid.
20. J.E. Jones, *Wales and the War* (Caernarfon: Swyddfa'r Blaid 1940), p. 8.
21. Saunders Lewis, *To the Electors of the University of Wales* (Denbigh: Gee and Son), 1942, p.4.
22. Ibid.
23. Michael Freeden, *Ideologies and Political Theory* (Oxford: Clarendon Press, 1996), p. 544.
24. Ibid., pp. 544–545.
25. Carwyn Fowler and Rhys Jones, 'Locating and Scaling the Welsh Nation', University of Lincoln, Political Studies Association paper, 2004, p. 12.
26. Ibid.
27. Elin Jones, interview, 16 October 2002.
28. Ibid.
29. Ibid.
30. Ibid.
31. D. Hywel Davies, *The Welsh Nationalist Party 1925–1945*, p. 167.
32. David Adamson, *Class, Ideology and the Nation: A Theory of Welsh Nationalism* (Cardiff: University of Wales Press, 1991), p. 127.
33. Michael Freeden, *Ideology*, p. 20.
34. Ibid., p. 57.
35. In various interviews conducted with party members (see Bibliography).
36. Ieuan Wyn Jones, interview with tribancoch.com, 30 December 2002.
37. Ibid.
38. Rhodri Glyn Thomas, interview, 14 May 2001.
39. Ibid.
40. Leanne Wood, 'US dire straits', tribancoch.com, 10 December 2003.
41. Plaid Cymru, *A Billion Ways to Build a New Wales – Plaid Cymru's Alternative Budget*, 11 April 2002.
42. Vaclav Havel, *Summer Meditations* (London: Faber & Faber, 1992), p. 44.
43. Laura McAllister, *Plaid Cymru*, p. 47.
44. D.J. and Noelle Davies, *Wales: The Land of Our Children* (Caernarfon: Swyddfa'r Blaid, 1942), p. 3.
45. Michael Freeden, *Ideologies and Political Theory*, p. 168.
46. D.J. and Noelle Davies, *Wales: The Land of Our Children*, 1942, p. 3.
47. Ibid.
48. Dai Lloyd, 'Spreading the wealth', *Swansea West News*, Spring, 2003, p. 2.
49. Elin Jones, 'More jobs for rural Wales', press release, 29 November 2001.
50. John Ball, interview, 16 March 1999.
51. Phil Williams, *The Psychology of Distance*, p. 8.
52. Phil Williams, interview, 25 September 2001.
53. Michael Freeden, *Ideologies and Political Theory*, p. 533.
54. Plaid Cymru, *Working for the New Wales* (Cardiff: Plaid Cymru, 1999), p. 29.
55. D.J. and Noelle Davies, *Wales: The Land of Our Children*, p. 25.
56. Ibid., p. 28.
57. Plaid Cymru, *Summer School and Conference*, 1959, Llangefni.
58. Laura McAllister, *Plaid Cymru*, p. 48.
59. Phil Williams, interview, 25 September 2001.

60. Alison Griffiths, 'Ethnography and popular memory: postmodern configurations of Welsh identities', *Continuum: The Australian Journal of Media and Culture*, vol. 7, no. 2, 1994, p. 1.
61. Michael Freeden, *Ideologies and Political Theory*, p. 63.
62. Rhodri Glyn Thomas, interview, 14 May 2001.
63. Ibid.
64. Ibid.
65. Phil Williams, interview, 25 September 2001.
66. Plaid Cymru, *How Much Policy?*, 1967, p. 1.
67. Plaid Cymru, *Annual Conference*, 1968.
68. Laura McAllister, *Plaid Cymru*, p. 78.
69. Plaid Cymru: www.plaidcymru.org.uk.
70. Dave Adamson, *Class, Ideology and the Nation*, p. 135.
71. Plaid Cymru, *Summer School and Conference*, 1959, Llangefni, p. 17.
72. Ibid., p. 73.
73. Ibid., p. 87.
74. J.E. Daniel, *Welsh Nationalism: What it Stands For*, p. 61.
75. Plaid Cymru, *The New Wales* (Caernarfon: Swyddfa'r Blaid, 1939), p. 14.
76. Wynne Samuel, *Transference Must Stop* (Caernarfon: Gwenlyn Evans 1943), p. 11.
77. Charlotte Davies, *Welsh Nationalism in the Twentieth Century* (Connecticut: Praeger, 1989), p. 76.
78. Michael Freeden, *Ideology*, p. 56.
79. Michael Freeden, *Ideologies and Political Theory*, p. 248.
80. Geraint H. Jenkins, 'Terminal decline: the Welsh language in the twentieth century', *North American Journal of Welsh Studies*, vol. 1, no. 2, 2001, p. 63.
81. Jane Aaron, 'Women in search of a Welsh identity', *Hard Times*, vol. 63, Summer 1998, p. 14.
82. Laura McAllister, 'The perils of community as a construct for the political ideology of Welsh nationalism', *Government and Opposition*, vol. 33, 1998, p. 501.
83. Ibid., p. 500.
84. Gwynfor Evans, *They Cry Wolf: Totalitarianism in Wales and the Way Out*, (Caernarfon: Nationalist Offices, 1944), p. 5.
85. Ibid., p. 5.
86. Michael Freeden, 'Confronting the chimera of a "post-ideological" era', paper presented at ECPR Joint Sessions of Workshops, Uppsala University, April 2004, p. 8.
87. Laura McAllister, *Plaid Cymru*, p. 44.
88. Ibid., p. 45.
89. Ibid., p. 48.
90. Plaid Cymru, *Annual Conference*, 1970, p. 31.
91. Plaid Cymru: www.plaidcymru.org.uk.
92. Dafydd Wigley, speech at Theatr Gwynedd, Bangor, 18 January 1999.
93. Ibid.
94. Plaid Cymru, *The Peaceful Road to Self-Government* (Cardiff: Plaid Cymru, 1969), p. 19.
95. Plaid Cymru, *The New Wales* (Cardiff: Plaid Cymru, 1939), p. 12.
96. Ibid.
97. Jill Evans, *Manifesto for the election of President of Plaid Cymru*, 2000.

98. Ibid., p. 3.
99. Ibid.
100. Darren Price, interview, 11 June 2002.
101. Will Kymlicka, *Multicultural Citizenship: A Liberal Theory of Minority Rights* (Oxford: Oxford University Press, 1996).
102. Freeden, *Ideologies and Political Theory*, p. 39.
103. Ibid., p. 107.
104. Plaid Cymru: www.plaidcymru.org.uk.
105. Michael Freeden, *Ideologies and Political Theory*, p. 108.
106. Colin Williams, *Revival of the Welsh Language: Economy, Planning and Territory*, Plaid Cymru discussion paper, 2003.
107. Ibid.
108. Geraint H. Jenkins, 'Terminal decline: the Welsh language in the twentieth century', *North American Journal of Welsh Studies*, vol. 1, no. 2, 2001, p. 61.
109. Carwyn Fowler and Rhys Jones, *Locating and Scaling the Welsh Nation*, p. 6.
110. Plaid Cymru, *The New Wales: Synopsis of the Policy of the Welsh Nationalist Party*, p. 6.
111. Colin Williams, *Revival of the Welsh Language*, p. 19.
112. Dafydd Iwan, 'Plaid Cymru announces new vice president', press release, 10 April 2002.
113. Dafydd Wigley, speech at Theatr Gwynedd, Bangor, 18 January 1999.
114. Plaid Cymru, *Annual Report 1967/68*, p. 5.
115. Rhodri Glyn Thomas, interview, 14 May 2001.
116. D. Hywel Davies, *The Welsh Nationalist Party 1925–1945*, p. 180.
117. Ibid., p. 183.
118. Eurig Wyn, 'MEP's Kurdish pledge', press release, 8 February 2002.
119. Michael Freeden, *Ideologies and Political Theory*, p. 65.
120. Cynog Dafis, *The Presidency of Ieuan Wyn Jones*, tribancoch.com, 20 December 2002.
121. Helen Mary Jones, *Plaid Cymru in Opposition*, tribancoch.com, 21 December 2002.
122. Rhodri Glyn Thomas, interview, 14 May 2001.
123. Michael Freeden, *Ideologies and Political Theory*, p. 390.
124. Plaid Cymru, *Working for the New Wales*, p. 4.
125. J.E. Daniel, *Welsh Nationalism: What it Stands For*, p. 60.
126. Ibid., p. 21.
127. Michael Hechter, *Internal Colonialism: The Celtic Fringe in British National Development, 1536–1966* (Berkely: University of California Press, 1975).
128. Charlotte Davies, *Welsh Nationalism in the Twentieth Century*, Chapter 4.
129. Michael Freeden, *Ideologies and Political Theory*, p. 420.
130. Ibid., p. 425.

VII

IDEOLOGICAL DEBATES WITHIN
PLAID CYMRU

Introduction

It is important to recognise that although all ideologies and ideological concepts are, initially at least, the products of the thoughts of individuals, and Plaid Cymru's ideology is no different in this respect, there is evidence that groups promoting varying ideological positions have been operating within Plaid Cymru since its inception. Attention, therefore, will be drawn to one specific example of this ideological factionalism within Plaid Cymru. This example is proffered primarily because it occurred at a time of widespread ideological debate across British politics and because the outcome of this ideological dialectic within Plaid Cymru opened the pathway to the configuration of the party's contemporary thought-practices.

This collective ideological confrontation within Plaid Cymru took place in the early 1980s: an era in which the New Right ideology, embraced in Britain by leading Conservative thinkers and condensed in the term 'Thatcherism', was approaching its apex and the Labour Party was involved in an orientation to the left. Both of these external occurrences undoubtedly had an influence on the thought-practices of Plaid Cymru's membership. As, over the past two decades or so, Thatcherism and any sense of a socialist essence within the Labour Party have both faded, Plaid Cymru's construction, or re-evaluation, of its ideology at that time may actually prove to be the most enduring of these epochal ideological turns: even though, in terms of popular awareness and public salutation, it was not particularly far-reaching. Nevertheless, this was a crucial period for Plaid Cymru's thought-practices, the after-effects of which are still resonating today.

The rationale for including this assessment is an attempt to show how the ideological dialectic within a party can surface at certain periods within that party's history. Also, the reasoning behind focusing on this at a late stage in the exploration is that, having covered the ideologies and ideological concepts evident within Plaid Cymru's thought-practices, this ideological dispute should now prove to be more amenable to interpretation and understanding.

'Hydro and the National Left': Plaid Cymru's Key Factional Ideological Battle

The election of the Conservative Party in the 1979 General Election almost certainly had a massive effect on how Plaid Cymru saw itself as a party of opposition – not just to the party's customary foe in Wales, the Labour Party, but also to the perceived Englishness of a Conservative government that had very little sympathy with what it believed to be the atavistic principles and policies that were being put forward at that time by Plaid Cymru. Hence, Plaid Cymru found itself in the situation that, if the party was to propel itself forward as a realistic challenger to the policies and the perspectives held by both the Labour Party and the Conservative Party, a redefinition of its political position was deemed necessary. This need for a repositioning and redefinition was heightened by the Welsh public's rejection of the Labour Party's proposals for political devolution in 1979 – a defeat that was undeniably felt harder amongst the membership of Plaid Cymru than it was within the rank and file of the Labour Party who had actually instigated the proposals in the first place.

Around the time of these events, two diametrically opposed factions emerged within Plaid Cymru. One, the Hydro group, focused on what they perceived to be the traditional party strengths, such as its commitment to rurbanisation and the safeguarding of the Welsh language. The other faction, who became known as the National Left, sought to formulate an agenda that would build on the Welsh social and political tradition of radicalism in order to challenge the New Right-inspired Thatcherite ideology. These progressives within the National Left thus intended to situate Plaid Cymru, once and for all, as a socialist political party. Once again, comparisons could be made at this point to the ideological debates taking place within the SNP in Scotland in the 1980s and early 1990s over whether to plump for a fast-moving and dynamic campaign to secure independence or whether a steadier, piecemeal approach would be the most realistic option.[1]

Hydro, Ideology and Dogma

The Hydro group was set up at the 1982 Llandudno conference.[2] Its name derives from a local hotel where some delegates were staying.

One of Hydro's chief instigators, Keith Bush, has contended that the objective of Hydro was to 're-establish self-government for Wales, unqualified by ideological dogma, as the main aim of Plaid Cymru.'[3] Hydro's argument on this point was that 'Plaid's nationalism required no qualifying or explanatory terms.'[4] Plaid Cymru's nationalism, as far as advocates of the Hydro position were concerned, was incontestable. It was, they maintained, the established form of nationalism that was identifiable through association with Plaid Cymru.

Two points that relate to ongoing discussions within this examination are of note in these statements. First, the idea that re-establishing self-government for Wales – an act that would demand enormous change to the social and political landscape in Wales – is somehow non-ideological and can be achieved through a few minor technical adjustments here and there, as opposed to recourse to the thought-practices of the party, is staggering. This approach does, nevertheless, present a picture of how the nature of ideology is misunderstood not only by people within Plaid Cymru, it has to be said, but also by the public at large. Furthermore, it also brings to light the attitude of conservatives – conservative traditionalists in this instance – to ideology. Both small and large 'c' conservatives view their political beliefs as being innate dispositions that are not constructed and do not subsist on dogmatic positions. Hydro's view of self-government for Wales as somehow being the natural, evolutionary course down which Welsh society is charted displays all of these conservative tendencies. Similarly, Hydro's disdain for the variety of socialism that it saw operating within Plaid Cymru would also fit into this anti-dogmatic position, even though its refusal to enter into a dialectic process with those advocating socialism amounted to a dogmatic position in itself. Erroneously, the Hydro group argued for an ideological stasis when what it really wanted, if it genuinely sought a substantial transference of power to enable Wales to have self-government, was a paradigmatic shift.

The National Left: Plaid Cymru's Socialist Front

The National Left was formed two years before Hydro at Plaid Cymru's 1980 Porthcawl conference. The founders of the National Left included committed socialists and radical thinkers such as Robin Reeves, Phil Cooke, Janet Davies and Dafydd Elis-Thomas.[5] The National Left's remit was that it should be 'a broad-based movement representing all strands of left opinion in Wales, including members of other parties, and those without party affiliation.'[6] Although, being a scion of the party, it was inevitably dominated by Plaid Cymru activists, the National Left's ambitious intention was to build a socialist front on an all-Wales level so that a future self-governing Wales could introduce a full raft of socialist policies. At its heart was the philosophy of the New Left, an inspiration for Elis-Thomas and other students of the 1960s.

The National Left's stance on socialism tied in to Plaid Cymru's 1981 conference decision to adopt decentralist socialism, albeit after a nine-hour debate on the findings of the Commission of Inquiry. This internal Commission of Inquiry had looked in some considerable detail at the party's ideology. However, Phil Williams, who himself wrote a minority report at the time, raised some serious questions about the 'practicality of the decentralist socialism advocated in the main report.'[7] Williams later remarked that the commitment to decentralist socialism was acceptable to him but 'I was aware that no deep thought had gone into it.'[8] In a sense, herein lies Plaid Cymru's ideological dilemma. A concept, decentralist socialism, was recommended by the Commission of Inquiry, accepted by conference and welcomed by the socialist-minded National Left without, it appeared, any great understanding of what the actual concept entails. Hence, it is fair to assert that decentralist socialism had not been decontested within Plaid Cymru's ideological arena.

Furthermore, it could be argued that the entire internecine ideological battle of the early 1980s between Hydro and the National Left was conducted on a level in which the thought-practices of the two factions were either in denial, in the case of Hydro, or, in the instance of the National Left, suffering from a distinct lack of clarity, with concepts that they sought to introduce, such as decentralist socialism and, arguably, the ideology of socialism itself, remaining decontested within Plaid Cymru's ideational process. Yet the perceived understanding of the use of the terminology of decentralist socialism, self-government, and even nationalism, proved sufficient for advocates of these ideological concepts and ideologies to insert them into their general political discourse. The development of the National Left, for instance, can thus be seen through the growth in personal and group statements and rhetoric that included references to decentralist socialism, community socialism and the coalescence of socialist and nationalist elements within the party.

Tracing the ideological line adopted by the party, since this period of factionalism in the 1980s, it would be accurate to describe the National Left as having had far more of an impact on the party's thought-practices and policy direction than Hydro managed. Moreover, the legacy of the National Left could also be seen in the articles conveying socialist and republican themes that were available on the Plaid Cymru-supporting left-wing website tribancoch.com, whose former editor was Rhondda activist and erstwhile Plaid Cymru chairman, Syd Morgan, one of the National Left's founder members. The traditionalism represented by Hydro, on the other hand, though not entirely expunged, is very much a perimeter position within the party today.

Plaid Cymru's Ideological Modifications

The importance of highlighting this collective ideological struggle is to ensure that it is appreciated that there is an internal dialectic within Plaid Cymru that is not merely the product of lone voices – those lone voices being, more often than not, people who hold, or have held, strategic positions within the party. Through the creation of ideological factions at sporadic intervals throughout the party's history, Plaid Cymru has reasserted the openness of its internal space for discussion and it has managed, simultaneously, to disparage any sceptics who may have sought to portray the ideological and policy pronouncements of the party as top-down in their nature. As Rhodri Glyn Thomas observed, 'it has always been part of the party's philosophy that there are groups who try to move the agenda on.'[9] As simplistic as this statement may appear to be, it does acknowledge that political discourse within Plaid Cymru is fluidic and that the party's internal reasoning has not been left to simply stagnate.

One contemporary example of this agenda setting can be seen with the establishment of a pressure group entitled Dewis (Choice) set up by Plaid Cymru's former leader, Dafydd Wigley, and the party's former policy director, Cynog Dafis. Dewis arrived in the wake of the party's disappointing showing at the 2005 British General Election, and the group has added to the evolving dialectic within Plaid Cymru. Dewis wanted to see Plaid Cymru adopting a position of principled pragmatism[10] so that the party can explore ways in which to end Labour's political hegemony in Wales through the establishment of some form of political coalition or alliance: something that came about, to an extent, in 2007 with the coalition in Cardiff Bay, though this outcome was somewhat different from that envisaged by the founders of Dewis. Cynog Dafis, at the time, argued that Plaid Cymru must consider 'a real historic compromise in which Plaid, the Liberal Democrats and Welsh Conservatives, along with others such as Forward Wales, work together to transform Welsh politics.'[11] This bold initiative, however, did not have universal support throughout the party as it called for talks with the Conservative Party. For a party espousing socialist principles and policies to consider any form of alliance with an avowedly anti-socialist party, such as the Conservatives, appears impractical. Interestingly, Dafydd Iwan, Plaid Cymru's president at that time, immediately described the proposals put forward by Dewis as a 'huge political mistake,'[12] and the message advanced by Dewis did not appear to have impacted on party thinking to any great extent until, that is, Plaid Cymru was forced into considering coalition politics after the 2007 Assembly Election. Of overarching interest to this particular examination, however, is the fact that Plaid Cymru's internal ideological debates continue apace. This is important because it further exemplifies the aforementioned fluidic nature of the party's thought-practices.

Despite the occasional arrival of pressure groups which attempt to promote certain ideological or policy positions, what is evident for all to see is that, as with most other political parties, Plaid Cymru has a leadership tradition that has carved its own niche on the ideology of the party. However, as it has evolved into a vibrant democratic forum, Plaid Cymru has produced through its ranks people who have challenged the prevailing orthodoxies of the party. Thus, as a consequence, some intriguing ideological directions have been unveiled. The fact that the party of 2010 is a completely transformed political animal and a markedly, though not entirely, different ideological force from that which first met at Pwllheli in 1925 proves that most of the ideological shifts that have occurred within the party have not been parentheses but have had a lasting effect.

Also, the party's thought-practices in its early and modern modes emphasise these shifts and show the maturing of the party on a variety of levels. In terms of straightforward ideological taxonomy, early Plaid Cymru symbolised a romantic nationalist vision of a Wales that has long disappeared, and in some instances, like all nationalisms, it celebrated a Wales that never existed. In some of its political dealings, during a time of major social, economic and political upheavals, it displayed a pathetic naivety. Eventually, within the general process of introspection that happens in all political parties, the relinquishing of the Plaid Cymru leadership by Saunders Lewis in 1939 allowed a recalculation of the party's objectives and its direction to occur.

It was during this period of recalculation that modern Plaid Cymru began to take shape. The party, after much contemplation, tightened its political image – both inwardly and outwardly – during the years of the post-war consensus and, over time, Plaid Cymru began to drift leftward as the realisation that the welfarist settlement devised by the 1945 Labour government did not turn out to be the panacea that many on the left in Wales envisaged. In conspicuous ideological terms, as noted earlier, matters came to a head with the battle for the soul and direction of the party that occurred around the early to mid 1980s.

When considering the possible longevity of modern Plaid Cymru, contemporary Plaid Cymru – certainly that is the party that has come through the devolutionary process and is now, through its position within the Welsh Assembly Government, very much centre-stage in Welsh politics – could be said to be in the last stages of modernity. This is because further ideological shifts may be required if the party is to achieve its *raison d'être* and attain a form of autonomous rule that would prioritise the safeguarding and promotion of all things Welsh. What is clear, however, is that the thought-practices of Plaid Cymru have not stagnated and are thus bound to create fresh avenues down which the party will inevitably travel in the years ahead.

Notes

1. Jonathan Hearn, *Claiming Scotland: National Identity and Liberal Culture* (Edinburgh: Polygon, 2000), pp. 53–56.
2. Laura McAllister, *Plaid Cymru: The Emergence of a Political Party* (Seren: Bridgend, 2001), p. 173.
3. Ibid.
4. Ibid.
5. Ibid., p. 175.
6. Ibid., p.174.
7. Charlotte Davies, *Welsh Nationalism in the Twentieth Century* (Connecticut: Praeger, 1989), p. 79.
8. Phil Williams, interview, 25 September 2001.
9. Rhodri Glyn Thomas, interview, 14 May 2001.
10. Cynog Dafis, 'Wales and Plaid Cymru face clear choices', *Western Mail*, 21 May 2005, p. 18.
11. Ibid.
12. Dafydd Iwan, *BBC Wales Today*, 16 May 2005.

VIII

CONCLUSION: A NEW IDEOLOGICAL FRAMEWORK

Constructing an Ideological Model for Plaid Cymru

Having assessed the concepts and ideologies existing within Plaid Cymru's morphology, a picture emerges of what exactly the party's ideological make-up is. With this in mind, a model of Plaid Cymru's ideology can be constructed in order for a new definition of the party's ideology to be enunciated. Hopefully, this innovative model could be used by people engaged in research into the thought-practices, or the public persona, of Plaid Cymru in order to further the debate regarding, and the subsequent understanding of, the ideational configuration of the party. The taxonomy for the model will be along Michael Freeden's classification of core, peripheral and adjacent concepts. It is worth recalling here how Freeden saw these concepts operating within a political party's morphology. As he declared, core concepts are 'ineliminable key concepts'[1] that provide 'a minimum kit'[2] without which any particular ideology would cease to exist. Hence, Plaid Cymru must have some core ideological concepts in order to have a considerable, and vital, degree of substance to its thought-practices.

Peripheral concepts, on the other hand, are 'situated on the perimeter of an ideology.'[3] These peripheral concepts bolster the core concepts without being an essential part of an ideology's corpus. For this reason, they tend to have a more fluidic persona than core concepts. Plaid Cymru requires a certain number of peripheral concepts to stimulate the ideational process. Ideological concepts that may at one time have been core concepts, such as, for instance, nationalisation or universal state welfare in the case of the Labour Party, may now be registered as peripheral concepts or even, in the former case, adjacent concepts. This could be down to the fact that peripheral concepts such as universal state welfare still generate ideas that add to the morphology of the ideology of which they are constituents, but they are no longer perceived to be or, alternatively, never have been perceived as being imperative core components of the conceptual framework. Hence, using examples such as the above, it is possible to relate how the fluidic nature of ideological concepts is personified through the ebbing and flowing of concepts, over space and time, between the core, peripheral and adjacent positions.

Further to the two aforementioned categories of concepts, adjacent concepts are also part of an ideology's make-up. Adjacent concepts act to restrict the core's 'capacity for multiple interpretations.'[4] Therefore, if democracy were estimated to be an adjacent concept within the ideology of environmentalism, for example, then environmentalism's capacity to adopt anti-democratic tendencies or anti-democratic concepts, such as imprisonment without trial or denial of basic human rights, would be eliminated or, at the very minimum, severely restricted. Further to this, when applied to political parties, such as Plaid Cymru, adjacent concepts should enable party members to embrace ideological concepts, or political themes, that may not necessarily be part of the party's main ideological corpus – in terms of its core and peripheral concepts – but which, nevertheless, do not in any shape or form impinge in a negative sense upon the spirit or general mood of the party's ideological perspective. Indeed, adjacent concepts should always complement, and add extra dimensions to, a political party's thought-practices.

After these ideological concepts are presented, in the upcoming model, they will then be collated in order to judge whether they fit into a pattern associated with any standard political ideology, or whether, as will probably be the case, Plaid Cymru's ideology is a distinctive set of thought-practices that does not sit comfortably under any one recognisable ideological banner. This examination will attempt to resist placing the exact same concepts that have appeared in the previous chapters into this original model, as the purpose of constructing this new paradigm is to offer innovative approaches to the study of Plaid Cymru's ideology. Although this model will undoubtedly fall short of covering every minute aspect of the party's ideology, it should, by re-classifying some concepts and forging some fresh ones, at least enable a more accurate description of the actual content of the ideological concepts that make up the thought-practices of Plaid Cymru to emerge. However, a word of caution must be noted at this juncture as some overlap in description, and a certain degree of similarity of content to that previously exhibited, is almost inevitable. Nevertheless, in attempting to proffer original thoughts, this examination will try to keep any repetition to an absolute minimum.

A New Model of Core Concepts

To commence, therefore, Plaid Cymru's core concepts – remembering that these are the essential ideas at the heart of the party, and without which there would be not be a political entity known as Plaid Cymru – could be arranged as follows.

An Acknowledgement of, and Promotion of, Welsh Identity

This, debatably, is the sine qua non of Plaid Cymru's ideology. From the outset, in 1925, the party has been very specific in its commitment to preserve and enhance traditions and vernacular activities. These activities would include the promotion of not only the Welsh language but also the prolongation of corresponding Welsh customs such as the Eisteddfod, the Welsh poetic and folk traditions, and so forth. However, in acknowledging that there is a conspicuous thing that can be labelled Welsh identity, there is also a stress on the fact that the Welsh nation – the breeder and feeder of this Welsh identity – is no better or no worse than any other nation or group of people on earth. To this extent, therefore, Plaid Cymru does not in any way represent any ultra nationalistic or xenophobic line in which, invariably, preference is always given to one's own nation over and above any concern that may be expressed about the fate or condition of others. The acknowledgement of, and promotion of, Welsh identity is thus a non-imperialistic celebration of existing literature, culture, language and social traditions. Hence, it falls short of being a possible core concept of nationalism in that it does not emphasise 'its superiority over other national identities.'[5]

The Legitimacy and Centrality of the Nation

This is the proposition that the nation, in the eyes of Plaid Cymru, acts as the focal point towards which all political, social and cultural ideas gravitate. Likewise, it is the location from which political ideas, aims and objectives can be disseminated back into the public arena. Hence, it acts as a two-way magnet. The nation is also the unit from which socio-economic, as well as political, subsidiarity derives. Although it is the entity, or the centralised machinery, that is recognised as the nation that is the focus for this distributive network, this top-down course of action is not necessarily a nationalist assumption and it should not be taken as one. What it does denote, however, is a sense of identification with a geographical entity – Wales – within whose boundaries multifarious layers of power are acknowledged as existing. In the meantime, also, new layers and networks are constantly evolving, in a Foucauldian sense.[6] Hence, the legitimacy and centrality of the nation is not a centralising concept. It is, in point of fact, almost the complete opposite as it is interwoven with, and can be identified through, the adjacent concept of decentralisation. This is because Plaid Cymru maintains that a substantial degree of power – power that other ideologies seek to hold at the centre – should be imparted to these various decentred layers of authority.

Vicinity as the Primary Source of Solidarity

This entails a belief in localism as a positive rather than a negative concept. One of the ideas cherished within this concept is that local communities are organic, and part of their function is to absorb and to reflect the concerns of people in Wales. Thus, bonding and social transaction on a localised, face-to-face basis is encouraged within Plaid Cymru's thought-practices. This nurtures a sense of solidarity that Plaid Cymru contends is a viable one as it does not demand day-to-day allegiance to any abstract constructs; hence, the party maintains that the vicinity around you is there to be experienced as you go about your routine and, over time, a rapport and sense of togetherness is established, often subconsciously, with your neighbours.

This is the type of communal identification and allegiance that people such as Saunders Lewis and Gwynfor Evans believed actually energised the people of Wales within their locales. The solidarity that arises from the sense of calm assurance that people can discover in their local areas feeds into a lot of Plaid Cymru's rhetoric about communityism. However, where vicinity may differ from communityism, and these are important spatial and philosophical points, is that individuals can experience this form of localised harmonisation without any of the commitment attached to forging strong community links. This belief in vicinity as the primary source of solidarity could therefore be seen as thin communityism, and it may find backing from more liberally inclined Plaid Cymru members who are attracted by libertarian values and who, while still accepting the fact that human beings operate in a social environment, may wish to take a concept such as decentralisation down to its lowest possible level. This examination would conclude, therefore, that vicinity as the primary source of solidarity presents an avenue for those seeking to maximise personal freedom whilst, simultaneously, offering a safety net in order for them to engage with, and possibly endorse, community values and actions. In a liberal sense, therefore, these chosen courses of action should be undertaken on a strictly voluntary as opposed to an obligatory basis.

Encouraging the Ubiquity of Spirituality

It is important to emphasise from the offset that this concept is not necessarily an adherence to any given religion or religious order. What it is, nonetheless, is a belief in a certain degree of decorum and tranquillity within society. It is fair to assert that spirituality has the advantage over any set religion, as it is able to locate itself within a predominantly secular polity without having to seek approval from any theocratic body; spirituality, as a concept of a non-religiously based party such as Plaid Cymru, would thus be used in a corporeal, rather than a metaphysical, setting. Furthermore, this advocating of spirituality does not alienate potential supporters of the party who already hold religious views. This is because this spirituality would not be seen as being antithetical to any other religious creed and it would not seek to implant any fundamental religious principles or practice. On an empirical basis, a historical precedent for this encouraging the ubiquity of spirituality is evidenced by the fact that it was from this general disposition of spirituality within Wales, plus the allied desire to attain a more self-possessed and serene existence, that Plaid Cymru's scepticism towards the dehumanisation of Welsh society – a dehumanisation process that the party maintains came about through industrialisation – stemmed. This ideological concept, therefore, has a genealogy within the party's thought-practices and, moreover, spirituality represents the party's engagement in an ongoing struggle against both dehumanisation, in its various guises, and the excessive devotion of some people within society to materialistic values.

The Endorsing of Negotiation over Disruption

Plaid Cymru's concerns for non-violence as a general rule of life, non-violent direct action as a campaigning tool and pacifism as a general philosophical position all fit into this category. These three components of the core concept of negotiation over disruption furnish Plaid Cymru with a complete counterbalance to any allegations or insinuations that the party is a belligerent political force – a belligerent force, its critics may imply, that, in its desire to defenestrate the British state system, would one day be tempted to take up arms and operate along the same parameters as some of the more aggressive elements of nationalist or liberationist parties visible elsewhere. Plaid Cymru has consistently rejected any suggestions that it would contemplate any such action. Moreover, Plaid Cymru's, and in particular Adam Price's, persistent voicing of its disapproval of the actions of the US and UK administrations in Afghanistan and Iraq, and the party's concern for the indigenous peoples displaced by conflict in these, and other, lands, further exemplifies that the endorsing of negotiation over disruption should be considered as a core concept within Plaid Cymru's thought-practices.

Without this concept at its core, remembering that Plaid Cymru is desirous of structural and constitutional change, the party could feasibly lay itself open to influences of a more extreme type; the type, indeed, that may seek to promote a more hard-line insurrectionary approach. Hence, negotiation over disruption, as it currently operates, anchors the party's thoughts and actions through the employment of a conciliatory methodology. This anchoring, and the party's general stance on violence of any kind, affirms this concept as a core component of Plaid Cymru's ideology. In addition, the endorsing of negotiation over disruption could also be portrayed as being an adjacent concept to the previous core concept of spirituality; although it must be acknowledged that the two are stand-alone concepts that are not necessarily mutually interwoven.

A New Model of Peripheral Concepts

This analysis will now move on to contend that Plaid Cymru's peripheral concepts – concepts that support and enliven a party's ideology without having the burden of being indispensable to the central workings, or the heartbeat, of an ideology – could be the following.

Holistic Assessment

Holistic assessment is an ability to look beyond Wales's borders for an appreciation of matters political, cultural and philosophical. Central to this concept, therefore, is the mode of thinking – evident within Plaid Cymru – which asserts that an internationalist agenda is an indispensable element for a modern political party that has to function in a rapidly evolving global society. Added to this, there is a conviction within Plaid Cymru that maintains that a credible attentiveness towards cross-border solidarity and equality – both internally, in a UK sense, and externally, in a global sense – is a vital instrument for attaining conceptions of how the good life can be achieved. All of this is then immersed in an environmentally friendly ethos.

Taken as a whole, this holistic assessment, when contrasted with narrow, insular nationalism, can be viewed as a 'binary opposite'.[7]

This is because, although some critics have claimed that Plaid Cymru's political standpoint is representative of the insularity typified by the narrow nationalist position, the truth of the matter is that the binary opposite of narrow nationalism, what this analysis has termed holistic assessment, is far more symbolic of the party's ideological outlook. Moreover, placing holistic assessment as a peripheral concept within Plaid Cymru's ideology also reinforces the link between this particular aspect of the party's thought-practices and Plaid Cymru's aforementioned commitment to harmony through non-violence. Subsequently, by adopting holistic assessment as a peripheral concept, this may culminate in pushing Plaid Cymru further away from its, misleading, categorisation as a nationalist political party.

Social Fairness

This peripheral concept is, prima facie, similar to social justice, although replacing fairness with justice is not strictly compatible as justice may be seen as too legalistic a term for this concept's philosophical basis. The concept of social fairness can be linked to the core concept of spirituality through the implication, within some of Plaid Cymru's rhetoric, that there is a sense – albeit a naïve one, it may be correct to say – that within Wales there is an inherent responsiveness to fair play that is juxtaposed with a high degree of mutual aid among people. The belief in being a good citizen – celebrated not only by Plaid Cymru members but by communitarians and Third Way advocates alike – could also enter the discussion at this point. Nevertheless, the unique Plaid Cymru concept of social fairness, in terms of a style of good citizenship and acknowledgement of fair play, can be viewed in the personal philosophies and convictions of party theoreticians such as Gwynfor Evans.

Further to the above, the peripheral concept of social fairness bolsters Plaid Cymru's core concepts of vicinity as solidarity and spirituality in the manner that it concludes that breaking down the causes of alienation within society will lead to the formation of enriched individuals and communities. Interestingly, Laura McAllister, remarking on Gwynfor Evans's thoughts in this ideational arena, argued that they owed a lot to guild socialism.[8] By eradicating alienation through the breeding and application of social fairness, Plaid Cymru may seek to contend that everybody would wish to help others, be it in their immediate vicinities or beyond. Yet again, the core concept of spirituality can be brought into play here as a belief in moral goodness, impartiality and integrity, on an individual and collective basis, would tie in with Plaid Cymru's credence that, given the right conditions, respect and fairness, like communities themselves, can evolve organically in a caring environment.

The Redistribution of Wealth

It may be misleading to assume that, within Plaid Cymru's ideology, the redistribution of wealth should be read as a strictly socialist concept. This is down to the fact that schemes to apportion wealth more evenly are not uncommon within non-right-wing political parties the world over. In Britain, for example, the centrist Liberal Democrats – not generally regarded as being a socialist organisation – have pursued various types of redistributive schemes since the party's formation in 1988. What an analysis of Plaid Cymru's particular interpretation of the concept of the redistribution of wealth could conclude, however, is that the party has made a number of commitments in its manifestos to raising the economic and social profile of the poorest in society through, for example, redistributive and egalitarian policies.[9] To this extent, the concept of the redistribution of wealth should be included as a peripheral concept in any list of Plaid Cymru's thought-practices. This is because it adds an important economic element to some of the more philosophical concepts, both core and peripheral.

Furthermore, contained within this peripheral concept, as Plaid Cymru would see it, is the acceptance that in any decent society the more affluent citizens of that society have a duty to help to ameliorate the living conditions experienced by the poorest citizens. However, Plaid Cymru would argue that this duty to organise redistributive services, and to adequately resource this distribution network, cannot remain the preserve of charities or philanthropists. Hence, once more, the moral and economic duty falls on the individual acting on an equal basis with others in his or her community. Thus, the concept of the redistribution of wealth, as interpreted within Plaid Cymru's ideology, is a commitment on both the individual and the community to bring to fruition practical economic cooperative action to ensure a fairer redistribution of resources, goods and services. This would all be underpinned by a philosophical position stemming from another peripheral concept, social fairness.

Freedom as a Frame of Mind

The peripheral concept of freedom as a frame of mind represents the inculcating of the idea that people in Wales, and indeed worldwide, should be at liberty to express their views and feelings and to act with the maximum amount of autonomy possible in any given scenario. A belief in freedom of thought and expression is seen as an imperative within this concept and the act of suppression – be it government inspired or emanating from another individual – is not to be regarded as an option. Indeed, any form of suppression is frowned upon not only because it is ethically wrong but also because freedom of thought and expression acts as a driver for the societal dialectic that is required if the entity that is Wales, with all its constituent parts, is to progress.

What is of interest in this concept is not just how it could sit with adjacent concepts such as democracy, liberty or even existentialism but how, through the discourse of freedom that runs throughout Plaid Cymru's thought-practices, the party has opened up fresh ideological avenues that other parties which have been labelled nationalist, such as the SNP in Scotland or the SDLP in the north of Ireland, do not appear to have explored. Here, it is appropriate to add that this could be seen as a criticism rather than a compliment, as it may be construed as being another version of romanticism that steers Plaid Cymru away on a different ideological course and, in so doing, further removes it from the more prosaic everyday political practice of the aforementioned parties. Whether true or not, it is probably reasonable to declare that this peripheral concept of freedom as a state of mind heads towards a libertarian position – though not in an unfettered Nozickean New Right sense[10] – but it stops short as cultural constraints and the formality of community succeed in keeping a check on any unbridled actions.

A New Model of Adjacent Concepts

In addition to the above, and recalling that adjacent concepts are concepts that can be adopted to support an ideology, and to offer different interpretations and angles for manoeuvring within that ideology, adjacent concepts that have a bearing on Plaid Cymru's core and peripheral concepts could be as follows.

Democracy

Plaid Cymru has always maintained a commitment to both a democratic system of government in Wales and the proliferation of democratic values throughout society at large. Plaid Cymru's affirmation that the party would not engage in undemocratic practices to achieve its stated aims is identified here by positioning democracy as an adjacent concept to the entire breadth of the party's core and peripheral concepts. As a party that seeks to change the social and political structure within Wales through support garnered through the ballot box, Plaid Cymru's embedding within the mainstream of democratic party politics within Britain was secured at the party's inception in 1925. Since then, no indication of undemocratic practice, or any conspicuous anti-democratic rhetoric, has been observed within party pronouncements or literature. Thus, although talk of democracy certainly does not dominate Plaid Cymru's thought-practices in any way, positing democracy as an adjacent concept is important to the party's morphology because 'the existence of concepts adjacent to the ideological core is essential to the formation of the ideology.'[11]

If democracy were not an adjacent concept for Plaid Cymru's thought-practices then it would disrupt the party's conception of its role in the Welsh, British and European political processes, as all of these are based on the principles of liberal democracy. Excluding democracy from any of the concepts that constitute Plaid Cymru's ideology would also reposition the party, and it would alter the channels through which the party's policies, which were designed to achieve autonomous rule, could pass. Whereas, under democracy, the party has to go through a conventional formal procedure, wherein it attempts to persuade the electorate to grant it a minimum winning margin, if it was to stand outside of the standard routes of democracy, and therefore not contest elections, it would inevitably operate in a more informal setting in which it would, in essence, become a political pressure group. Under these circumstances the methods employed by the party to secure its aims and objectives would undoubtedly be modified. Hence, the concept of democracy, though rarely mentioned or discussed by the party, is nevertheless vital to the ideology of Plaid Cymru, and to its image as a conformist party within a multilevel democratic political system.

Equality

Opposition to all forms of inequality can be registered as an adjacent concept to the peripheral concept of social justice, as seen in the previous chapter, and social fairness, as presented in this prototype. This is because, in familial, local, communal, national and international settings, the philosophical notion of equality pervades Plaid Cymru's thinking. Dispensing with the theoretical underpinning that the concept of equality brings could leave the party open to sexist, homophobic, racist or other non-egalitarian or chauvinistic tendencies. Although many of these biases could be countered by practical action, both at the policy-making and the grass-roots levels, the fact that commitments to the creation of an equitable Welsh, and global, society are embedded within the party's ideology enables the party to refute criticisms and accusations that may come its way. Hence, it is important to observe the concept of equality in operation on an everyday basis as an adjacent concept within the thought-practices of Plaid Cymru.

Indigenous Entrepreneurialism

Indigenous entrepreneurialism should be viewed as an adjacent concept to the concepts of communityism, decentralisation and vicinity as the primary source of solidarity. Indigenous entrepreneurialism represents both the spirit and the practicality of enticing home-grown talent in the cultural, social, political and, above all else, economic fields. This adjacent concept has evolved gradually over the course of the party's history. For example, whereas early Plaid Cymru sought to foster localised skills and community-based crafts, modern, and certainly contemporary, Plaid Cymru has chosen to encourage the development of indigenous small and medium-sized enterprises in order for them to supply, first and foremost, the Welsh market, but then to expand their range within Europe and beyond.

In a practical and philosophical sense, some within Plaid Cymru may have been tempted to maintain that inducing indigenous talent and entrepreneurial skills would ensure that the culture and heritage of Wales – the country's innateness – seeps through. As this occurs, any unnecessarily extraneous or ill-fitting ideas, such as industrialisa-tion if Saunders Lewis's line of reasoning were to be highlighted, could be rejected as being contrary to more conducive and inherent Welsh practices. Indigenous entrepreneurialism, therefore, is open to several interpretations and may be visible in several guises. Nonetheless, it should not be interpreted as one of Plaid Cymru's ideological drivers, its role as an adjacent concept being one of offering space and ideas that other core and peripheral concepts can then borrow from in order to further develop and enhance the clarity of Plaid Cymru's ideology.

Attaching Labels to Plaid Cymru: More Socialist than Nationalist?

Arguably the key finding or recommendation to be extrapolated from this exploration is that, if it is necessary to classify Plaid Cymru's thought-practices in terms of the existing and standardised politi-cal ideologies, then it would be far more accurate to describe Plaid Cymru's ideology as being akin to socialist ideology than it would be to match the party to a nationalist ideological standpoint. Whereas this may cause dismay among some party traditionalists, and it would cause confusion among observers of both ideologies and the Welsh political scene, for Plaid Cymru this would be more beneficial in practical terms, as socialism is a full ideology that is comprehensive in its ideational scope. Nationalism is not a full ideology in that its core and peripheral concepts do not furnish it with the complete range of viewpoints and opportunities for developing policies that full ideologies require. As this analysis would contend that Plaid Cymru's ideology is also not a full ideology, in the sense that, over time, the party's political pronounce-ments and manifestos have had to broaden the range of policies and ideological concepts that they have featured – borrowing unashamedly from other parties and ideologies on occasions – it may be useful if the party added further components of socialism in order to augment its existing thought-practices. This would then make Plaid Cymru a party with a clear and precise socialist ideology.

If some form of synthesis was to be concocted between Plaid Cymru's current thought-practices and socialist thought-practices – ideological positions that are partly overlapping but which remain suf-ficiently diverse enough to stand alone – then a type of spatial socialist patriotism could well be the resulting ideology; indeed, this may not be too far removed from the stated opinion of Adam Price, who cites Marx as a major influence and who envisages a decentralised libertarian socialism as the way ahead for Plaid Cymru and Wales.[12]

However, whatever shape the party's ideology takes in the years ahead, Plaid Cymru's thought-practices will remain unique – as, it could be argued, all ideologies are anyway – and the party's ideology may well continue to defy conventional classification. Plaid Cymru's ideology, like all ideologies that are not full, is a palimpsest. This means that, rather than being set in stone, it is continuously evolv-ing and expanding, and it is overwritten by each new generation of politicians and theoreticians. Although some people within the party may not be too happy with this interpretation, it should be viewed in a positive light. This is because the present morphology of Plaid Cymru's thought-practices allows scope for the type of ideational development that full ideologies tend to stifle.

This examination started out to analyse whether Plaid Cymru's ideology could be equated to nationalism, as Plaid Cymru is invariably regarded as a party that exudes nationalist thought and nationalistic intentions. The conclusion arrived at is that, rather than just applying the simplistic, and inaccurate, label of nationalism to Plaid Cymru's ideol-ogy, the actual thought-practices of the party, certainly at this present moment in time, could in fact be the spatial socialist patriotism that was cited earlier. Whether or not this is acceptable to party members, Plaid Cymru's ideology is undoubtedly unclassifiable in conventional terms. However, one thing that is certain, and one thing that this examination has hopefully revealed, is that the party's ideology cannot simply be labelled as nationalist. Whatever descriptive terms are used to sum up Plaid Cymru's thought-practices, Plaid Cymru is not a nationalist party, in its purest sense, as it is not a conduit for, and breeder of, nationalist ideology alone.

Notes

1. Michael Freeden, *Ideology: A Very Short Introduction* (Oxford: Oxford University Press, 2003), p. 61.
2. Ibid., p. 62.
3. Ibid.
4. Ibid., p. 63.
5. Ibid., p. 98.
6. Eric Matthews, *Twentieth Century French Philosophy* (Oxford: Oxford University Press, 1996), p. 149.
7. Jim Powell, *Derrida for Beginners* (London: Writers and Readers Limited, 1997), p. 23.
8. Laura McAllister, 'The perils of community as a construct for the political ideology of Welsh nationalism', *Government and Opposition*, vol. 33, no. 4, 1998, p. 505.
9. See, for example, Plaid Cymru, *Manifesto 1999*, and Plaid Cymru, *Manifesto 2001*.
10. Robert Nozick, *Anarchy, State, and Utopia* (Oxford: Blackwell Publishers, 1974).
11. Michael Freeden, *Ideologies and Political Theory* (Oxford: Clarendon Press, 1996), pp. 77–78.
12. Adam Price, 'The passion of price', *Western Mail*, 13 September 2004, p. 15.

BIBLIOGRAPHY

Plaid Cymru: Party Documents

A Billion Ways to Build a New Wales – Plaid Cymru's Alternative Budget, 11 April 2002.

A Future for Wales: Plaid Cymru Election Manifesto, 1979.

A Teaching Profession for Wales, A Plaid Cymru – Party of Wales discussion paper, 2003.

A Voice for Wales in Europe, 1984.

Agenda Wales: Peace, Jobs and Justice: General Election Manifesto, 1983.

Annual Conference, Aberystwyth, 1968.

Annual Conference, Aberystwyth, 1970.

Annual Report 1967/8.

Breton Nationalism, 1946.

'Buffer zone needed to protect homes and schools', press release, 10 May 2005.

'Dafydd Iwan: Plaid Cymru announces new vice president', press release, 10 April 2002.

Fighting Hard for Communities: A Manifesto for the Local Government Election, 2004.

Fighting Hard for Wales: A Manifesto for the European Parliament Election, 2004.

Free Wales: Plaid Cymru Policy, 1959.

Gweithio dros Gymru: Action for Wales, 1966

Health and Health Services for Wales, A Plaid Cymru – Party of Wales discussion paper, 2003.

How Much Policy?, 1967.

Make a Difference – National Assembly Manifesto, 2007.

Manifesto 2001.

Manifesto 2003 – Plaid Cymru: The Party of Wales, 2003.

'MEP launches scathing attack on "duplicitous Labour"', press release, 17 September 2005.

Power for Wales: General Election Manifesto, November 1974.

Protest against the Establishment of a Bombing School at Porth Neigwl, Lleyn Peninsula, 1936.

Reviving the Welsh Language: Policy for Wales, 2003–2007, 2003.

South West Wales Election Package, April 2006.

Summer School and Conference, Dolgellau, 1967.

Summer School and Conference, Llangefni, 1959.

Summer School and Conference, Pontarddulais, 1962.

Ten Points of Policy, 1934.

The New Wales: Synopsis of the Policy of the Welsh Nationalist Party, 1939.

The Peaceful Road to Self-Government, 1969.

The Principles of Nationalism, 1926.
The Wages of Servitude: Wales' Reward for Collaboration with the English Government, 1946.
Towards 2000: Plaid Cymru's Programme for Wales in Europe, 1994
Wales in Europe: A Community of Communities, 1989.
We Can Build a Better Wales: Westminster Election Manifesto, 2005.
Winning for Wales: General Election Programme, 1987.
Working for Wales: County Council Election Manifesto, 1985.
Working for the New Wales: The Manifesto of Plaid Cymru, 1999.

Plaid Cymru: Primary Literature and Resources

Anon., *Plan Electricity for Wales* (London: London Branch of the Welsh Nationalist Party, 1944).
Bowen Rees, Ioan, *The Welsh Political Tradition* (Cardiff: Plaid Cymru, 1961).
Collins, R.C., *Workers Control in Wales* (Caernarfon: Plaid Cymru, 1967).
Dafis, Cynog, 'Migration, identity and development', *Agenda* (Institute of Welsh Affairs), Summer 2004.
Dafis, Cynog, 'The presidency of Ieuan Wyn Jones', tribancoch.com, 20 December 2002.
Dafis, Cynog, 'The choice – inept Labour or bold Plaid', *The Welsh Nation*, September/October 2005, p. 3.
Dafis, Cynog, 'Wales and Plaid Cymru Face Clear Choices', *Western Mail*, 21 May 2005, p. 18.
Daniel, J.E., *Wales: Make or Break?* (Caernarfon: Welsh Nationalist Party, 1943).
Daniel, J.E., *Welsh Nationalism: What it Stands For* (London: Foyle's, 1937).
Davies, D.J., 'The insufficiency of cultural nationalism', *The Welsh Nationalist*, March 1932.
Davies, D.J., 'The national spirit in economics', *Y Ddraig Goch*, December 1930.
Davies, D.J., 'The way to real co-operation', *The Welsh Nationalist*, May 1932.
Davies, D.J., *Towards an Economic Democracy* (Cardiff: Plaid Cymru, 1949).
Davies, D.J., *Towards Welsh Freedom: 27 Articles* (Cardiff: Plaid Cymru, 1958).
Davies, D.J., and Davies, Noelle, *Can Wales Afford Self-Government?* (Caernarfon: Swyddfa'r Blaid, 1939).
Davies, D.J., and Davies, Noelle, *Wales: The Land of Our Children* (Caernarfon: National Office, 1942).
Davies, John, *The Green and the Red: Nationalism and Ideology in Twentieth Century Wales* (Aberystwyth: Adran Cyhoeddiadau Plaid Cymru, 1982).
Davies, Noelle, *Connolly of Ireland: Patriot and Socialist* (Caernarfon: Swyddfa'r Blaid, 1946).
Dixon, John, 'Let's accentuate the positive', *The Welsh Nation*, September/October, 2005, p. 4.

Dixon, John, 'We welcome new thinking', *The Welsh Nation*, September/ October 2005, p. 8.

Evans, Gwynfor, *End of Britishness* (Cardiff: Plaid Cymru, 1981).

Evans, Gwynfor, *For the Sake of Wales: The Memoirs of Gwynfor Evans* (Cardiff: Welsh Academic Press, 2001).

Evans, Gwynfor, *Nonviolent Nationalism* (New Malden: Fellowship of Reconciliation, 1973).

Evans, Gwynfor, *Plaid Cymru and Wales* (Llandybie: Llyfrau'r Dryw, 1950).

Evans, Gwynfor, *They Cry Wolf: Totalitarianism in Wales and the Way Out* (Caernarfon: Nationalist Offices, 1944).

Evans, Gwynfor, *Voice of Wales: Parliamentary Speeches (26 July 1966–8 December 1967)* (Cardiff: Plaid Cymru, 1968).

Evans, Jill, *Manifesto for the election of President of Plaid Cymru*, July 2000 (www.jill2000.co.uk/manifesto-e.html).

Evans, Jill, 'Turkey and the European Union', *Cambria*, January/February 2005, p. 17.

Islam, Mohammed-Saru, 'Welsh so vital for our nation's future', *The Welsh Nation*, November/December, 2005, p. 7.

Iwan, Dafydd, interview, *BBC Wales Today*, 16 May 2005.

Iwan, Dafydd, 'Who needs a Tory government when we have this lot?', *The Welsh Nation*, November/December, 2005, p. 2.

Jones, Elin, 'More jobs for rural Wales', press release, 29 November 2001.

Jones, Helen Mary, 'Plaid Cymru in opposition', tribancoch.com, 21 December 2002.

Jones, Ieuan Wyn, 'The actual gap between the richer and poorer parts of Wales is ever-widening', *Western Mail*, 16 November 2005, p. 7.

Jones, J.E., *The Welsh Nationalist Party Aims* (Caernarvon: Nationalist Party Offices, 1929).

Jones, J.E., *Wales and the War* (Caernarfon: Swyddfa'r Blaid, 1940).

Lewis, Roy, *Nation without a Government: Twenty Five Years of Misgovernment in Wales* (Cardiff: Plaid Cymru, 1950).

Lewis, Saunders, *Local Authorities and Welsh Industry* (Caernarfon: Swyddfa'r Blaid, 1934).

Lewis, Saunders, *To the Electors of the University of Wales* (Denbigh: Gee and Son, 1942).

Lewis, Saunders, *Wales after the War* (Caernarfon: Swyddfa'r Blaid, 1942).

Lewis, Saunders, and Daniel, J.E, *The Party of Wales* (Caernarfon: National Office, 1942).

Lewis, Saunders, and Valentine, Lewis, *Why We Burnt the Bombing School* (Caernarfon: Welsh Nationalist Party, 1936).

Lloyd, Dai, 'Spreading the wealth', *Swansea West News*, Spring 2003.

Matthews, Gwyn, *This is Plaid Cymru* (Cardiff: Plaid Cymru, 1969).

Nosworthy, Colin, 'Welsh mirror rules', tribancoch.com, 10 July 2003.

Packer, Anthony, 'Tough choices as Lithuania leads the way', *Welsh Nation*, Summer 2004, pp. 3–4.

Price, Adam, 'Democratic deficit', *Agenda*, Spring 2005, pp. 27–28.

Price, Adam, 'Global crisis: UK parties reject Plaid lead', *The Welsh Nation,* September/October 2005, pp. 1 and 4.

Samuel, Wynne, *Local Government and Wales* (Cardiff: Plaid Cymru, 1945).

Samuel, Wynne, *Must the Welsh Pits Close?: A Constructive Policy for the Welsh Coalfields* (Cardiff: Swyddfa'r Blaid, 1948).

Samuel, Wynne, *Save the Welsh Tinplate Area* (Cardiff: Plaid Cymru, 1941).

Samuel, Wynne, *The Political Betrayal of Wales* (Caernarfon: Swyddfa'r Blaid, 1943).

Samuel, Wynne, *Transference Must Stop* (Caernarfon: Gwenlyn Evans, 1943).

Titherington, Ian, 'Calling all trade unionists', *Swansea West News*, Spring 2003.

Wigley, Dafydd, *Democratic Wales in a United Europe* (Cardiff: Plaid Cymru, 1995).

Williams, Colin, *Revival of the Welsh Language: Economy, Planning and Territory*, Plaid Cymru discussion paper, 2003.

Williams, Dafydd, *The Story of Plaid Cymru: The Party of Wales* (Aberystwyth: Plaid Cymru, 1990).

Williams, Phil, *The Assembly Years 1999–2003* (Cardiff: Plaid Cymru – The Party of Wales, 2004).

Williams, Phil, *The Psychology of Distance* (Cardiff: Welsh Academic Press, 2003).

Williams, Phil, *Voice from the Valleys* (Bridgend: Seren, 1981).

Wood, Leanne, 'Social justice failures revealed in Plaid dossier', press release, 20 September 2005.

Wood, Leanne, 'US dire straits', tribancoch.com, 10 December 2003.

Wyn, Eurig, 'MEP's Kurdish pledge', press release, 8 February 2002.

Plaid Cymru: Secondary Literature

Anon., 'The passion of price', *Western Mail*, 13 September 2004.

Balsom, Denis, *The Nature and Distribution of Support for Plaid Cymru* (Glasgow: University of Strathclyde, Centre for the Study of Public Policy, 1979).

Christiansen, Thomas, *Plaid Cymru in the 1990s: Dilemmas and Ambiguities of Welsh Regional Nationalism* (Florence: European University Institute, 1995).

Combs, Thomas, 'The Party of Wales, Plaid Cymru: Populist Nationalism in Contemporary British Politics', PhD thesis, University of Connecticut, 1977.

Davies, D. Hywel, *The Welsh Nationalist Party 1925–1945: A Call to Nationhood* (Cardiff: University of Wales Press, 1983).

Ifans, Dafydd (ed.), *Annwyl Kate, Annwyl Saunders: Gohebiaeth 1923–1983* (Aberystwyth: Llyfrgell Genedlaethol Cymru, 1992).

Jones, Alun R., and Thomas, Gwyn (eds), *Presenting Saunders Lewis* (Cardiff: University of Wales Press, 1983).

Levy, Roger, 'Finding a place in the world-economy: party strategy and party

vote: the regionalisation of SNP and Plaid Cymru support, 1979–1992',
Political Geography, vol. 14, no. 3, 1995, pp. 295–308.

McAllister, Laura, 'Plaid Cymru' in John Osmond and J. Barry Jones (eds)
*Birth of Welsh Democracy: The First Term of the National Assembly for
Wales* (Cardiff: Institute of Welsh Affairs, 2003), pp. 322–338.

McAllister, Laura, 'Plaid Cymru's coming of age', *Contemporary Wales*, vol.
14, 2001, pp. 109–114.

McAllister, Laura, *Plaid Cymru: The Emergence of a Political Party* (Bridgend:
Seren, 2001).

McAllister, Laura, 'The perils of community as a construct for the political
ideology of Welsh nationalism', *Government and Opposition*, vol. 33, no. 4,
Autumn 1998, pp. 497–517.

Stephens, Meic, 'Gwynfor', *Cambria*, May–June 2005, pp. 14–26.

Turner, Caroline, 'Plaid Cymru and European Integration: An Empirical Study
of Multi-Level Governance', PhD thesis, University of Wales, Aberystwyth,
1998.

Works by Michael Freeden

'Confronting the chimera of a "post-ideological" age', paper prepared for the
ECPR Joint Sessions of Workshops, Uppsala, April 2004.

'Essential contestability and effective contestability' (editorial), *Journal of Political Ideologies*, vol. 9, no. 4, 2004, pp. 3–11.

'Fundaments and foundations in ideologies' (editorial), *Journal of Political
Ideologies*, vol. 10, no. 1, 2005, pp. 1–9.

Ideologies and Political Theory (Oxford: Clarendon Press, 1996).

'Ideological boundaries and ideological systems', *Journal of Political Ideologies*, vol. 8, no. 1, 2003, pp. 3–12.

'Ideologies as communal resources', *Journal of Political Ideologies*, vol. 4, no.
3, 1999, pp. 411–417.

Ideology: A Very Short Introduction (Oxford: Oxford University Press, 2003).

'Is nationalism a distinct ideology?', *Political Studies*, XLVI, 1998, pp. 748–
765.

Liberalism Divided: A Study in British Political Thought 1914–1939 (Oxford:
Clarendon Press, 1998).

'Practising ideology and ideological thought practices', *Political Studies*, vol.
48, 2000, pp. 302–322.

Reassessing Political Ideologies: The Durability of Dissent (London:
Routledge, 2001).

'Stormy relationships: ideologies and politics' (editorial), *Journal of Political
Ideologies*, vol. 3, no. 1, 1998, pp. 5–11.

'Understanding liberalism: between liberalism and philosophy', Manchester,
Political Studies Association conference paper, April 2001.

'What is special about ideologies?' (editorial), *Journal of Political Ideologies*,
vol. 6, no. 1, 2001, pp. 5–12.

'What should the "political" in political theory explore?', *Journal of Political Philosophy*, vol. 13, no. 2, June 2005, pp. 113–134.

Writings on Ideology and Political Philosophy

Adams, Ian, *The Logic of Political Belief* (Hemel Hempstead: Harvester Wheatsheaf, 1989).

Archibugi, Daniele, 'The language of democracy: vernacular or Esperanto? A comparison between the multiculturalist and cosmopolitan perspectives', *Political Studies*, vol. 53, no. 3, 2005, pp. 537–555.

Ball, Terence, 'From "core" to "sore" concepts: ideological innovation and conceptual change', *Journal of Political Ideologies*, vol. 4, no. 3, 1999, pp. 391–396.

Bevir, Mark, 'Socialism, civil society, and the state in modern Britain', *Socialist History*, vol. 20, 2001, pp. 1–18.

Binkley, Luther, *Conflict of Ideals: Changing Values in Western Society* (New York: Van Nostrand Reinhold, 1969).

Danaher, Geoff, Schirato, Tony, and Webb, Jen, *Understanding Foucault* (London: Sage, 2000).

De-Shalit, Avner, 'Political philosophy and empowering citizens', *Political Studies*, vol. 52, no. 4, 2004, pp. 802–818.

Drucker, Henry Matthew, *The Political Uses of Ideology* (London: Macmillan, 1974).

Enloe, Cynthia, *Bananas, Bases and Beaches: Making Feminist Sense of International Politics* (Berkeley: University of California Press, 2000).

Evans, Jocelyn, *Conceptualising the Left–Right Continuum as an Enduring Dimension of Political Competition* (Florence: European University Institute, 1996).

Firestone, Shulamith, *The Dialectic of Sex: The Case for Feminist Revolution* (London: Women's Press, 1979).

Fanon, Frantz, *The Wretched of the Earth* (New York: Grove Press, 1963).

Farr, James, 'Social capital: a conceptual history', *Political Theory*, vol. 32, no. 1, 2004, pp. 6–33.

Finlayson, Alan, 'Third Way theory and social policy: a rhetorical analysis of a political argument', University of Leeds, Political Studies Association conference paper, 7 April 2005.

Griffin, Roger, 'Between politics and the apoliteia: the New Right's strategy for conserving the fascist vision in the "interregnum"' (www.brookes.ac.uk/schools/humanities/Roger/apoliteia.part1.htm!).

Griffiths, Dylan, *Thatcherism and Territorial Politics* (Aldershot: Avebury, 1996).

Groth, Alexander, *Major Ideologies: An Interpretive Survey of Democracy, Socialism, and Nationalism* (New York: John Wiley, 1971).

Haddock, Bruce, 'Contingency and judgement in Oakeshott's political thought', *European Journal of Political Theory*, vol. 4, no. 1, 2005, pp 7–21.

Hampsher-Monk, Iain, *A History of Modern Political Thought: Major Political Thinkers from Hobbes to Marx* (Oxford: Blackwell Publishers, 1992).

Havel, Vaclav, *Summer Meditations: On Politics, Morality and Civility in a Time of Transition* (London: Faber & Faber, 1992).

Hobbes, Thomas, *Leviathan* (London: Penguin, 1993).

Kymlicka, Will, *Multicultural Citizenship: A Liberal Theory of Minority Rights* (Oxford: Oxford University Press, 1996).

Levine, Andrew, *The Future for Marxism? Althusser, the Analytical Turn and the Revival of Socialist Theory* (London: Pluto Press, 2003).

Love, Nancy S., *Dogmas and Dreams: A Reader in Modern Political Ideologies*, 3rd edn (Washington: CQ Press, 2005).

Lukacs, Georg, *History and Class Consciousness* (London: Merlin Press, 1990).

Mackay, Fiona, *Love and Politics: Women Politicians and the Ethics of Care* (London: Continuum, 2001).

Mackay, Fiona, 'Gender and political representation in the UK: the state of the "disciple" ', *British Journal of Politics and International Relations*, vol. 2, no. 1, 2004, pp. 99–120.

McLaughlin, Janice, *Feminist Social and Political Theory* (Basingstoke: Palgrave, 2003).

McLellan, David, *Ideology* (Milton Keynes: Open University Press, 1986).

McLellan, David, *Karl Marx: Selected Writings* (Oxford: Oxford University Press, 1988).

Manning, David. J (ed.), *The Form of Ideology* (London: George Allen and Unwin, 1980).

Marx, Karl, and Engels, Friedrich, *The Communist Manifesto* (New York: Vanguard Press, 1926).

Matthews, Eric, *Twentieth Century French Philosophy* (Oxford: Oxford University Press, 1996).

Morrow, John, *History of Western Political Thought: A Thematic Introduction*, 2nd edn (Basingstoke: Palgrave, 2005.

Novack, George, *Polemics in Marxist Philosophy* (New York: Pathfinder, 1996).

Nozick, Robert, *Anarchy, State and Utopia* (Oxford: Blackwell Publishers, 1974).

O'Sullivan, Noel, 'Preface' and 'The politics of ideology', in Noel O'Sullivan (ed.), *The Structure of Modern Ideology* (Aldershot: Edward Elgar, 1989), pp. i–ix and pp. 26–38.

Parker, Stan, *Stop Supporting Capitalism! Start Building Socialism!* (Wrexham: Bridge Books, 2002).

Powell, Jim, *Derrida for Beginners* (London: Writers and Readers Limited, 1997).

Redhead, Brian, *Political Thought from Plato to Nato* (London: Ariel, 1984).

Sorel, Georges, *Reflections on Violence* (New York: Collier Books, 1961).

Smith, Dai, 'Left historic: Dai Smith on Eric Hobsbawm's interesting times', *New Welsh Review*, no. 59, Spring 2003, pp. 11–19.

Sparks, Chris, and Isaacs, Stuart, *Political Theorists in Context* (London: Routledge, 2004).

Talib, Ismail S., *The Language of Postcolonial Literatures: An Introduction* (London: Routledge, 2002).

Tholfsen, Trygve, *Ideology and Revolution in Modern Europe: An Essay in the History of Ideas* (New York: Columbia University Press, 1984).

Torrance, John, *Karl Marx's Theory of Ideas* (Cambridge: Cambridge University Press, 1995).

Vincent, Andrew, 'Ideology and the politics of community', *Journal of Political Ideologies*, vol. 4, no. 3, 1999, pp. 403–410.

Vincent, Andrew, *Political Theory: Tradition and Diversity* (Cambridge: Cambridge University Press, 1997).

Wolff, Jonathan, *An Introduction to Political Philosophy* (Oxford: Oxford University Press, 1996).

Writings on Welsh Nationalism

Adamson, David, *Class, Ideology and the Nation: A Theory of Welsh Nationalism* (Cardiff: University of Wales Press, 1991.

Berresford Ellis, Peter, *Wales – A Nation Again: The Nationalist Struggle for Freedom* (Letchworth: Garden City Press, 1968).

Butt Philip, Alan, *The Welsh Question: Nationalism in Welsh Politics 1945–1970* (Cardiff: University of Wales Press, 1975).

Curtice, John, 'Is devolution succouring nationalism?', *Contemporary Wales*, vol. 14, 2001, pp. 80–103.

Darlington, Thomas, *Welsh Nationality and its Critics: A Lecture* (Wrexham: Hughes and Son, 1895).

Davies, Charlotte Aull, 'Ethnic Nationalism in Wales: An Analysis of the Factors Governing the Politicization of Ethnic Identity', PhD thesis, Duke University, 1978.

Davies, Charlotte Aull, *Welsh Nationalism in the Twentieth Century: The Ethnic Option and the Modern State* (New York: Praeger, 1989).

Davies, Charlotte Aull, *Welsh Nationalism and the British State* (Swansea: Swansea University Press, 1983).

Davies, Charlotte Aull, *Two Tongues, One Voice* (Swansea: Swansea University Press, 1989).

Davies, Charlotte Aull, 'Women, nationalism and feminism', in Jane Aaron, Teresa Rees, Sandra Betts and Moira Vincentelli (eds), *Our Sisters' Land: The Changing Identities of Women in Wales* (Cardiff: University of Wales Press, 1994), pp. 247–251.

Evans, Gwynfor, *Land of My Fathers* (Talybont: Y Lolfa, 1992).

Evans, Gwynfor, *The Fight for Welsh Freedom* (Talybont: Y Lolfa, 2000).

Fowler, Carwyn, 'A durable concept: Anthony Smith's concept of "national identity" and the case of Wales', University of Aberdeen, Political Studies Association conference paper, 5 April 2002.

Fowler, Carwyn, 'A typology of nationalism in Welsh language folk and rock music', University of Leeds, Political Studies Association conference paper, 7 April 2005.

Griffith, Gwilym O., *The New Wales: Some Aspects of National Idealism, with a Plea for Welsh Home Rule* (Liverpool: Hugh Evans and Son, 1913).

Hearne, Derrick, *The Rise of the Welsh Republic* (Talybont: Y Lolfa, 1975).

Hughes Jones, William, *What is Happening in Wales? An Open Discussion on the National Awakening* (London: Foyles, 1937).

Jones, Richard Wyn, 'From community socialism to quango Wales', *Planet: The Welsh Internationalist*, 118, August/September 1996, pp. 59–70.

Kohr, Leopold, *An Austrian Looks at Welsh Nationalism* (Cardiff: J.E. Jones, 1960).

Thomas, Ned, *The Welsh Extremist: Modern Welsh Politics, Literature and Society*, new edition (Talybont: Y Lolfa, 1994).

Williams, Colin, 'Language Decline and Nationalist Resurgence in Wales', PhD thesis, University College Swansea, 1978.

Williams, Hefin, 'Devolution and Other Issues in Welsh Nationalist Politics between 1966 and 1986', MA thesis, University of Wales, 1986.

Writings on Nationalism

Alcock, Antony, *A History of the Protection of Regional Cultural Minorities in Europe: From the Edict of Nantes to the Present Day* (Basingstoke: Macmillan, 2000).

Alter, Peter, *Nationalism* (London: Arnold, 1994).

Anderson, Benedict, *Imagined Communities* (London: Verso, 1991).

Aughey, Arthur, *Nationalism, Devolution and the Challenge to the United Kingdom* (London: Pluto Press, 2001).

Averill, Kenelm, 'Nationalism and narcissistic injury: affect and contemporary nationalist discourse in Britain', University of Leeds, Political Studies Association conference paper, 5 April 2005.

Benner, Erica, 'Is there a core national doctrine?', *Nations and Nationalism*, vol. 7, no. 2, 2001, pp. 155–174.

Benner, Erica, 'Nationality without nationalism', *Journal of Political Ideologies*, vol. 2, no. 2, 1997, pp. 189–206.

Billig, Michael, *Banal Nationalism* (London: Sage, 1995).

Bond, Ross, McCrone, David, and Brown, Alice, 'National identity and economic development: reiteration, recapture, reinterpretation and repudiation', *Nations and Nationalism*, vol. 9, no. 3, 2003, pp. 371–391.

Butt Philip, Alan, 'European nationalism in the nineteenth and twentieth centuries', in Rosalind Mitchison (ed.), *The Roots of Nationalism* (Edinburgh: John Donald, 1980), pp. 45–59.

Cederman, Lars-Erik, *Nationalism and Bounded Integration: What it Would Take to Construct a European Demos* (Florence: European University Institute, 2000).

Day, Graham and Thompson, Andrew, *Theorizing Nationalism* (London: Palgrave, 2004).

Echeverria, Begona, 'Privileging masculinity in the social construction of Basque identity', *Nations and Nationalism*, vol. 7, no. 3, 2001, pp. 339–363.

Fevre, Ralph, and Thompson, Andrew (eds), *Nation, Identity and Social Theory* (Cardiff: University of Wales Press, 1999).

Finlayson, Alan, 'Ideology, discourse and nationalism', *Journal of Political Ideologies*, vol. 3, no. 1, 1998, pp. 99–118.

Green, David Michael, 'The end of identity? The implications of postmodernity for political identification', *Nationalism and Ethnic Politics*, vol. 6, no. 3, 2000, pp. 68–90.

Hagendoorn, Louk, Csepeli, Gyorgy, Dekker, Henk, and Farnen, Russell (eds), *European Nations and Nationalism: Theoretical and Historical Perspectives* (Aldershot: Ashgate, 2000).

Hamilton, Paul, 'Converging nationalisms: Quebec, Scotland, and Wales in comparative perspective', *Nationalism and Ethnic Politics*, vol. 10, 2004, pp. 657–685.

Hearn, Jonathan, *Claiming Scotland: National Identity and Liberal Culture* (Edinburgh: Polygon, 2000).

Hechter, Michael, *Internal Colonialism: The Celtic Fringe in British National Development, 1536–1966* (Berkely: University of California Press, 1975).

Hobsbawm, Eric, *Nations and Nationalism since 1780: Programme, Myth, Reality*, 2nd edn (Cambridge: Cambridge University Press, 1992).

Hoppe, Marcus, 'Nationalist parties and Europeanisation', University of Budapest ECPR conference paper, 11 September 2005.

James, Paul, *Nation Formation: Towards a Theory of Abstract Community* (London: Sage, 1996).

Jones, R. Tudur, *The Desire of Nations* (Landybie: C. Davies, 1974).

Kamenka, Eugene, *Nationalism* (London: Edward Arnold, 1973).

Kellas, James G., *The Politics of Nationalism and Ethnicity* (London: Macmillan, 1991).

Lazar, Michelle, 'For the good of the nation: "strategic egalitarianism" in the Singapore context', *Nations and Nationalism*, vol. 7, no. 1, 2001, pp. 59–74.

Lynch, Peter, *Minority Nationalism and European Integration* (Cardiff: University of Wales Press, 1996).

Miller, David, 'Crooked timber or bent twig? Isaiah Berlin's nationalism', *Political Studies*, vol. 53, no. 1, 2005, pp. 100–123.

Miller, David, *On Nationality* (Oxford: Clarendon Press, 1995).

Mitchison, Rosalind, 'Some conclusions' in Rosalind Mitchison (ed.), *The Roots of Nationalism* (Edinburgh: John Donald, 1980), pp. 160–169.

Muro, Diego, 'Spanish nationalism: civic or ethnic?', *Ethnicities*, vol. 5, no. 1, March 2005, pp. 9–29.

Penrose, Jan, 'Nations, states and homelands: territory and territoriality in nationalist thought', *Nations and Nationalism*, vol. 8, no. 3, 2002, pp. 277–297.

Sleeboom, Margaret, 'The power of national symbols: the credibility of a dragon's efficacy', *Nations and Nationalism*, vol. 8, no. 3, 2002, pp. 299–313.

Smith, Anthony D., *Nations and Nationalism in a Global Era* (London: Polity, 1995).

Smith, Anthony D., *Theories of Nationalism* (London: Duckworth, 1971).

Stewart-Leigh, Murray, 'Political representations of national identity in

Scotland during the latter 20th century', University of Leeds, Political Studies Association conference paper, 6 April 2005.

Tamir, Yael, *Liberal Nationalism* (Princeton: Princeton University Press, 1993).

Vincent, Andrew, *Nationalism and Particularity* (Cambridge: Cambridge University Press, 2002).

Wilson, Robin, 'The politics of contemporary ethno-nationalist conflicts', *Nations and Nationalism*, vol. 7, no. 3, 2001, pp. 365–384.

Yiangou, George, 'Analysing the prospects of forging an overarching European collective identity', *Studies in Ethnicity and Nationalism*, vol. 1, no. 2, 2001, pp. 37–49.

Writings on Devolution, Welsh Politics and Welsh Society

Aaron, Jane, *The Welsh Survival Gene: The 'Despite' Culture in the Two Language Communities in Wales* (Cardiff: Institute of Welsh Affairs, 2003).

Aaron, Jane, Rees, Teresa, Betts, Sandra, and Vincentelli, Moira (eds), *Our Sisters' Land: The Changing Identities of Women in Wales* (Cardiff: University of Wales Press, 1994.

Aaron, Jane, 'Women in search of a Welsh identity', *Hard Times*, no. 63, 1998, pp. 11–16.

Aughey, Arthur, *Nationalism, Devolution and the Challenge to the United Kingdom State* (London: Pluto, 2001).

Ballard, Paul H., and Jones, D. Huw (eds), *This Land and People = Y Wlad a'r Bobl Hyn: A Symposium on Christian and Welsh National Identity* (Cardiff: Collegiate Centre of Theology, 1979).

Balsom, Denis, 'The first Welsh general election', in J.B. Jones and D. Balsom (eds), *The Road to the National Assembly for Wales* (Cardiff: University of Wales Press, 2000), pp. 109–125.

Beddoe, Deirdre, *Out of the Shadows: A History of Women in Twentieth Century Wales* (Cardiff: University of Wales Press, 2000).

Bogdanor, Vernon, *Devolution in the United Kingdom* (Oxford: Oxford University Press, 1998).

Bradbury, Jonathan, 'The political dynamics of sub-state regionalisation: a neo-functionalist perspective and the case of devolution in the UK', *British Journal of Politics and International Relations*, vol. 5, no. 4, 2003, pp. 543–575.

Bradbury, Jonathan, and Mawson, John, *British Regionalism and Devolution: The Challenge of State Reform and European Integration* (London: Regional Studies Association, 1997).

Bradbury, Jonathan, Mitchell, James, and Russell, Meg, 'The constituency role of members of the Scottish Parliament and Welsh Assembly: representation and party interest', University of Leeds, Political Studies Association conference paper, 5 April 2005.

Davies, John, *A History of Wales* (London: Penguin, 1993).

Day, Graham, *Making Sense of Wales: A Sociological Perspective* (Cardiff: University of Wales Press, 2002).

Deacon, Russell, *The Governance of Wales: The Welsh Office and the Policy Process 1964–1999* (Cardiff: Welsh Academic Press, 2002).

Dunkerley, David, and Thompson, Andrew (eds), *Wales Today* (Cardiff: University of Wales Press, 1999).

Dyer, Ian, *The Nationalist Road to Socialism: With Supplementary Welsh Road to Socialism* (Bridgend: Plaid Gwerin Cymru, 1990).

Edwards, Aled, *Transforming Power: A Christian Reflection on Welsh Devolution* (Bangor: Cyhoeddiadau'r Gair, 2001).

Edwards, Julia, and McAllister, Laura, 'One step forward, two steps back? Women in the two main political parties in Wales', *Parliamentary Affairs* no. 55, 2002, pp. 154–166.

Edwards, Sian, 'Danger – revolution in progress', in Deirdre Beddoe (ed.), *Changing Times: Welsh Women Writing on the 1950s and 1960s* (Dinas Powys: Honno, 2003), pp. 35–40.

Fowler, Carwyn, 'Nationalism and the Labour Party in Wales', *Llafur: Journal of Welsh Labour History*, vol. 8, no. 4, 2003, pp. 97–105.

Fowler, Carwyn, and Jones, Rhys, 'Locating and scaling the Welsh nation', University of Lincoln, Political Studies Association paper, April 2004.

Griffiths, Alison, 'Ethnography and popular memory: postmodern configurations of Welsh identities', *Continuum: The Australian Journal of Media and Culture*, vol. 7, no. 2, 1994, pp. 1–14.

Griffiths, Bethan, 'The Welsh language and the New Europe', *Cambria*, March–April, 2005, pp. 39–41.

Harries, Peter: 'Cwmllynfell colliery: an early attempt to form a workers co-operative', *Llafur: Journal of Welsh Labour History*, vol. 7, no. 2, 2002, pp. 40–51.

Jones, J. Barry, and Balsom, Denis (eds), *The Road to the National Assembly for Wales* (Cardiff: University of Wales Press, 2000).

Jones, Richard Wyn, 'On process, events and unintended consequences: national identity and the politics of Welsh devolution', *Scottish Affairs*, no. 37, Autumn 2001, pp. 34–57.

Kimber, Charlie, *Wales: Class Struggle and Socialism* (London: Socialist Workers Party, 1999).

Legonna, John, *Celtic Odyssey* (Cardiff: Roger Boore, 2001).

Lewis, Iain, 'The Welsh elite', *Planet: The Welsh Internationalist*, 156, December 2002/January 2003, pp. 9–18.

Llewelyn, Dorian, *Sacred Place, Chosen People: Land and National Identity in Welsh Spirituality* (Cardiff: University of Wales Press, 1999).

McAllister, Laura, 'The new politics in Wales: rhetoric or reality?', *Parliamentary Affairs*, vol. 53, 2000, pp. 591–604.

Mackay, Fiona, 'Women's representation in Wales and Scotland', *Contemporary Wales*, vol. 17, 2004, pp. 140–161.

Miles, Gareth, and Griffiths, Rob, *Socialism for the Welsh People* (Cardiff: Y Faner Goch, 1979).

Morgan, Kenneth O., 'Wales in British politics: forty years on', *Llafur: Journal of Welsh Labour History*, vol. 9, no. 1, 2004, pp. 19–25.

Osmond, John, *Creative Conflict: The Politics of Welsh Devolution* (Llandysul: Gomer Press, 1978).

Osmond, John, *New Politics in Wales* (London: Charter 88, 1998).

Osmond, John, *The National Question Again: Welsh Political Identity in the 1980s* (Llandysul: Gomer, 1985).

Osmond, John, *Welsh Europeans* (Bridgend: Seren, 1995).

Osmond, John, and Jones, J. Barry (eds), *Birth of Welsh Democracy: The First Term of the National Assembly for Wales* (Cardiff: Institute of Welsh Affairs, 2003).

Taylor, Bridget, and Thomson, Katarina (eds), *Scotland and Wales: Nations Again?* (Cardiff: University of Wales Press, 1999).

Thomas, R.S., *Cymru or Wales?* (Llandysul: Gwasg Gomer, 1992).

Webb, Harri, *A Militant Muse: Selected Literary Journalism 1948–80* (Bridgend: Seren, 1998).

Williams, Chris, *Democratic Rhondda: Politics and Society 1885–1951* (Cardiff: University of Wales Press, 1996).

Williams, Gwyn Alf, *Peace and Power: Henry Richard – A Radical for Our Times* (Cardiff: CND Cymru, 1988).

Williams, Gwyn Alf, *The Search for Beulah Land* (New York: Holmes and Meier, 1980).

Williams, Gwyn Alf, *When Was Wales? A History of the Welsh* (London: Penguin, 1985).

Speeches, Lectures and Public Meetings

Elis-Thomas, Dafydd, 'Wales – a new constitution', Cardiff University, Welsh Centre for Governance, 1 March 2000.

Jenkins, Simon, 'Welsh devolution through London eyes', Institute of Welsh Politics Annual Lecture, Aberystwyth, 2003.

Wigley, Dafydd, Speech at Theatr Gwynedd, Bangor, 18 January 1999.

Williams, Chris, 'A post-national Wales', University of Glamorgan, Inaugural Lecture, 14 October 2003.

Williams, Richard, Hustings meeting, County Hall, Swansea, 26 October 2002.

Interviews

Ackerman, Lyn, 6 March 2003 and 24 October 2008 at University of Wales Institute Cardiff.

Ball, John, 16 March 1999 at Swansea Metropolitan University.

Davies, Karl, 9 October 2001 at Ty Gwynfor (Plaid Cymru's Head Office), Cardiff.

Elis-Thomas, Dafydd, 12 November 2002 at the National Assembly for Wales, Cardiff.

Evans, Jill, 18 May 2002 via e-mail.

Evans, Nerys, 8 October 2008 at the National Assembly for Wales, Cardiff.
Haines, Lila, 4 March 2003 at Ty Gwynfor, Cardiff.
Jones, Elin, 16 October 2002 at the National Assembly for Wales, Cardiff.
Llwyd, Elfyn, 21 October 2002 at the House of Commons, London.
Morgan, Keith, 19 November 2001 at the Guildhall, Swansea.
Price, Darren, 11 June 2002 at University of Wales, Swansea.
Pritchard, Gareth, 7 October 2002 at University of Wales, Swansea.
Thomas, Rhodri Glyn, 14 May 2001 at the National Assembly for Wales, Cardiff.
Trystan, Dafydd, 8 March 2003 at Ty Gwynfor, Cardiff.
Wigley, Dafydd, 25. February 2002 at the National Assembly for Wales, Cardiff.
Williams, Phil, 25 September 2001 at the National Assembly for Wales, Cardiff.
Wood, Leanne, 8 October 2008 at the National Assembly for Wales, Cardiff.
Wyn, Eurig, 22 October 2002 at Transport House, Cardiff.

Web Resources

www.brookes.ac.uk/schools/humanities/Roger/apoliteia.part1.htm!
www.jill2000.co.uk/manifesto-e.html
www.plaidcymru.org.uk
www.tribancoch.com

INDEX

A

Aaron, Jane, 48–49
active citizenship, 19
Act of Union (1536), 35, 68
Adamson, Dave
    Class, Ideology and the Nation, 97
    gwerin, 84
    non-violent direct action, 153
adjacent concepts
    definition, 200
    identification, 16–18
    nationalism, exposure of, 25–26
    new models, 207–209
    religion, 70
    see also specific concepts
Alter, Peter, 29
Anderson, Benedict, 47
antidogma (conservative) ideology, 12
anti-industrialisation
    Lewis, 60–63, 66–68
    The Ten Points of Policy, 60
anti-materialism
    working classes, 61–62
anti-modernist discourse, 60–63
Aughey, Arthur, 94

B

Ball, John, 160–161
Barres, Maurice, 51–52
Bebb, Ambrose, 64
    militaristic views, 65
Beddoe, Deidre, 126
Benner, Erica, 42
A Billion Ways to Build a New Wales,
    156
bonedd (bond), 83
Bradbury, Jonathan, 95
Burke, Edmund, 28

C

Can Wales Afford Self-Government
    (1939), 68–69, 72–75
capitalism, 185–188

interpreters, 186–187
Lewis, 71–72
causal determinants, 8–9
Christianity, 145–146
    Egwyddorion Cenedlaetholdeb
        (The Principles of Nationalism)
        (1926), 69
citizenship
    active, 19
    definition, 19
Class, Ideology and the Nation (Adam-
    son), 97
collective liberty, 124–125
Collins, R. C.
    Liberal Party, views on, 124
    socialism, 102–103
    Workers Control in Wales, 102–103
Combs, Thomas
    Labour Party phase, 34–35, 45
    Liberal Party phase *see* Liberal
        Party phase
    nationalism, development of, 34
    pre-political phase, 34–36, 39
Common Market
    entry into, 89
communitarianism
    cydweitbrediad, 170–171
    identification, 173–174
concepts
    adjacent *see* adjacent concepts
    core *see* core concepts
    perimeter, 16
    peripheral *see* peripheral concepts
    see also specific concepts
conservatism, 12, 27–30, 44–45, 82
    Egwyddorion Cenedlaetholdeb (The
        Principles of Nationalism), 54
    Freeden's views, 54–57
    Lewis, 53–54
Cooke, Phil, 194
cooperativism, 167–177
    community socialism, 174–176
    cydweitbrediad, 169–170

freedom, 171–173
oppression *vs.* solidarity, 176–177
polyarchic systems, 171–173
Power for Wales (1974), 109–110
see also communitarianism
core concepts
definition, 15–16, 199
new models, 201–204
pacifism/non-violence, 156–157
socialism, 45–46
see also specific concepts
Le Cultes du Moi (Barres), 51–52
Cwm Tryweryn, 153
cydweitbrediad
communitarianism, 170–171
cooperativism, 169–170
Davies, D. J. & Noelle, 83
Cymdeithas yr Iaith Gymraeg (Welsh
Language Society), 182

D
Dafis, Cynog
Dewis (Choice), 196
green issues, 150
social justice, 183
Daniel, J. E.
capitalism, 185–186
cooperativism, 168
religion, 146
David, Wayne, 63
Davies, Charlotte
capitalism, 186–187
cooperativism, 169
historical role of women, 126, 127
internationalism, 88
Lewis, views on, 52
Liberal Party, views on, 123
religion, 143–144, 147
socialism, 113
Davies, D. J. & Noelle
conservatism, views on, 55
cydweitbrediad, 83
decentralisation, 158
economic policies, 72
Lewis, opposition to, 58
price of self-government, 72–75
rurbanisation, 162
socialism, 61, 102, 117
Davies, Gwilym, 146

Davies, Hywel
fascism, views on, 65
language, 181
pacifism/non-violence, 149
Davies, Janet, 194
Davies, Karl
liberalism, 121
socialism, 103–104, 105, 107
Davies, Kitchener
Labour Party condemnation, 62
Lewis, views on, 60–61
Day, Graham
feminism, views on, 129–130
Y Ddraig Goch (The Red Dragon), 132
Marxism, attacks on, 60
decentralisation, 157–167
green issues, 161–163
initialization, 158–159
polyarchic approach, 163–165
Power for Wales (1974), 109–110
in practice, 159–160
rurbanisation, 161–163
socialism, 165
decentralised socialism, 165
evolution of, 166–167
non-nationalist concept, 167
decontested nation
socialism, 117–119
democracy, 207–208
Derfel, R. J., 170
Deutsch, Karl, 22
development (of Plaid Cymru), 5–6
cultural constraints, 63
early period, 33–80
modern times, 81–101
pre-1925, 45
see also specific people
devolution, 114–115
Dewis (Choice), 196
direct action, 48
non-violent, 153–154
disruption
over negotiation, 203–204
distinct ideology, 17
duwiol
Welsh Mam, 134

E
eco-feminism, 137

economic policies, 72
Egwyddorion Cenedlaetholdeb (The Principles of Nationalism), 68–69
  Christian principles, 69
  conservatism, 54
  internationalism, 56
  language, 69
Elis-Thomas, Dafydd
  core concepts, 97–98
  feminism, 136, 137
  internationalism, 88, 90
  National Left, 194
  post-nationalism, 95–96, 97–99
  self-determination, 92
  socialism, 105, 107, 117, 138
Ellis, Peter Beresford, 39
Enloe, Cynthia, 130–131
entrepreneuralism, 209
equality, 208
established ideology, 16–17
Etzioni, Amitai, 171
Eurig, Aled, 137
European Economic Community, 112
European Union, 151–152
Evans, Gwynfor
  communal identification, 202
  communitarianism, 171
  decentralisation, 157, 165
  Fighting for Wales, 91
  gwerin, 85
  historical role of women, 127
  internationalism, 91–92
  Lewis, opposition to, 58
  liberalism, 119–120, 121
  nationalism, 50
  pacifism/non-violence, 155
  as party president, 81
  religion, 147
  self-identification, 94–95
  socialism, 105, 107, 108
Evans, Jill
  community socialism, 175
  internationalism, 88
  self-determination, 92
  socialism, 117
Evans, Nerys, 117

F
family *see teulu* (family)

Y Faner, 132
Fanon, Franz, 14
fascism, 28
  Lewis, 57–59, 62
  support, supposed, 63–66, 76–77
  totalitarian organicism, 58
feminism, 81, 126–138
  historical aspects, 136–137
  historical role of women, 126–129
  ideology, 136–137
  left-liberalism, 135–136
  placement, 130–131
  symbolism, 133–134
  universalism–particularism debate, 135
Fighting for Wales, 120
Finlayson, Alan, 28
Firestome, Shulamith, 129
Foley, Kathleen, 126–127
formation (of Plaid Cymru), 4, 33, 50
Fowler, Carwyn
  fascism, views on, 65
  language debate, 179
Freeden, Michael
  analysis choice, 12–13
  capitalism, 187
  ideological distinctions, 15–16
  see also specific theories
freedom
  as frame of mind, 206–207
  Lewis, views of, 70–71
Frost, John, 48
full ideology, 18–19

G
Gahan, Carmel, 127–128
Gramsci, Antonio, 74
green issues
  decentralisation, 161–163
  pacifism/non-violence, 150–151
green leftism, 97
Griffiths, Rob, 39
ap Gruffydd, Llywelyn, 35
gwerin, 84–87

H
Haines, Lila, 108
Havel, Vaclav, 157
Hechter, Michael, 186

hiraeth, 39
historical continuity, 27–30
history
    conception of, 47–48
    feminism, 136–137
Hobbes, Thomas, 13
Hobhouse, L. T., 69
holism, 67
holistic assessment, 204–205
home rule
    Lloyd George, 43
host-vessels, 26–27
    Liberal Party phase, 42
How Much Policy?, 166
human rights, 122
Hydro, 193–197

I
identification
    communitarianism, 173–174
ideology
    categorisation, 9
    conservative interpretation, 11–12
    debates within, 192–198
    feminism, 136–137
    frameworks of, 199–211
    full, 18–19
    modifications in, 196–198
    pejorative views, 11–12
    perimeter, 16
    see also specific types
Ignatieff, Michael, 96
inclusivist position, nationalism, 28
indigenous entrepreneuralism, 209
individual liberty, 124–125
internationalism, 87–90
    Common Market, entry into, 89
    Egwyddorion Cenedlaetholdeb (The
        Principles of Nationalism), 56
    Fianna Fail, relationship with, 91
    language, 181–182
    Lewis, 56–57
Iwan, Dafydd
    ideological changes, 196–197
    language debate, 179

J
Jarman, Pauline, 133
Jenkins, Bethan, 117
Jenkins, Dafydd, 106–107

Jenkins, Geraint H, 179
Jones, Elin
    decentralisation, 159–160
    internationalism, 88
    pacifism/non-violence, 151
    rurbanisation, 162
Jones, Helen Mary
    feminism, 133
    social justice, 183, 184
Jones, Ieuan Gwynedd
    anti-materialism, 61
    nationalism, 49
Jones, Ieuan Wyn
    pacifism/non-violence, 155
    socialism, 108
    social justice, 183. 184
Jones, Rhys, 179
Jones, Richard Wyn
    Elis-Thomas, views on, 97
    fascism, views on, 62–63

K
Kedourie, Elie, 59

L
Labour Party
    competition with, 105
    Power for Wales, attack on, 109
    relationship with, 2
Labour Party phase, 34–35, 45
language *see* Welsh language
left-liberalism
    feminism, 135–136
legitimacy, 9–10
Lewis, Saunders, 33
    anti-industrialisation, 60–63, 66–68
    capitalism, views on, 71–72, 187
    Catholicism, 146
    communal identification, 202
    communitarianism, 171
    conservatism, 53–54, 56
    decentralisation, 165
    in development of party, 51
    fascism, 57–59, 62
    freedom, views on, 70–71
    internationalism, 56–57
    language debate, 179
    Marxism, attacks on, 60
    militaristic views, 65
    nationalism, 51–53, 56, 84

pacifism/non-violence, 149
religion, 52–53, 54, 55–56
rurbanisation, 162
liberal ideology, 12, 19
liberalism, 81, 119–125
coalitions, 122–124
Liberal Party phase, 34, 38–40
as host-vessel, 42
Lloyd George, 39
role of, 42–43
liberty, 124–125
collective, 124–125
nationalism, 26
Llandudno conference (1982), 193–194
Lloyd, Dai, 159
Lloyd George, David
home rule, calls for, 43
Liberal Party phase, 39
UK, concentration on, 50
Llwyd, Elfyn
historical role of women, 127–128
nationalism, views on, 83
religion, 144
Lukacs, George, 17–18

M
McAllister, Laura
communitarianism, 171, 173–174
Davies, views on, 73
Elis-Thomas, views on, 97
feminism, 132–133, 136
historical role of women, 127
internationalism, 88
liberalism, 119–120
nationalism, 86
religion, 144–145
social fairness, 205
socialism, 102, 105
Manifesto 2001, 114–117
liberalism, 121–122
mutualism, 114
manifestos
socialism, 108–109
see also specific manifestos
Marxism, 12
Lewis, attacks of, 60
Marx, Karl, 12, 47, 60
Merched Y Wawr (The Women's
Movement), 86
Middle East issues, 151

Miles, Gareth, 38–39
Minogue, Ken, 11
minorities, 152
Morgan, Keith, 88
Morgan, Syd, 117
Morgannwg, Iolo, 37
mutualism
Manifesto 2001, 114
myth-making, 36–38, 58–59
National Eisteddfod, 37

N
nation
centrality, 201–202
cognisant change, 76
definition of, 21–22
legitimacy, 201–202
positive valorisation of, 22–23
recognition of, 22
National Assembly 2007
feminism, 128–129
National Eisteddfod
myth-making, 37
nationalism, 81, 82–84
adjacent concept exposure, 25–26
as core concept, 21–26
as distinct ideology, 14–15
fascism, 28
historical continuity, 27–30
inclusivist position, 28
language, 23
liberty, 26
modern labelling, 209–211
morphology evaluation, 20–21
as motif, 3
peripheral concept exposure, 25–26
policy matters, 21
sense of belonging, 24
sentiment, 24–25
social identity, 23
socialism problems, 104–106
as thought-practice, 13–14
National Left, 194–196
negotiation
disruption, over, 203–204
*New Wales: synopsis of the policy of
the Welsh Nationalist Party*, 82
non-Christian faiths, 146–147
non-violence *see* pacifism/non-violence
non-violent direct action, 153–154

O

Oakeshott, Michael, 53
oppression
  solidarity *vs.,* 176–177
organisational structure
  The Ten Points of Policy, 72
origins (of Plaid Cymru), 34
Owens, D. E., 94

P

pacifism/non-violence, 148–157
  as core concept, 156–157
  green issues, 150–151
  hegemony, 154–156
  Middle East issues, 151
  as peripheral concept, 156–157
Packer, Anthony, 90
parch
  Welsh Mam, 134
The Party for Wales
  religion, 146
The Peaceful Road to Self-Government,
  175
perchentyaeth, 83, 121
perimeter concepts, 16
peripheral concepts
  definition, 199–200
  nationalism, exposure of, 25–26
  new model, 204–207
  pacifism/non-violence, 156–157
  see also specific concepts
Philips, Thomas, 48
placement
  feminism, 130–131
politics of direct action, 48
Porthcawl conference (1980), 194
post-nationalism, 95–97
Power for the People, 84
Power for Wales (1974), 109–112
  cooperativism, 109–110
  decentralisation, 109–110
  Labour Party, attack on, 109
  social justice, 110
  Welsh language, 110–111
pragmatism, 97
pre-political phase
  Welsh language, 36
Price, Adam
  religion, 144

socialism, 117
Price, Darren, 175–176
The Principles of Nationalism see
  Egwyddorion Cenedlaetholdeb (The
  Principles of Nationalism)
Proudhon, Pierre-Joseph, 103

Q

qualitative human lifestyles, 67–68

R

racial discrimination, 122
radicalism
  Welsh language, 48–50
Radical Wales
  launch of, 113
The Red Dragon see Y Ddraig Goch
  (The Red Dragon)
redistribution of wealth, 115–116,
  183–184, 206
Reeves, Robin, 194
Reeves, Roseanne, 127–128
Reflections on the Revolution in France
  (Burke), 28
Reform Act (1868), 47–48
regionalism, 97
religion, 143–148
  as adjacent concept, 70
  as core concept, 147
  Lewis, views on, 52–53, 54, 55–56
  non-Christian faiths, 146–147
  see also Christianity
rhydid (freedom), 153
Richard, Henry, 41
Roberts, Kate
  economic policies, 72
  feminism, 132
  Lewis, opposition to, 58
  socialism, 117
Roberts, Mai
  feminism, 133
  historical role of women, 126
rurbanisation
  decentralisation, 161–163

S

Samuel, Wynne
  conservatism, views on, 55
  cooperativism, 168

Lewis, opposition to, 58
self-determination, 92
self-identification, 94–95
sense of belonging
    nationalism, 24
sentiment, 37
    nationalism, 24–25
sexual discrimination, 122
Sianel Pedwar Cymru, 154
social fairness, 205
social identity
    nationalism, 23
socialism, 81, 102–119
    as core concept, 45–46
    decontested nation, 117–119
    depth of, 117
    history, 106–108
    as host-vessel, 29
    manifestos, 108–109
        see also specific manifestos
    modern labelling, 209–211
    nationalism problems, 104–106
    social justice, 183–185
social justice, 182–185
    Power for Wales (1974), 110
    socialism, 183–185
solidarity
    oppression *vs.*, 176–177
    vicinity, 202–203
spirituality, 203
Statute of Rhuddlan (184), 35–36
Stephens, Meic, 173
Summer Meditations (Havel), 157
symbolism
    feminism, 133–134

T
The Ten Points of Policy, 68–69, 71–72
    anti-industrialisation, 60
    organisational structure, 72
teulu (family), 83
Thatcherism, 192
Thomas, Ben Bowen, 50
Thomas, Rhodri Glyn
    decentralised socialism, 165
    ideological changes, 193
    language, 181
    redistribution of wealth, 115–116,
        183

religion, 144
    social justice, 183, 184
Thomas, R. S., 96
Thomas, Simon, 41
Thompson, Andrew, 129–130
thought practices, 8–11
totalitarian organicism
    fascism, 58
Y Traethodydd
    religion, 146
Trystan, Dafydd
    liberalism, 120–121
    nationalism, views on, 83
    socialism, 138
Tudur Jones, R. 59

U
unilingual country
    Welsh language, 59
universalism–particularism debate
    feminism, 135
Urdd Gobiath Cymru (Welsh Youth
    Organization), 86

V
Valentine, Lewis
    language debate, 179
    pacifism/non-violence, 149
vicinity
    solidarity, 202–203
A Voice for Wales in Europe, 112–114

W
Wales and the War, 149
*Wales in Europe: A Community of
    Communities,* 107
wealth
    redistribution of, 115–116,
        183–184, 206
Webb, Harri, 48
welfare policies, 20
Welsh identity, 201
Welsh language, 36–38, 177–182
    debate evolution, 179–180
    development, 178
    *Egwyddorion Cenedlaetholdeb (The
        Principles of Nationalism),* 69
    internationalism, 181–182
    in nationalism, 23

party dilemma, 180–181
Power for Wales (1974), 110–111
pre-political phase, 36
radicalism, 48–50
unilingual country, 59
Welsh Language Act (1993), 35
Welsh Mam, 134
Welsh Nationalist, 107
Weltanschauung, 93–94, 152
Western Mail, 64
Wigley, Dafydd
    community socialism, 174–175
    Dewis (Choice), 196
    internationalism, 90
    language, 180
    Liberal Party coalition, 123
    nationalism, views on, 83
    socialism, 107, 108
Williams, D. J.
    language debate, 179
    Lewis, views on, 52
    pacifism/non-violence, 149
Williams, Gwyn Alf, 37
    internationalism, 41, 57
Williams, Mallt, 133
Williams, Phil

decentralisation, 161, 163
decentralised socialism, 166
gwerin, 85
Liberal Party coalition, 123
Liberal Party, views on, 124
National Left, 195
rurbanisation, 161
Towards 2000: Plaid Cymru's Programme for Wales in Europe, 89
Williams, Raymond, 170
Williams, Richard, 116
The Women's Movement (Merched Y Wawr), 86
Wood, Leanne
    pacifism/non-violence, 156
    socialism, 117
Workers Control in Wales (Collins), 102–103
working classes
    anti-materialism, 61–62
    demography of, 47
Wyn, Eurig
    internationalism, 87
    liberalism, 121
    self-determination, 92